MICROWAVE
COOKING

WITH
CHEF POL MARTIN

BRIMAR·PUBLISHING

The author wishes to thank
Melissa du Fretay
for her invaluable assistance.

Photographs: Pol Martin (Ontario) Ltd Studio

French version of this book titled
«L'Encyclopédie micro-ondes Pol Martin»
published by Les Éditions La Presse.

ISBN: 2-920845-04-7

Contents

Introduction

Dear Friends:

Welcome to microwave cooking! For years I have ignored this modern type of oven. But through my demonstrations I was asked repeatedly: "Is it possible to create delicious dishes in a microwave?" Your persistence concerning this matter convinced me that it was due time to explore the possibilities.

I must confess that in the beginning I approached my new task with some scepticism. My education as a gourmet chef hindered my acceptance of this revolutionary device, but today after much experiment, I can assure you there is no reason to ignore the microwave. Paired with a conventional oven, the microwave becomes an unmeasurable asset in today's kitchen.

The recipes included in this book are all delicious and quite simple to prepare. If you have not already, take some time to carefully read your microwave manufacture's guide booklet, before you tackle a recipe.

Good luck,

Pol Martin

What are microwaves?

Microwaves, as the world implies, are very short waves of energy that work on the same principle as radio or television.

Microwaves used for cooking are produced by a magnetron tube which converts household electricity into microwaves. The waves then bounce off the metal walls of the oven and pass through substances such as glass, plastic, and paper, thus cooking the food. It should be noted that metal is an unacceptable substance. As the waves are generated, food is cooked from the outside with remaining cooking processed by heat conduction towards the centre.

As soon as the cooking time has elapsed or the oven door is opened, the magnetron tube relinquishes therefore failing to continue producing microwaves.

With every new cooking appliance it is essential to understand it's functions and capabilities. Therefore, study the manufacture's guide booklet until familiar with the controls and settings. Remember that all microwaves work the same, though designs and recommendations may differ slightly.

Differences often occur according to wattage and electrical power in your region. For this reason, we have devised a chart that you can follow to set your microwave correctly for our recipes.

Settings	% of high settings	watts
HIGH	100%	650
MEDIUM-HIGH	75%	485
MEDIUM	50%	325
LOW	25%	160

If your microwave has a wattage of less than 650 watts, cooking time should be increased.

For unthawing foods, consult your guide booklet for best results.

Points to remember

— Cooking time will vary according to the volume and density of the food.

— Cooking time will also vary depending on food temperature and quantity.

— The cooking process will continue after food is removed from the oven. In certain recipes, you will find it necessary to allow the dish to stand before serving.

— To obtain uniform cooking, cut ingredients into equal pieces.

— To obtain best results with meat and large food, occasionally turn during the cooking process.

— As microwave cooking begins from the outside, placing food correctly in the utensil is important. Place the thickest or largest part of the food towards the outside of the dish and the thinnest or smallest part towards the middle of the dish.

— Since cooking is far quicker around the exterior of the dish, stir ingredients towards the middle for even cooking.

— When cooking eggs, gently prick the egg yolk to prevent the egg from exploding during cooking process. Important: Do not attempt to cook hard boiled eggs in the microwave.

— To brown meat, brush with a mixture of soya sauce and maple syrup.

Covering food

To conserve moisture in food, cover with a sheet of plastic wrap. Pierce wrap to allow excess steam to escape.

Should you prefer, a corner of the plastic wrap may be turned up obtaining the same result.

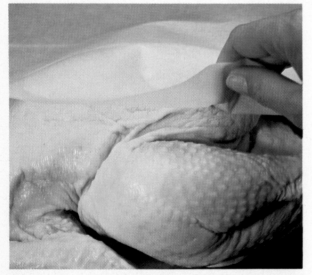

To retain a little less moisture, cover food lightly with a sheet of wax paper. To absorb grease or fat, cover with a sheet of paper towel. This technique can be used when reheating food and will prevent splashing.

Utensils

Avoid cooking with metal substances as the microwaves will not penetrate this material. The only exception to this rule, is the use of aluminium foil, which will decrease the cooking process of a roast or chicken.

Generally glass products are most commonly used and plastic utensils for short cooking times only.

Most likely there are many other types of utensils already in your kitchen that can be used for microwave cooking. To accurately test their durability follow this technique:

Place the empty utensil in your microwave and set at HIGH for 1 minute. If the article becomes hot, it should not be used. But remember, when in doubt, refer to your guide booklet.

Variety of casserole dishes

Here are a selection of Pyrex dishes that can be purchased at your local department store.

1 2 L square casserole dish

2 1.5 L pie plate

3 2 L round casserole dish with cover

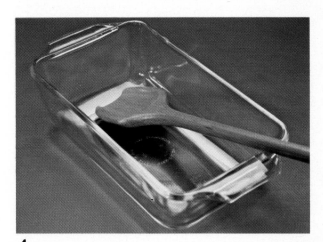

4 Rectangular casserole dish; available in different sizes.

Butters and Sauces

Garlic Butter

227 g	*(½ lb) soft butter*
2	*garlic cloves, smashed and chopped*
1	*shallot, chopped*
15 mL	*(1 tbs) chopped parsley*
	several drops lemon juice
	several drops Worcestershire sauce
	salt and cayenne pepper

Combine all ingredients in bowl; correct seasoning.

Place garlic butter on a sheet of aluminium foil. Roll and twist ends shut.

Refrigerate.

Note: Butter can also be frozen.

Mustard Butter

45 mL	*(3 tbs) butter*
15 mL	*(1 tbs) Dijon mustard*
1	*garlic clove, smashed and chopped*
	several drops lemon juice

Blend all ingredients together in bowl, using spatula.

Refrigerate.

Garlic-mustard Butter

45 mL	*(3 tbs) butter*
15 mL	*(1 tbs) Dijon mustard*
1	*garlic clove, smashed and chopped*
5 mL	*(1 tsp) Worcestershire sauce*
	salt and pepper

Blend all ingredients together in bowl, using spatula.

Refrigerate.

Horseradish Butter

Serve with roast pork.

45 mL	*(3 tbs) butter*
5 mL	*(1 tsp) Dijon mustard*
5 mL	*(1 tsp) horseradish*
5 mL	*(1 tsp) Worcestershire sauce*
	pepper from mill

Blend all ingredients together in bowl, using spatula.

Refrigerate.

Anchovy Butter

1	small can anchovy filets, washed and dried
227 g	(½ lb) soft butter
15 mL	(1 tbs) minced chives
	several drops lemon juice
	several drops Worcestershire sauce
	several drops Tabasco sauce

Purée anchovy filets in mortar. Strain through a fine sieve.

In bowl, combine anchovies with butter.

Sprinkle with lemon juice and add remaining ingredients. Mix well.

Place anchovy butter on sheet of aluminium foil. Roll and twist ends shut.

Refrigerate.

Serve with salmon steaks, sole filets, etc.

Clarified Butter

Setting:	MEDIUM-HIGH
Cooking time:	4 minutes
Utensil:	Microwave bowl

500 mL	(2 cups) butter

Place butter in bowl. Microwave 2 minutes. Stir well and microwave 2 more minutes.

Pass butter through cheesecloth set in strainer.

Note: Butter must be completely melted.

Devil Sauce

(serves 4)
Serve with pork, beef, and leftovers.

Setting:	HIGH
Cooking time:	9 minutes
Utensil:	2 L casserole

5 mL	(1 tsp) butter
3	shallots, chopped
250 mL	(1 cup) dry white wine, reduced by ½ on stove top
50 mL	(¼ cup) wine vinegar, reduced by ¾ on stove top
300 mL	(1¼ cups) hot beef stock
15 mL	(1 tbs) soya sauce
30 mL	(2 tbs) tomato paste
45 mL	(3 tbs) cornstarch
60 mL	(4 tbs) cold water
15 mL	(1 tbs) chopped parsley
15 mL	(1 tbs) Dijon mustard
	several drops Worcestershire sauce
	salt and pepper

Place butter and shallots in casserole. Cover with sheet of plastic wrap; microwave 2 minutes.

Remove casserole from microwave. Stir, then add wine, vinegar, beef stock, soya sauce, and tomato paste. Mix well.

Mix cornstarch with water; incorporate to sauce. Season to taste.

Microwave, uncovered, 7 minutes. Stir every 2 minutes with whisk.

Remove from microwave. Add parsley and Worcestershire sauce. Mix in mustard.

Serve.

Italian Sauce

Italian Sauce

(serves 4)

Setting:	HIGH
Cooking time:	25 minutes
Utensil:	2 L casserole

5 mL	*(1 tsp) olive oil*
1	*onion, peeled and chopped*
2	*garlic cloves, smashed and chopped*
1	*celery stalk, diced*
454 g	*(1 lb) ground beef*
45 mL	*(3 tbs) tomato paste*
1	*796 mL (28 oz) can tomatoes, drained and chopped*
1 mL	*(¼ tsp) nutmeg*
1 mL	*(¼ tsp) clove*
1	*bay leaf*
2 mL	*(½ tsp) oregano*
250 mL	*(1 cup) hot beef stock*
	salt and pepper

Place oil, onion, garlic, and celery in casserole. Season with salt and pepper.

Cover with sheet of plastic wrap; microwave 4 minutes.

Add beef, mix and continue to microwave 3 minutes.

Add tomato paste; mix well.

Add tomatoes and spices; mix well.

Add beef stock and season with pepper. Microwave, uncovered, 18 minutes.

Stir twice during cooking.

Serve sauce with pasta or hamburger steaks.

Technique

1 Place oil, garlic, onion, and celery in casserole.

2 Add meat and mix.

Technique : Italian Sauce (continued)

3   The meat after 3 minutes in microwave.

4   Add tomato paste.

5   Add tomatoes and spices.

6   Add beef stock.

Curry Sauce

(serves 4)
Serve with lamb chops and steaks.

Setting:	HIGH
Cooking time:	9 minutes
Utensil:	2 L round casserole

15 mL	*(1 tbs) butter*
1	*onion, peeled and chopped*
30 mL	*(2 tbs) curry powder*
375 mL	*(1½ cups) hot chicken stock* *
30 mL	*(2 tbs) cornstarch*
45 mL	*(3 tbs) 18% cream or milk*
	salt and pepper

Place butter, onion, and curry powder in casserole. Cover with sheet of plastic wrap; microwave 3 minutes.

Remove from microwave and stir. Add chicken stock; mix well.

Mix cornstarch with cream; incorporate to sauce. Season lightly with salt and pepper.

Microwave, uncovered, 6 minutes. Stir every 2 minutes with whisk.

Serve.

* See page 55.

Mushroom Sauce

(serves 4)
Serve with beef and veal.

Setting:	HIGH
Cooking time:	11 minutes
Utensil:	2 L round casserole

5 mL	*(1 tsp) butter*
30 mL	*(2 tbs) chopped onion*
227 g	*(½ lb) fresh mushrooms, washed and thinly sliced*
375 mL	*(1½ cups) hot beef stock*
15 mL	*(1 tbs) soya sauce*
15 mL	*(1 tbs) tomato paste*
45 mL	*(3 tbs) cornstarch*
60 mL	*(4 tbs) cold water*
	pinch tarragon
	pinch thyme
	several drops Tabasco sauce
	several drops lemon juice
	salt and pepper

Place butter, onion, and mushrooms in casserole. Season with salt and pepper; sprinkle with lemon juice.

Cover with sheet of plastic wrap; microwave 4 minutes.

Remove from microwave and stir.

Add beef stock, soya sauce, tomato paste, and spices; mix well.

Mix cornstarch with water; incorporate to sauce. Mix well with whisk.

Microwave, uncovered, 7 minutes. Stir every 2 minutes with whisk.

Correct seasoning and serve.

Green Peppercorn Sauce

(serves 4)
Serve with steaks, veal, and chicken.

Setting: HIGH
Cooking time: 9 minutes
Utensil: 2 L round casserole

5 mL	(1 tsp) butter
2	shallots, chopped
30 mL	(2 tbs) crushed green peppercorns
375 mL	(1½ cups) hot beef stock
15 mL	(1 tbs) soya sauce
15 mL	(1 tbs) tomato paste
45 mL	(3 tbs) cornstarch
60 mL	(4 tbs) cold water
30 mL	(2 tbs) 35% cream
15 mL	(1 tbs) chopped parsley
	salt

Place butter, shallots, and peppercorns in casserole. Cover and microwave 2 minutes.

Remove from microwave and stir. Add beef stock, soya sauce, and tomato paste. Mix well and season lightly.

Mix cornstarch with water; incorporate to sauce. Microwave, uncovered, 7 minutes. Stir every 2 minutes with whisk.

2 minutes before end of cooking, add cream and parsley. Mix well.

Serve.

Bearnaise Sauce

Setting: HIGH
Cooking time: 2 minutes
Utensil: Pyrex measuring cup

45 mL	(3 tbs) dry white wine
30 mL	(2 tbs) wine vinegar
2	shallots, chopped
5 mL	(1 tsp) tarragon
300 mL	(1¼ cups) unsalted butter
4	egg yolks
	several drops lemon juice
	pepper from mill

Pour wine into small saucepan. Add vinegar, shallots, and tarragon. Place on stove top and reduce by 2/3.

Rapidly mix egg yolks into liquid. Remove saucepan from heat.

Place butter in measuring cup and microwave 2 minutes.

Incorporate melted butter to egg mixture, mixing constantly with electric beater at medium speed.

Once mixture thickens, add lemon juice and pepper.

Serve.

White Sauce

(serves 4)

Setting: HIGH
Cooking time: 7 minutes
Utensil: Bowl or 2 L casserole

45 mL	*(3 tbs) butter*
15 mL	*(1 tbs) chopped onion*
15 mL	*(1 tbs) chopped parsley*
52 mL	*(3½ tbs) flour*
500 mL	*(2 cups) milk*
	pinch nutmeg
	salt and pepper

Place butter, onion, and parsley in bowl or casserole. Cover with sheet of plastic wrap; microwave 1 minute.

Add flour; mix with whisk. Incorporate milk slowly, stirring with whisk.

Season with nutmeg, salt, and pepper.

Microwave, uncovered, 6 minutes. Stir every minute.

Serve.

Sauce Bordelaise

(serves 4)
Serve with filet mignons and steaks.

Setting: HIGH
Cooking time: 9 minutes
Utensil: 2 L round casserole

5 mL	*(1 tsp) butter*
2	*dry shallots, chopped*
1	*,garlic clove*
250 mL	*(1 cup) dry red wine, reduced by ½ on stove top*
375 mL	*(1½ cups) hot beef stock*
15 mL	*(1 tbs) soya sauce*
15 mL	*(1 tbs) chopped parsley*
15 mL	*(1 tbs) tomato paste*
45 mL	*(3 tbs) cornstarch*
60 mL	*(4 tbs) cold water*
	pinch thyme
	pinch tarragon
	salt and pepper

Place butter, shallots, and garlic in casserole. Cover with sheet of plastic wrap; microwave 2 minutes.

Remove casserole from microwave and stir well.

Add wine, beef stock, soya sauce, parsley, tomato paste, and spices. Season with salt and pepper; mix well.

Mix cornstarch with water; incorporate to sauce.

Microwave, uncovered, 7 minutes. Stir every 2 minutes.

Season to taste and serve.

Brown Sauce

(serves 4)

Setting:	HIGH
Cooking time:	9 minutes
Utensil:	2 L bowl

5 mL	*(1 tsp) butter*
30 mL	*(2 tbs) chopped onion*
1	*small garlic clove, smashed and chopped*
375 mL	*(1½ cups) hot beef stock*
15 mL	*(1 tbs) soya sauce*
15 mL	*(1 tbs) tomato paste*
30 mL	*(2 tbs) cornstarch*
45 mL	*(3 tbs) cold water*
	pinch thyme
	pinch oregano
	salt and pepper

Place butter, onion, and garlic in bowl. Cover with sheet of plastic wrap; microwave 3 minutes.

Remove bowl and season with salt and pepper. Mix well.

Add remaining ingredients and season to taste.

Microwave, uncovered, 6 minutes. Stir every 2 minutes with whisk.

Pass sauce through sieve; season to taste.

Serve.

Technique

1 Place butter, onion, and garlic in bowl. Cover with sheet of plastic wrap; microwave 3 minutes.

4 You can also force vegetables through sieve using a pestle.

2 Add remaining ingredients. Microwave, un-covered, 6 minutes.

3 Pass sauce through sieve.

5 Finished product. The sauce has been thickened with cornstarch.

Fish Sauce

Setting: HIGH
Cooking time: 10 minutes
Utensil: 2 L casserole

60 mL	*(4 tbs) butter*
2	*shallots, chopped*
60 mL	*(4 tbs) flour*
500 mL	*(2 cups) hot fish stock*
50 mL	*(¼ cup) 18% cream*
	salt and pepper

Place butter and shallots in casserole. Cover with sheet of plastic wrap; microwave 2 minutes.

Add flour, mixing between spoonfuls.

Incorporate fish stock; mix well with whisk.

Microwave, uncovered, 4 minutes. Stir every minute.

Season to taste. Continue to microwave 3 minutes.

Add cream, stir, and microwave 1 minute.

Serve with sole filets, lobster, shrimp, etc.

Fish Stock

Setting: HIGH
Cooking time: 10 minutes
Utensil: 2 L casserole

15 mL	*(1 tbs) butter*
5	*mushrooms, washed and sliced*
2	*shallots, sliced*
3	*parsley sprigs*
125 mL	*(½ cup) dry white wine*
2	*sole filets*
1 L	*(4 cups) water*
1	*bay leaf*
	several drops lemon juice
	salt and pepper from mill

Place butter, mushrooms, shallots, and parsley in casserole. Pepper well and sprinkle with lemon juice.

Add wine and sole filets; season with salt. Add water and bay leaf.

Cover with sheet of plastic wrap; microwave 10 minutes.

Remove casserole from microwave and let stand 7 to 8 minutes.

Pass stock through sieve. Refrigerate.

Portuguese Sauce

(serves 4)
Serve with chicken, pork, and pasta.

Setting: **HIGH**
Cooking time: **17 minutes**
Utensil: **2 L round casserole**

5 mL	*(1 tsp) olive oil*
1	*onion, peeled and chopped*
1	*garlic clove, smashed and chopped*
3	*tomatoes, chopped*
30 mL	*(2 tbs) tomato paste*
375 mL	*(1½ cups) hot beef stock*
15 mL	*(1 tbs) soya sauce*
15 mL	*(1 tbs) chopped parsley*
45 mL	*(3 tbs) cornstarch*
45 mL	*(3 tbs) cold water*
	pinch oregano
	pinch sugar
	several drops Tabasco sauce
	salt and pepper

Place oil, onion, garlic, and tomatoes in casserole. Season with salt and pepper. Cover with sheet of plastic wrap; microwave 7 minutes.

Remove from microwave and mix with whisk.

Add tomato paste, beef stock, soya sauce, sugar, parsley, and oregano. Sprinkle with Tabasco sauce.

Mix cornstarch with water; incorporate to sauce. Microwave, uncovered, 10 minutes. Stir every 2 minutes.

Note: For smoother sauce, pass through food mill.

Tomato Sauce

(serves 4)
Serve with meat and veal.

Setting: **HIGH**
Cooking time: **11 minutes**
Utensil: **2 L round casserole**

5 mL	*(1 tsp) butter*
1	*onion, peeled and chopped*
1	*garlic clove, smashed and chopped*
2	*tomatoes, diced*
45 mL	*(3 tbs) tomato paste*
15 mL	*(1 tbs) soya sauce*
375 mL	*(1½ cups) hot beef stock*
30 mL	*(2 tbs) cornstarch*
45 mL	*(3 tbs) cold water*
1 mL	*(¼ tsp) basil*
1 mL	*(¼ tsp) thyme*
	salt and pepper

Place butter, onion, garlic, and tomatoes in casserole. Cover with sheet of plastic wrap; microwave 4 minutes.

Remove casserole from microwave and mix well.

Add tomato paste, soya sauce, and beef stock; mix well. Season lightly.

Mix cornstarch with water; incorporate to sauce. Add spices.

Microwave, uncovered, 7 minutes. Stir every 2 minutes.

Serve.

Lyonnaise Sauce

(serves 4)
Serve with chicken, beef, veal, etc.

Setting: **HIGH**
Cooking time: **13 minutes**
Utensil: **2 L round casserole**

15 mL	*(1 tbs) butter*
1	*Spanish onion, peeled and sliced*
30 mL	*(2 tbs) soya sauce*
15 mL	*(1 tbs) chopped parsley*
375 mL	*(1½ cups) hot beef stock*
15 mL	*(1 tbs) tomato paste*
5 mL	*(1 tsp) Worcestershire sauce*
30 mL	*(2 tbs) cornstarch*
45 mL	*(3 tbs) cold water*
	salt and pepper

Place butter, onion, 15 mL (1 tbs) soya sauce, and parsley in casserole.

Season with salt and pepper. Cover with sheet of plastic wrap; microwave 6 minutes.

Remove casserole from microwave and mix well.

Add beef stock, tomato paste, and Worcestershire sauce; mix well.

Mix cornstarch with water; incorporate to sauce. Add remaining soya sauce and season.

Microwave, uncovered, 7 minutes. Stir every 2 minutes with whisk.

Pass sauce through sieve.

Serve.

Mornay Sauce *

(serves 4)

Setting: **HIGH**
Cooking time: **8 minutes**
Utensil: **2 L casserole or bowl**

45 mL	*(3 tbs) butter*
15 mL	*(1 tbs) chopped onion*
15 mL	*(1 tbs) chopped parsley*
52 mL	*(3½ tbs) flour*
500 mL	*(2 cups) milk*
1	*egg yolk*
30 mL	*(2 tbs) 35% cream*
125 mL	*(½ cup) grated mozzarella cheese*
	pinch nutmeg
	salt and pepper

Place butter, onion, and parsley in casserole. Cover with sheet of plastic wrap; microwave 1 minute.

Add flour and mix with whisk.

Incorporate milk slowly, while mixing with whisk. Season with salt and pepper; add nutmeg.

Microwave, uncovered, 6 minutes. Stir every minute. Set aside.

Place egg yolk in a mixing bowl. Add cream and mix well. Incorporate to white sauce.

Add cheese to sauce and correct seasoning. Microwave 30 seconds.

* Serve with crepes, asparagus, endives, broccoli, leeks, poached eggs, mushrooms, fish, chicken, etc.

Sweet and Sour Sauce

Setting: HIGH
Cooking time: 6 to 7 minutes
Utensil: 2 L casserole

40 mL	(2½ tbs) cornstarch
50 mL	(¼ cup) sugar
175 mL	(¾ cup) cold chicken stock *
45 mL	(3 tbs) white vinegar
15 mL	(1 tbs) soya sauce
125 mL	(½ cup) pineapple juice
125 mL	(½ cup) chopped pineapples
	pepper

Mix cornstarch with sugar in mixing bowl. Add chicken stock, vinegar, soya sauce, and pineapple juice.

Transfer mixture to casserole. Mix well and microwave, uncovered, 5 minutes.

Stir well, add pineapples and continue to microwave 1 to 2 minutes.

Season with pepper. Serve.

* See page 55.

Tangy Sauce

(serves 4)
Serve with beef, pork, and chicken breasts.

Setting: HIGH
Cooking time: 8 minutes
Utensil: 2 L round casserole

5 mL	(1 tsp) butter
3	dry shallots, chopped
250 mL	(1 cup) dry white wine, reduced by ½ on stove top
125 mL	(½ cup) wine vinegar, reduced by ¾ on stove top
250 mL	(1 cup) hot beef stock
15 mL	(1 tbs) soya sauce
15 mL	(1 tbs) tomato paste
30 mL	(2 tbs) cornstarch
45 mL	(3 tbs) cold water
2	pickles, finely chopped
15 mL	(1 tbs) chopped parsley
15 mL	(1 tbs) chopped tarragon
	salt and pepper

Place butter and shallots in casserole. Cover with sheet of plastic wrap; microwave 2 minutes.

Remove casserole from microwave and mix with wooden spoon.

Add wine, vinegar, beef stock, soya sauce, and tomato paste. Mix well with whisk. Season to taste.

Mix cornstarch with water; incorporate to sauce.

Microwave, uncovered, 6 minutes. Stir every 2 minutes with whisk.

Remove from microwave. Add pickles, parsley, and tarragon.

Serve.

Chasseur Sauce

(serves 4)
Serve with chicken, veal, and pork.

Setting: HIGH
Cooking time: 11 minutes
Utensil: 2 L round casserole

5 mL	(1 tsp) butter
2	dry shallots, chopped
114 g	(¼ lb) fresh mushrooms, washed and sliced
250 mL	(1 cup) dry white wine, reduced by ¾ on stove top
375 mL	(1½ cups) hot beef stock
15 mL	(1 tbs) soya sauce
15 mL	(1 tbs) tomato paste
45 mL	(3 tbs) cornstarch
60 mL	(4 tbs) cold water
	salt and pepper

GARNISH:

15 mL	(1 tbs) chopped parsley
15 mL	(1 tbs) chopped chives

Place butter, shallots, and mushrooms in casserole.

Season with salt and pepper. Cover with sheet of plastic wrap; microwave 4 minutes.

Remove casserole from microwave and mix well.

Add wine, beef stock, soya sauce, and tomato paste; mix well.

Mix cornstarch with water; incorporate to sauce.

Microwave, uncovered, 7 minutes. Stir every 2 minutes with whisk.

Remove from microwave, add garnish and serve.

Creole Sauce

Setting: HIGH
Cooking time: 11 minutes
Utensil: 2 L casserole

15 mL	(1 tbs) olive oil
50 mL	(¼ cup) chopped onion
1	garlic clove, smashed and chopped
1	celery stalk, diced
2	tomatoes, peeled and diced
114 g	(¼ lb) fresh mushrooms, washed and diced
375 mL	(1½ cups) hot, thick tomato sauce *
2 mL	(½ tsp) basil
15 mL	(1 tbs) chopped parsley
	salt and pepper

Pour oil into casserole. Add onion, garlic, and celery; season with salt and pepper.

Cover and microwave 4 minutes.

Add tomatoes and mushrooms; cover and microwave 4 minutes.

Add tomato sauce, basil, and parsley. Season well and microwave, uncovered, 3 minutes.

Serve with chicken, veal, and meat.

* See page 25.

Duxelles Sauce

(serves 4)
Serve with chicken breasts, veal, and pork filets.

Setting: HIGH
Cooking time: 11 minutes
Utensil: 2 L round casserole

15 mL	(1 tbs) butter
30 mL	(2 tbs) chopped onion
114 g	(½ lb) fresh mushrooms, washed and chopped
15 mL	(1 tbs) chopped parsley
30 mL	(2 tbs) dry white wine
300 mL	(1¼ cups) hot beef stock
15 mL	(1 tbs) soya sauce
15 mL	(1 tbs) tomato paste
45 mL	(3 tbs) cornstarch
60 mL	(4 tbs) cold water
	salt and pepper

Place butter, onion, mushrooms, and parsley in casserole. Season with salt and pepper. Cover with sheet of plastic wrap; microwave 4 minutes.

Remove casserole from microwave and mix well.

Add wine, beef stock, soya sauce, and tomato paste. Season and mix well.

Mix cornstarch with water; incorporate to sauce.

Microwave, uncovered, 7 minutes. Stir every 2 minutes with whisk.

Serve.

Spicy Sauce

Setting: HIGH
Cooking time: 6 minutes
Utensil: 2 L casserole

250 mL	(1 cup) chili sauce
15 mL	(1 tbs) olive oil
2	garlic cloves, smashed and chopped
125 mL	(½ cup) thick brown sauce *
5 mL	(1 tsp) brown sugar
5 mL	(1 tsp) Worcestershire sauce
5 mL	(1 tsp) soya sauce

Mix all ingredients together in a glass bowl.

Transfer mixture to casserole. Cover and microwave 3 minutes.

Stir well, cover and continue to microwave 3 minutes. Cool.

* See page 22.

Hollandaise Sauce

Setting: HIGH
Cooking time: 2 minutes
Utensil: 2 L casserole

125 mL	(½ cup) melted butter
2 mL	(½ tsp) dry mustard
3	egg yolks, beaten
	juice ¼ lemon
	white pepper

Mix butter and mustard together; pour into casserole. Microwave 2 minutes. (The butter should bubble.)

Place egg yolks in hot stainless steel bowl. Mix with electric beater.

Add hot butter, in thin stream, while mixing with electric beater at medium speed.

When sauce begins to thicken, add lemon juice. Season to taste and serve.

Appetizers

Spicy Meatballs

(serves 4)

Technique

Setting :	HIGH
Cooking time :	8 to 9 minutes
Utensil :	30 × 20 × 5 cm (11¾ × 7½ × 1¾ in) casserole

680 g	*(1½ lb) lean ground beef*
1	*celery stalk, chopped*
2	*garlic cloves, smashed and chopped*
30 mL	*(2 tbs) chopped onion*
15 mL	*(1 tbs) horseradish*
30 mL	*(2 tbs) soya sauce*
50 mL	*(¼ cup) breadcrumbs*
½	*beaten egg*
30 mL	*(2 tbs) maple syrup*
	salt and pepper

Place beef, celery, garlic, onion, horseradish, 15 mL (1 tbs) soya sauce, and breadcrumbs in mixing bowl. Season with salt and pepper. Add egg and incorporate well.

Shape mixture into meatballs and place in casserole.

Mix remaining soya sauce with maple syrup; brush over meatballs.

Cover and microwave 8 to 9 minutes. Turn meatballs twice during cooking.

Serve with spicy sauce.*

* See page 29.

1 Place beef, celery, garlic, onion, horseradish, 15 mL (1 tbs) soya sauce, and breadcrumbs in mixing bowl.

4 Brush meatballs with soya sauce and maple syrup mixture.

2 Season with salt and pepper. Add egg.

3 Incorporate well and shape mixture into meatballs. Place in casserole.

5 Cover and microwave.

6 Turn meatballs during cooking.

Sweet and Sour Meatballs

(serves 4)

Setting: HIGH
Cooking time: 8 to 9 minutes
Utensil: 30 × 20 × 5 cm (11¾ × 7½ × 1¾ in) casserole

680 g	*(1½ lb) lean ground beef*
1	*celery stalk, chopped*
2	*garlic cloves, smashed and chopped*
15 mL	*(1 tbs) teriyaki sauce*
5 mL	*(1 tsp) Worcestershire sauce*
50 mL	*(¼ cup) slivered almonds*
45 mL	*(3 tbs) breadcrumbs*
50 mL	*(¼ cup) chopped nuts*
1	*beaten egg*
	several drops Tabasco sauce
	salt and pepper

Mix all ingredients together in mixing bowl. Shape into meatballs.

Place meatballs in casserole. Cover and microwave 8 to 9 minutes. Turn twice during cooking.

Serve with sweet & sour sauce.*

* See page 27.

Cheese Fondue

(serves 4)

Setting: MEDIUM
Cooking time: 4 minutes
Utensil: 2 L casserole

750 mL	*(3 cups) grated cheddar cheese*
15 mL	*(1 tbs) 35% cream*
15 mL	*(1 tbs) Madeira wine*
15 mL	*(1 tbs) chopped fresh parsley*
15 mL	*(1 tbs) chopped chives*
	several drops Tabasco sauce

Place all ingredients in casserole. Microwave 2 minutes.

Stir well and continue to microwave 2 minutes.

Note: The cheese must be completely melted.

Cheese Surprise

(serves 4)

Setting: MEDIUM
Cooking time: 2 minutes
Utensil: Large dish or plate

24	*Melba toast rounds*
24	*slices zucchini*
250 mL	*(1 cup) grated mozzarella cheese*
	pepper from mill

Place sheet of wax paper on dish. Arrange Melba toasts on top.

Add zucchini slices and sprinkle with cheese. Generously season with pepper.

Microwave 2 minutes.

Note: The cheese must be completely melted.

Welsh Rarebit

(serves 4)

Setting:	MEDIUM
Cooking time:	8 minutes
Utensil:	2 L casserole

50 mL	(¼ cup) beer
454 g	(1 lb) cheddar cheese, cubed
2 mL	(½ tsp) dry mustard
30 mL	(2 tbs) cold water
2 mL	(½ tsp) Worcestershire sauce
2	egg yolks
8	slices toasted bread

Place beer and cheese in casserole.

Mix mustard with water; incorporate to beer mixture. Add Worcestershire sauce. Microwave 3 minutes.

Stir well and continue to microwave 3 minutes.

Add egg yolks, mix, and microwave 2 minutes.

Pour cheese mixture over toasted bread and serve.

Shrimp Cocktail

(serves 4)

Setting:	HIGH
Cooking time:	4 to 5 minutes
Utensil:	2 L casserole

24	medium size shrimps, washed and deveined
50 mL	(¼ cup) cold water
	juice 1 lemon

Place shrimps in casserole. Add water and lemon juice; cover and microwave 3 minutes.

Stir, cover, and continue to microwave 1 to 2 minutes.

Remove casserole and allow shrimps to stand in hot liquid 7 to 8 minutes.

Cool shrimps under cold water, drain well, and set aside.

KETCHUP SAUCE:

75 mL	(1/3 cup) mayonnaise
75 mL	(1/3 cup) ketchup
75 mL	(1/3 cup) chili sauce
15 mL	(1 tbs) Madeira wine
	several drops lemon juice
	several drops Tabasco sauce
	pinch dry mustard
	pepper from mill

Incorporate all ingredients in mixing bowl. Season to taste.

Serve with shrimps.

Shrimp and Cheese Spread

Shrimp and Cheese Spread

(serves 4)

Setting:	HIGH
Cooking time:	6 to 7 minutes
Utensil:	2 L casserole

500 mL	*(2 cups) cold water*
454 g	*(1 lb) medium size shrimps*
227 g	*(8 oz) soft cream cheese*
30 mL	*(2 tbs) grated onion*
2 mL	*(½ tsp) Worcestershire sauce*
	lemon juice
	salt and pepper

Pour water into casserole. Add shrimps and sprinkle with lemon juice. Cover and microwave 6 to 7 minutes. Stir once or twice during cooking.

Remove casserole and allow shrimps to stand in liquid 2 to 3 minutes. Drain well, devein, and chop.

Place chopped shrimps in mixing bowl. Mix in remaining ingredients. Serve on crackers or toasted bread.

Technique

1 Pour water into casserole. Add shrimps and sprinkle with lemon juice. Cover and microwave.

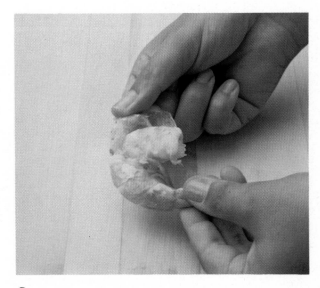

2 Devein shrimps.

→

Technique : Shrimp and Cheese Spread (continued)

3 Chop shrimps and place in mixing bowl. Add remaining ingredients.

4 Blend well.

Crab and Shrimp Surprise

(serves 4)

Setting :   **HIGH**
Cooking time : **8 to 9 minutes**
Utensil :   **2 L casserole**

15 mL	**(1 tbs) olive oil**
2	**shallots, chopped**
1	**garlic clove, smashed and chopped**
2	**tomatoes, peeled, seeded, and chopped**
30 mL	**(2 tbs) chopped capers**
2	**anchovy filets, chopped**
375 mL	**(1½ cups) mayonnaise**
250 mL	**(1 cup) cooked crab meat, chopped**
250 mL	**(1 cup) cooked shrimps, chopped**
	several drops wine vinegar
	salt and pepper

Pour oil into casserole. Add shallots and garlic ; cover and microwave 2 minutes.

Add tomatoes and vinegar ; mix well and season to taste. Cover and microwave 6 to 7 minutes.

Remove casserole and cool.

Transfer cooled mixture to mixing bowl. Add remaining ingredients ; blend well.

Serve on toasted bread.

Shrimp and Garlic Fondue

(serves 4)

Setting: HIGH
Cooking time: 7 minutes
Utensil: 2 L casserole and small Pyrex bowl

350 g	*(¾ lb) medium size shrimps, deveined and washed*
50 mL	*(¼ cup) cold water*
227 g	*(½ lb) butter*
1	*shallot, chopped*
3	*garlic cloves, smashed and chopped*
15 mL	*(1 tbs) chopped fresh parsley*
	juice 1½ lemons
	pepper from mill

Place shrimps in casserole. Add water and juice of 1 lemon. Cover and microwave 3 minutes.

Stir well and continue to microwave 3 minutes. Remove casserole and let shrimps stand in liquid 3 to 4 minutes.

Place butter, shallots, garlic, parsley, pepper, and remaining lemon juice in Pyrex bowl. Microwave 1 minute.

Dip shrimps in garlic butter and serve.

Shrimp Bouchées

(serves 4)

Setting: HIGH
Cooking time: 9 to 10 minutes
Utensil: 2 L casserole

350 g	*(¾ lb) shrimps, deveined and washed*
50 mL	*(¼ cup) cold water*
15 mL	*(1 tbs) butter*
114 g	*(¼ lb) fresh mushrooms, diced*
2	*shallots, chopped*
500 mL	*(2 cups) hot white sauce**
15 mL	*(1 tbs) chopped fresh parsley*
5 mL	*(1 tsp) chopped tarragon*
	juice ½ lemon
	salt and pepper
	paprika

Place shrimps in casserole. Add water and lemon juice; cover and microwave 3 minutes.

Stir well, cover and continue to microwave 3 minutes. Cool shrimps under cold water, drain, and chop.

Place butter in casserole. Add mushrooms and shallots; cover and microwave 3 to 4 minutes.

Drain mushrooms and replace in casserole. Add chopped shrimps, white sauce, parsley, and tarragon. Mix together well.

Stuff flakey pastry bouchées** with mixture. Sprinkle with paprika and serve.

* See page 21.
** Available in supermarkets.

Shrimp Catherine

Shrimp Catherine

(serves 4)

Setting:	HIGH
Cooking time:	9 to 11 minutes in microwave
Utensil:	2 L casserole

30 mL	*(2 tbs) olive oil*
1	*red pepper, thinly sliced*
3	*tomatoes, peeled and diced*
1	*garlic clove, smashed and chopped*
1 mL	*(¼ tsp) basil*
15 mL	*(1 tbs) chopped fresh parsley*
680 g	*(1½ lb) medium size shrimps, deveined*
	salt and pepper

Pour 15 mL (1 tbs) oil in casserole. Cover and microwave 1 minute.

Add red pepper and tomatoes; season with salt and pepper. Add garlic, basil, and parsley; cover and microwave 8 to 10 minutes.

Heat remaining oil in frying pan on stove top. When oil begins to smoke, add shrimps and cook 2 minutes. Do not stir.

Turn shrimps and continue cooking 1 minute.

Place shrimps on service platter and top with tomato mixture. Serve with rice.

Technique

1 Here is the tomato and pepper mixture after 8 to 10 minutes in microwave.

2 Sauté shrimps in hot oil.

→

Technique : Shrimp Catherine (continued)

3 Turn shrimps and continue cooking.

Shrimp Sandwiches

(serves 4)

Setting :	HIGH
Cooking time :	5 minutes
Utensil :	2 L casserole

350 g	*(¾ lb) medium size shrimps, deveined and washed*
50 mL	*(¼ cup) cold water*
½	*celery stalk, finely chopped*
1	*shallot, finely chopped*
15 mL	*(1 tbs) finely chopped parsley*
75 mL	*(1/3 cup) mayonnaise*
5 mL	*(1 tsp) curry powder*
	juice 1 lemon
	salt and pepper

Place shrimps in casserole. Add water and lemon juice ; cover and microwave 3 minutes.

Stir well and continue to microwave 2 minutes. Let shrimps stand in hot liquid 2 to 3 minutes.

Cool shrimps under cold water, drain, and chop. Place in mixing bowl.

Add celery, shallots, and parsley.

Mix mayonnaise with curry powder ; incorporate to shrimp mixture. Mix until well blended and season to taste.

Spread mixture over toasted bread and garnish with lettuce.

Serve.

Bacon Surprise

(serves 4)

Setting:	**HIGH**
Cooking time:	**9 minutes**
Utensil:	**Plate**

8	*bacon slices*
8	*commercial bread sticks*
125 mL	*(½ cup) grated cheese*

Coat bacon slices with cheese and wrap around bread sticks.

Set on plate and cover with sheet of paper towel. Microwave 9 minutes.

Remove and sprinkle with cheese. Serve.

Technique

1 Coat bacon slices with cheese and wrap around bread sticks.

2 Set on plate and cover with sheet of paper towel.

Ham and Asparagus with Hollandaise Sauce

(serves 4)

Technique

Setting:	HIGH
Cooking time:	4 minutes
Utensil:	30 × 20 × 5 cm (11¾ × 7½ × 1¾ in) rectangular casserole

8	*slices cooked ham*
125 mL	*(½ cup) grated mozzarella cheese*
32	*cooked asparagus**
375 mL	*(1½ cups) hot white sauce*** hollandaise sauce****

Sprinkle ham with grated cheese. Place 4 asparagus on each ham slice and roll. Place in casserole.

Pour white sauce over ham rolls, cover and microwave 3 minutes.

Top with hollandaise sauce. Microwave, uncovered, 1 minute.

Serve.

* See technique.   ** See page 21.   *** See page 29.

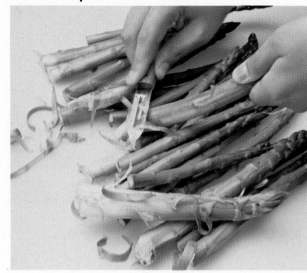

1 To cook asparagus, peel.

4 Sprinkle ham with grated cheese.

5 Place 4 asparagus on each ham slice.

2　Place asparagus in casserole. Add water and salt. Cover with sheet of plastic wrap; microwave 12 minutes at HIGH.

3　Prick asparagus with point of a knife to test if cooked. Drain well.

6　Roll and place in casserole.

7　Pour white sauce over ham rolls, cover and microwave 3 minutes.

Chicken Bouchées

(serves 4)

Setting:	HIGH and MEDIUM
Cooking time:	22 minutes in microwave
Utensil:	2 L casserole

30 mL	*(2 tbs) butter*
1	*chicken breast, skinned, deboned, and cut in 2*
227 g	*(½ lb) fresh mushrooms, washed and diced*
15 mL	*(1 tbs) chopped fresh parsley*
2	*shallots, chopped*
500 mL	*(2 cups) hot, thick white sauce ****
125 mL	*(½ cup) grated Gruyère cheese*
	pinch nutmeg
	salt and pepper

Place 15 mL (1 tbs) butter in casserole. Microwave 1 minute at HIGH.

Add chicken breast; season with salt and pepper. Cover and microwave 8 minutes at MEDIUM.

Turn chicken, cover and continue to microwave 7 minutes.

Remove chicken, cool and dice.

Add remaining butter to casserole. Add mushrooms and season with salt and pepper; cover and microwave 3 minutes at HIGH.

Add parsley, shallots, diced chicken, white sauce, and nutmeg. Mix well. Microwave 3 minutes at HIGH.

Stuff flakey pastry bouchées ** with mixture. Sprinkle with cheese. Melt cheese in conventional oven set at broil, for 2 minutes.

Serve.

 * See page 21.
** Available at supermarkets. Miniature vol-au-vent pastry can also be used.

Eggs Benedict

(serves 4)

Setting:	HIGH and MEDIUM
Cooking time:	5 minutes
Utensil:	30 × 20 × 5 cm (11¾ × 7½ × 1¾ in) rectangular casserole and 2 L casserole

4	*English muffins*
4	*slices ham*
750 mL	*(3 cups) water*
5 mL	*(1 tsp) vinegar*
4	*fresh eggs*
375 mL	*(1½ cups) hollandaise sauce ****
	salt and pepper

Place muffins in rectangular casserole. Place slice of ham on each and set casserole aside.

Pour water in 2 L casserole and bring to boil in microwave. Add salt and vinegar.

Break eggs, one at a time, in small bowl. Delicately pierce yolks and slowly slide eggs into boiling water. Cover and microwave 4 minutes at HIGH.

Let eggs stand in hot water 2 to 3 minutes.

Drain eggs well and place over ham. Top with hollandaise sauce and microwave 1 minute at MEDIUM.

* See page 29.

Technique

1 Place muffins in rectangular casserole. Place slice of ham on each.

2 Break eggs, one at a time, in small bowl. Delicately pierce yolk.

3 Place poached eggs over ham.

4 Top with hollandaise sauce.

Soups

Cream of Watercress

(serves 4)

Technique

Setting: HIGH
Cooking time: 23 minutes
Utensil: 3 L casserole

15 mL	*(1 tbs) butter*
2	*onions, peeled and sliced*
1 mL	*(¼ tsp) basil*
4	*potatoes, peeled and sliced*
1	*bunch watercress, well washed*
500 mL	*(2 cups) cold milk*
250 mL	*(1 cup) cold water*
	several drops Worcestershire sauce
	paprika to taste
	salt and pepper

Place butter, onions, basil, and Worcestershire sauce in casserole. Cover and microwave 3 minutes.

Add potatoes and season with salt and pepper. Sprinkle with paprika.

Add watercress, milk, and water; cover and microwave 15 minutes.

Remove casserole, mix well and cover. Continue to microwave 5 minutes.

Pass mixture through food mill, using attachment with medium size holes.

Serve.

1 Place butter, onions, basil, and Worcestershire sauce in casserole. Cover and microwave.

3 Add watercress.

Cream of Asparagus

(serves 4)

Setting:	**HIGH**
Cooking time:	**24 minutes**
Utensil:	**2 L round casserole**

50 mL	*(¼ cup) water*
454 g	*(1 lb) asparagus stems, washed*
15 mL	*(1 tbs) butter*
60 mL	*(4 tbs) flour*
750 mL	*(3 cups) hot chicken stock* *
30 mL	*(2 tbs) 35% cream*
	asparagus tips, diced for garnish

Pour water into casserole and bring to boil in microwave.

Add asparagus stems to water and season with salt. Add butter.

Cover with sheet of plastic wrap; microwave 7 minutes.

Turn casserole a ½ turn; continue to microwave 7 minutes.

Add flour, stirring between spoonfuls.

Mix well; microwave, uncovered, 2 minutes.

Mix in chicken stock with whisk. Microwave, uncovered, 4 minutes.

Stir well and continue to microwave 4 minutes.

Pass mixture through food mill, using attachment with large holes. Add cream, mix and correct seasoning.

Garnish with asparagus tips before serving.

* See page 55.

2 Add potatoes and season with salt and pepper. Sprinkle with paprika.

4 Add liquids, cover and microwave.

Cream of Vegetables

(serves 4)

Setting: HIGH
Cooking time: 24 minutes
Utensil: 2 L round casserole

2	*large potatoes, peeled and diced*
125 mL	*(½ cup) water*
2	*carrots, diced*
1	*celery stalk, diced*
5 mL	*(1 tsp) butter*
1 mL	*(¼ tsp) thyme*
2 mL	*(½ tsp) oregano*
½	*cucumber, peeled, seeded, and diced*
1	*green pepper, diced*
750 mL	*(3 cups) hot chicken stock* *
	dash crushed chillies
	salt and pepper

Place potatoes in casserole; season and add water.

Cover with sheet of plastic wrap; microwave 6 minutes.

Mix well and add carrots, celery, butter, and spices. Cover and microwave 6 minutes.

Add cucumbers, green pepper, and chicken stock. Correct seasoning, cover and microwave 12 minutes.

Remove vegetables from casserole and purée in blender. Transfer purée to mixing bowl. Add cooking liquid and stir well.

Season to taste and serve.

* See page 55.

Cream of Mushrooms

(serves 4)

Setting: HIGH
Cooking time: 20 minutes
Utensil: 2 L round casserole

454 g	*(1 lb) mushrooms, washed and sliced*
45 mL	*(3 tbs) chopped onion*
125 mL	*(½ cup) water*
15 mL	*(1 tbs) butter*
60 mL	*(4 tbs) flour*
500 mL	*(2 cups) hot chicken stock* *
30 mL	*(2 tbs) 35% cream*
	several drops lemon juice
	chopped parsley
	salt and pepper

Place mushrooms, onion, water, butter, and lemon juice in casserole. Season with salt and pepper.

Cover with sheet of plastic wrap; microwave 5 minutes.

Turn casserole a ½ turn; continue to microwave 5 minutes.

Add flour, mixing between spoonfuls. Microwave, uncovered, 2 minutes.

Add chicken stock and microwave 4 minutes.

Stir well and continue to microwave 4 minutes.

Remove casserole, mix rapidly, and add cream. Mix and season to taste.

Sprinkle with chopped parsley. Serve.

* See page 55.

Cream of Endives and Potatoes

(serves 4)

Setting: HIGH
Cooking time: 21 minutes
Utensil: 2 L round casserole

15 mL	*(1 tbs) butter*
30 mL	*(2 tbs) chopped onion*
3	*endives, washed, cut in 4, and sliced*
2	*potatoes, peeled and sliced*
5 mL	*(1 tsp) chopped parsley*
875 mL	*(3½ cups) hot chicken stock* *
30 mL	*(2 tbs) 35% cream*
125 mL	*(¼ cup) croutons*
	chopped chives
	salt and pepper

Place butter and onion in casserole; cover with sheet of plastic wrap and microwave 3 minutes.

Stir mixture well. Add endives and potatoes; season and add spices.

Cover and microwave 8 minutes.

Add chicken stock and season; microwave, uncovered, 10 minutes.

Pass mixture through sieve. Reserve stock and purée vegetables in blender.

Place purée vegetables with stock and add cream. Mix well and sprinkle with chives.

Garnish soup with croutons. Serve.

* See page 55.

Cream of Spinach

(serves 4)

Setting: HIGH
Cooking time: 14 minutes
Utensil: 2 L round casserole

2	*bunches fresh spinach, well washed*
1	*garlic clove, smashed and chopped*
15 mL	*(1 tbs) butter*
60 mL	*(4 tbs) flour*
1 mL	*(¼ tsp) nutmeg*
500 mL	*(2 cups) hot chicken stock* *
60 mL	*(4 tbs) 35% cream*
	several drops lemon juice
	pinch sugar
	salt and pepper

Place spinach, garlic, and butter in casserole. Press spinach with hands. Season with salt and pepper; sprinkle with lemon juice.

Cover with sheet of plastic wrap; microwave 6 minutes.

Remove spinach from casserole and chop. Replace spinach in cooking liquid.

Add flour, stirring between spoonfuls.

Add sugar and nutmeg; season with salt and pepper. Clean sides of casserole with spatula.

Microwave, uncovered, 3 minutes.

Add chicken stock, stir and microwave, uncovered, 5 minutes.

Purée mixture in blender and correct seasoning.

Add cream. Serve.

* See page 55.

Cream of Cauliflower

Cream of Cauliflower

(serves 4)

Setting: HIGH
Cooking time: 22 minutes
Utensil: 2.5 or 3 L round casserole

5 mL	*(1 tsp) butter*
45 mL	*(3 tbs) chopped onion*
1	*small cauliflower, cut into flowerets*
5 mL	*(1 tsp) chopped parsley*
75 mL	*(5 tbs) flour*
1.2 L	*(5 cups) hot chicken stock (recipe follows)*
	pinch thyme
	salt and pepper

Place butter, onions, cauliflower, parsley, and thyme in casserole. Season with salt and pepper; cover and microwave 10 minutes.

Add flour, mixing between spoonfuls.

Add half of chicken stock; mix well.

Add remaining chicken stock and mix well. Microwave, uncovered, 6 minutes.

Stir well and continue to microwave 6 minutes. Serve.

Chicken Stock

(quick method)

15 mL	*(1 tbs) oil*
1	*onion, peeled and sliced*
1	*celery stalk, sliced*
30 mL	*(2 tbs) chicken bouillon mix*
1.5 L	*(6 cups) cold water*
1	*bouquet garni*
	salt and pepper

Heat oil in saucepan over medium heat. When hot, add onion and celery; cook 3 minutes.

Add chicken bouillon mix and water; mix well. Season with salt and pepper; drop in bouquet garni.

Bring to boil and cook, over low heat, 7 minutes.

Pass stock through sieve and refrigerate.

Technique

1 Place butter, onion, cauliflower, parsley, and thyme in casserole. Season with salt and pepper; cover and microwave 10 minutes.

2 Add flour, mixing well.

Cream of Broccoli

(serves 4)

Setting: HIGH
Cooking time: 24 minutes
Utensil: 2 L round casserole

1	*small onion, peeled and chopped*
1	*head broccoli, washed and cut into flowerets*
15 mL	*(1 tbs) butter*
3	*potatoes, peeled and sliced*
15 mL	*(1 tbs) chopped parsley*
1 mL	*(¼ tsp) oregano*
125 mL	*(½ cup) water*
500 mL	*(2 cups) hot chicken stock**
125 mL	*(½ cup) 35% cream*
	pinch thyme
	salt and pepper

Place onion, broccoli, and butter in casserole. Cover with sheet of plastic wrap; microwave 2 minutes.

Add potatoes, parsley, thyme, and oregano. Season with salt and pepper; mix well.

Add water and cover with sheet of plastic wrap; microwave 5 minutes.

Stir and continue to microwave 5 minutes.

Add chicken stock and microwave 6 minutes.

Stir and continue to microwave 6 minutes.

Pass mixture through food mill. Mix with whisk and add cream.

Refrigerate 6 hours. Serve.

* See page 55.

Cream of Carrots

(serves 4)

Setting: HIGH
Cooking time: 24 minutes
Utensil: 2 L round casserole

1	*small onion, peeled and chopped*
3	*carrots, peeled and sliced*
15 mL	*(1 tbs) butter*
2	*potatoes, peeled and sliced*
15 mL	*(1 tbs) chopped parsley*
1 mL	*(¼ tsp) oregano*
125 mL	*(½ cup) water*
500 mL	*(2 cups) hot chicken stock**
125 mL	*(½ cup) 35% cream*
	pinch thyme
	salt and pepper

Place onion, carrots, and butter in casserole. Cover with sheet of plastic wrap; microwave 2 minutes.

Add potatoes, parsley, thyme, and oregano; season with salt and pepper. Mix well.

Add water and cover with sheet of plastic wrap; microwave 5 minutes.

Stir and continue to microwave 5 minutes.

Add chicken stock and microwave 6 minutes.

Stir and continue to microwave 6 minutes.

Pass mixture through food mill. Mix with whisk and add cream.

Refrigerate 6 hours. Serve.

* See page 55.

Cream of Cucumber

(serves 4)

Setting: HIGH
Cooking time: 20 minutes
Utensil: 2.5 or 3 L round casserole

5 mL	*(1 tsp) butter*
45 mL	*(3 tbs) chopped onion*
3	*potatoes, peeled and sliced*
1	*cucumber, peeled and sliced*
750 mL	*(3 cups) very hot chicken stock* *
50 mL	*(¼ cup) 35% cream*
	pinch tarragon
	pinch parsley
	salt and pepper

Place butter, vegetables, tarragon, and parsley in casserole. Cover and microwave 6 minutes.

Stir and continue to microwave 6 minutes.

Add chicken stock, stir and season to taste. Microwave 8 minutes.

Pass mixture through food mill. Add cream and stir.

Sprinkle with chopped parsley. Serve.

* See page 55.

Cream of Lentils

(serves 4)

Setting: HIGH
Cooking time: 48 minutes
Utensil: 3 L casserole

300 mL	*(1¼ cups) green lentils, washed*
15 mL	*(1 tbs) butter*
1	*onion, peeled and finely chopped*
1	*celery stalk, washed and diced*
1 L	*(4 cups) hot chicken stock* *
1	*bay leaf*
50 mL	*(¼ cup) 35% cream*
	pinch thyme
	pinch powdered anise seed
	salt and pepper

Place lentils in cold water for 30 minutes. Drain and set aside.

Place butter, onion, and celery in casserole. Add herbs, cover and microwave 3 minutes.

Add lentils, chicken stock, and bay leaf. Cover and microwave 45 minutes.

Pass mixture through food mill, using attachment with medium holes.

Add cream and stir well.

Serve with toasted French bread.

* See page 55.

Cream of Parsley

(serves 4)

Setting: **HIGH**
Cooking time: **23 minutes**
Utensil: **3 L casserole**

15 mL	*(1 tbs) butter*
1½	*onions, peeled and finely chopped*
¼	*bunch parsley, washed and drained*
½	*bunch watercress, washed and drained*
½	*turnip, peeled and sliced*
3	*potatoes, peeled and sliced*
750 mL	*(3 cups) hot chicken stock* *
1 mL	*(¼ tsp) savory*
3	*slices cooked ham, cut into julienne*
	salt and pepper

Place butter, onions, parsley, and watercress in casserole. Season with salt and pepper; cover and microwave 3 minutes.

Add turnip, potatoes, chicken stock, and savory. Season and mix well. Cover and microwave 20 minutes.

Pass mixture through food mill.

Garnish with sliced ham. Serve.

* See page 55.

Cream of Tomatoes

(serves 4)

Setting: **HIGH**
Cooking time: **16 minutes**
Utensil: **2 L round casserole**

5 mL	*(1 tsp) butter*
1	*onion, peeled and chopped*
1	*garlic clove, smashed and chopped*
1	*796 mL (28 oz) can tomatoes, drained and chopped*
45 mL	*(3 tbs) tomato paste*
5 mL	*(1 tsp) sugar*
2 mL	*(½ tsp) basil*
1 mL	*(¼ tsp) oregano*
30 mL	*(2 tbs) flour*
500 mL	*(2 cups) hot chichen stock* *
30 mL	*(2 tbs) 35% cream*
	dash crushed chillies
	pinch cloves
	several drops Tabasco sauce
	salt and pepper

Place butter, onion, and garlic in casserole. Cover with sheet of plastic wrap; microwave 2 minutes.

Add tomatoes, mix well, and add tomato paste. Mix again; season with salt and pepper.

Add sugar and spices; cover and microwave 4 minutes.

Incorporate flour. Add chicken stock; microwave, uncovered, 10 minutes.

Pass mixture through food mill and correct seasoning.

Add cream and serve.

* See page 55.

Potage Parmentier

(serves 4)

Setting: HIGH
Cooking time: 24 minutes
Utensil: 2 L round casserole

1	*small onion, peeled and chopped*
15 mL	*(1 tbs) butter*
3	*potatoes, peeled and sliced*
15 mL	*(1 tbs) chopped parsley*
1 mL	*(¼ tsp) oregano*
125 mL	*(½ cup) water*
500 mL	*(2 cups) hot chicken stock* *
45 mL	*(3 tbs) 35% cream*
	pinch thyme
	salt and pepper

Place onion and butter in casserole. Cover with sheet of plastic wrap; microwave 2 minutes.

Add potatoes, parsley, thyme, and oregano. Season with salt and pepper; mix well.

Add water, cover with sheet of plastic wrap and microwave 5 minutes.

Stir and continue to microwave 5 minutes.

Add chicken stock; microwave 6 minutes.

Stir and continue to microwave 6 minutes.

Pass mixture through food mill. Mix with whisk and add cream.

Garnish with chopped chives. Serve hot or cold.

* See page 55.

Garden Vegetable Soup

(serves 4)

Setting: HIGH
Cooking time: 27 minutes
Utensil: 3 L casserole

30 mL	*(2 tbs) butter*
1	*zucchini, sliced*
½	*green pepper, sliced*
2	*carrots, peeled and sliced*
2	*potatoes, peeled and sliced*
2 mL	*(½ tsp) oregano*
1 L	*(4 cups) hot chicken stock* *
	salt and pepper
	toasted rounds of bread with cheese for garnish

Place butter, zucchini, green pepper, carrots, and potatoes in casserole. Season with salt and pepper.

Add oregano; cover and microwave 15 minutes.

Add chicken stock and stir well. Correct seasoning, cover and microwave 12 minutes.

Arrange toasted bread in soup just before serving.

* See page 55.

Puréed Carrot and Potato Soup

Puréed Carrot and Potato Soup

(serves 4)

Setting: **HIGH**
Cooking time: **34 to 36 minutes**
Utensil: **2.5 or 3 L round casserole**

5 mL	*(1 tsp) butter*
1	*large onion, peeled and chopped*
5 mL	*(1 tsp) chopped parsley*
3	*large carrots, peeled and sliced*
3	*large potatoes, peeled and sliced*
1	*bay leaf*
1.1 L	*(4½ cups) hot chicken stock* *
50 mL	*(¼ cup) 15% or 10% cream*
	pinch thyme
	salt and pepper

Place butter, onion, and parsley in casserole. Season with salt and pepper; cover and microwave 4 minutes.

Add carrots, potatoes, and thyme; mix well. Add bay leaf and chicken stock; season with salt and pepper. Microwave, uncovered, 15 minutes.

Turn casserole a ½ turn and continue to microwave 15 to 17 minutes.

Pass mixture through food mill.

Add cream, stir well, and serve.

* See page 55.

Potage St-Germain

(serves 4)

Setting: **HIGH**
Cooking time: **30 minutes**
Utensil: **2.5 or 3 L round casserole**

15 mL	*(1 tbs) bacon fat*
1	*small onion, peeled and chopped*
1	*garlic clove, smashed and chopped*
5 mL	*(1 tsp) chopped parsley*
250 mL	*(1 cup) split green peas, soaked 8 hours in water*
1	*bay leaf*
1.1 L	*(4½ cups) hot chicken stock* *
	pinch thyme
	salt and pepper

Place bacon fat, onion, garlic, and parsley in casserole. Cover and microwave 3 minutes.

Drain peas well and add to casserole. Mix well and season with salt and pepper. Add thyme and bay leaf.

Stir in chicken stock. Cover and microwave 15 minutes.

Remove cover and microwave 12 minutes. Serve.

* See page 55.

Potage Flemish

(serves 4)

Setting:	HIGH
Cooking time:	27 minutes
Utensil:	3 L casserole

454 g	*(1 lb) Brussels sprouts, well washed*
15 mL	*(1 tbs) butter*
3	*potatoes, peeled and sliced*
750 mL	*(3 cups) hot chicken stock* *
2 mL	*(½ tsp) basil*
	pinch thyme
	salt and pepper

Trim Brussels sprouts and using sharp knife, form a cross on base.

Place Brussels sprouts in casserole. Add butter and potatoes; season with salt and pepper. Cover and microwave 12 minutes.

Add chicken stock and herbs; correct seasoning. Cover and microwave 15 minutes.

Pass mixture through food mill, using attachment with medium holes. Serve.

* See page 55.

Soupe Dauphinoise

(serves 4)

Setting:	HIGH
Cooking time:	19 minutes
Utensil:	3 L casserole

15 mL	*(1 tbs) butter*
½	*turnip, diced*
1	*zucchini, peeled and diced*
3	*potatoes, peeled and diced*
15 mL	*(1 tbs) chopped chives*
500 mL	*(2 cups) hot water*
500 mL	*(2 cups) hot milk*
¼	*bunch watercress, shredded*
	pinch thyme
	salt and pepper

Place butter, turnip, zucchini, potatoes, and herbs in casserole. Season with salt and pepper; cover and microwave 15 minutes.

Add water and milk. Stir and season to taste. Microwave, uncovered, 4 minutes.

Add watercress, stir well, and serve.

Soupe Aïgo

(serves 4)

Setting: **HIGH**
Cooking time: **38 minutes**
Utensil: **1 L casserole and 3 L casserole**

5 mL	*(1 tsp) oil*
1	*large onion, peeled and chopped*
1	*leek, white section only, washed and sliced*
2	*garlic cloves, smashed and chopped*
3	*potatoes, peeled and sliced*
1	*796 mL (28 oz) can tomatoes, drained and coarsely chopped*
750 mL	*(3 cups) water*
4	*poached eggs*
	zest ½ orange, cut in strips
	pinch fennel
	pinch saffron
	salt and pepper

In 1 L casserole, place orange zest. Cover with 50 mL (¼ cup) water. Cover and microwave 2 minutes. Drain and set aside.

Pour oil into 3 L casserole. Add onion, leek, garlic, and herbs. Season with salt and pepper; cover and microwave 6 minutes.

Add potatoes, tomatoes, and water. Correct seasoning, cover and microwave 30 minutes.

Pass mixture through food mill.

Ladle soup into bowls and delicately place poached egg on top.

Garnish with orange zest before serving.

Onion Soup

Onion Soup

(serves 4)

Setting:	HIGH
Cooking time:	25 minutes in microwave
Utensil:	2 L casserole

4	**large onions, peeled and finely sliced**
15 mL	**(1 tbs) butter**
15 mL	**(1 tbs) chopped parsley**
2 mL	**(½ tsp) oregano**
1	**bay leaf**
5 mL	**(1 tsp) soya sauce**
5 mL	**(1 tsp) maple syrup**
30 mL	**(2 tbs) cognac**
1 L	**(4 cups) hot beef stock**
4	**slices toasted French bread**
175 mL	**(¾ cup) grated Gruyère cheese**
	salt and pepper

Preheat conventional oven to grill (broil).

Place onions in casserole. Add butter, spices, and bay leaf.

Add soya sauce and maple syrup; correct seasoning.

Cover with sheet of plastic wrap; microwave 15 minutes.

Stir onions well. Add cognac and beef stock; mix well.

Microwave, uncovered, 10 minutes.

Ladle soup into bowls. Set toasted bread on top and sprinkle with grated cheese.

Place in conventional oven at grill (broil), 6 to 7 minutes. Serve.

Technique

1 Place onions in casserole. Add butter, spices, and bay leaf.

2 Add soya sauce and maple syrup, which will brown onions.

Technique : Onion Soup (continued)

3   Here are the cooked onions.

4   Add cognac.

5   Add hot beef stock.

6   Ladle soup into bowls, top with toasted bread and sprinkle with cheese.

Yellow Pea Soup

(serves 4)

Setting: **HIGH**
Cooking time: **49 minutes**
Utensil: **3 L casserole**

15 mL	*(1 tbs) butter*
1	*celery stalk, diced*
1	*onion, peeled and diced*
2	*carrots, peeled and diced*
1	*green pepper, diced*
1	*garlic clove, smashed and chopped*
250 mL	*(1 cup) split yellow peas, soaked 8 hours in cold water and drained*
1.2 L	*(5 cups) hot chicken stock* *
1	*bay leaf*
3	*parsley sprigs*
	pinch thyme
	salt and pepper

Place butter, celery, onion, carrots, green pepper, and garlic in casserole. Cover and microwave 4 minutes.

Add yellow peas, chicken stock, and herbs. Season with salt and pepper; stir well. Microwave, uncovered, 45 minutes.

Pass soup through food mill, using attachment with medium holes.

Serve.

* See page 55.

Tomato Soup

(serves 4)

Technique

1 The onion after 2 minutes in microwave.

Setting:	HIGH
Cooking time:	21 minutes
Utensil:	2.5 or 3 L round casserole

5 mL	*(1 tsp) butter*
5 mL	*(1 tsp) chopped parsley*
45 mL	*(3 tbs) chopped onion*
3	*large tomatoes, diced*
2 mL	*(½ tsp) oregano*
15 mL	*(1 tbs) tomato paste*
1.2 L	*(4 cups) very hot chicken stock* *
500 mL	*(2 cups) medium bow pasta*
	pinch sugar
	salt and pepper

Place butter, parsley, and onion in casserole. Cover and microwave 2 minutes.

Add tomatoes, oregano, and season with salt and pepper. Stir very well and sprinkle with sugar. Cover and microwave 4 minutes.

Add tomato paste and chicken stock. Stir and correct seasoning.

Add pasta, cover and microwave 6 minutes.

Stir and continue to microwave 6 minutes.

Stir well and continue to microwave 3 minutes. Serve.

* See page 55.

Fish Soup

(serves 4)

2 The tomatoes after 4 minutes in microwave.

3 Add pasta.

Setting: **HIGH**
Cooking time: **14 minutes**
Utensil: **2.5 or 3 L round casserole**

15 mL	*(1 tbs) butter*
1	*small onion, peeled and sliced*
5 mL	*(1 tsp) chopped parsley*
3	*medium size potatoes, peeled and finely sliced*
1	*large tomato, diced*
227 g	*(½ lb) turbot filets, cubed*
1 L	*(4 cups) hot, very light chicken stock* *
	pinch fennel
	salt and white pepper

Place butter, onion, parsley, and potatoes in casserole. Season with salt and pepper; add fennel. Cover and microwave 4 minutes.

Stir and continue to microwave 4 minutes.

Add tomato and fish; mix well.

Add chicken stock and stir well; microwave, uncovered, 6 minutes.

Serve.

* See page 55.

Chicken Soup with Vegetables

(serves 4)

Add celery; microwave 2 minutes.

Add pea pods, mushrooms, soya sauce, and thyme. Microwave 5 minutes.

Sprinkle with chopped parsley, pepper well, and serve.

* See page 55.

Setting:	HIGH
Cooking time:	25 minutes
Utensil:	2.5 or 3 L round casserole

1.2 L	(5 cups) chicken stock *
1	chicken breast, skinned, deboned, and cut in strips
½	celery stalk, sliced
8	pea pods, washed and trimmed
5	fresh large mushrooms, washed and sliced
5 mL	(1 tsp) soya sauce
5 mL	(1 tsp) chopped parsley
	pinch thyme
	pepper from mill

Pour chicken stock into casserole. Microwave, uncovered, 15 minutes.

Add chicken and stir with wooden spoon. Continue to microwave 3 minutes.

Pork and Soya Soup

(serves 4)

Setting:	HIGH
Cooking time:	9 minutes
Utensil:	2.5 or 3 L round casserole

5 mL	(1 tsp) butter
1	small garlic clove, smashed and chopped
½	green pepper, cut into julienne
½	celery stalk, cut into julienne
1	carrot, cut into julienne
1	pork filet, fat trimmed and sliced slantwise 1.2 cm (½ in) thick
1.2 L	(5 cups) hot chicken stock *
5 mL	(1 tsp) soya sauce
	salt and pepper

Place butter, garlic, and vegetables in casserole. Pepper well and cover; microwave 4 minutes.

Add sliced pork; continue to microwave 2 minutes.

Add chicken stock and soya sauce; microwave 3 minutes. Serve.

* See page 55.

→

Corn Soup

(serves 4)

Setting:	HIGH
Cooking time:	18 minutes
Utensil:	2.5 or 3 L round casserole

5 mL	*(1 tsp) butter*
5 mL	*(1 tsp) chopped parsley*
45 mL	*(3 tbs) chopped onion*
3	*ears fresh corn, kernels removed*
1	*celery stalk, diced*
60 mL	*(4 tbs) flour*
1 L	*(4 cups) very hot chicken stock* *
	pinch thyme
	pinch oregano
	salt and pepper

Place butter, parsley, onion, corn kernels, and celery in casserole. Season with salt and pepper; add herbs. Cover and microwave 8 minutes.

Add flour, mixing between spoonfuls. Microwave, uncovered, 2 minutes.

Stir well and add half of chicken stock. Mix until blended.

Add remaining stock, stir, and microwave 4 minutes.

Stir and continue to microwave 4 minutes.

Correct seasoning and serve.

* See page 55.

Minestrone

(serves 4)

Setting:	HIGH
Cooking time:	20 minutes
Utensil:	3 L casserole

15 mL	*(1 tbs) butter*
1	*onion, peeled and finely chopped*
2	*celery stalks, diced*
1	*large carrot, diced*
½	*turnip, diced*
1	*796 mL (28 oz) can tomatoes*
500 mL	*(2 cups) hot chicken stock**
125 mL	*(½ cup) medium bow pasta*
	pinch oregano
	pinch sugar
	salt and pepper

Place butter, onion, celery, carrot, turnip, and oregano in casserole. Season with salt and pepper; cover and microwave 5 minutes.

Add tomatoes, chicken stock, pasta, and sugar. Cover and microwave 15 minutes. Serve.

* See page 55.

Brabatine Soup

(serves 4)

Setting:	HIGH
Cooking time:	20 minutes
Utensil:	3 L casserole

3	*carrots, peeled and sliced*
1	*small turnip, sliced*
1	*leek, white section only, sliced*
30 mL	*(2 tbs) butter*
1	*small onion, peeled and chopped*
1 L	*(4 cups) hot milk*
	pinch thyme
	salt and pepper
	garlic croutons for garnish

Place carrots, turnip, and leek in mixing bowl. Cover with cold water and soak 10 minutes. Drain and set aside.

Place butter in casserole. Add onion and cover; microwave 3 minutes.

Add drained vegetables and herbs. Season with salt and pepper; cover and microwave 12 minutes.

Add milk; microwave, uncovered, 5 minutes.

Garnish with garlic croutons before serving.

Chinese Soup

(serves 4)

Setting: HIGH
Cooking time: 10 minutes
Utensil: 2 L round casserole

2	Chinese noodle nests
500 mL	(2 cups) water
15 mL	(1 tbs) oil
1	banana pepper, sliced
4	Chinese cabbage leaves, sliced
3	green onions, sliced
1	celery stalk, sliced
125 mL	(½ cup) hot chicken stock *
750 mL	(3 cups) hot chicken stock
5 mL	(1 tsp) soya sauce
	salt and pepper

Place noodles, water, and salt in casserole. Cover with sheet of plastic wrap; microwave 4 minutes.

Stir to separate noodles; cover and continue to microwave 1 minute.

Remove casserole and place noodles under cold water.

Place oil, banana pepper, cabbage, green onions, and celery in casserole. Season with salt and pepper.

Add 125 mL (½ cup) chicken stock; cover and microwave 5 minutes.

Place cooked vegetables in soup-tureen.

Add 750 mL (3 cups) hot chicken stock, soya sauce, and drained noodles.** Serve.

  * See page 55.
** Run hot water over noodles before adding to soup-tureen.

Vichyssoise

(serves 4)

Setting: HIGH
Cooking time: 24 minutes
Utensil: 2 L round casserole

1	small onion, peeled and chopped
2	leeks, white section only, washed and sliced
15 mL	(1 tbs) butter
3	potatoes, peeled and sliced
15 mL	(1 tbs) chopped parsley
1 mL	(¼ tsp) oregano
125 mL	(½ cup) water
500 mL	(2 cups) hot chicken stock *
125 mL	(½ cup) 35% cream
	pinch thyme
	salt and pepper

Place onion, leeks, and butter in casserole. Cover with sheet of plastic wrap; microwave 2 minutes.

Add potatoes, parsley, thyme, and oregano. Season with salt and pepper; mix well.

Add water; cover with sheet of plastic wrap and microwave 5 minutes.

Stir and continue to microwave 5 minutes.

Add chicken stock; microwave 6 minutes.

Stir again and microwave 6 minutes.

Pass mixture through food mill. Mix well with whisk and add cream.

Refrigerate 6 hours. Serve.

* See page 55.

Eggs
and
Quiches

Several Important Points Regarding Quiche

— We have given you a dough recipe, but you may use a commercial dough if desired. The cooking time will remain the same.
— Should you use a commercial dough, roll the dough to cover a 22 cm (9 in) microwave quiche plate.
— ATTENTION : Two settings, HIGH and MEDIUM, will be used for cooking quiche.
— Before cooking, prick dough with a fork.
— Brush dough with a mixture of : 1 egg yolk and 5 mL (1 tsp) soya sauce.
— For each quiche, it is necessary to pause 5 minutes before serving.
— To obtain a uniform cooking, heat the cream before using. However, do not allow the cream to boil.

Pie Dough

500 mL	(2 cups) all-purpose flour, sifted
250 mL	(1 cup) shortening, cut in pieces
60 to	
75 mL	(4 to 5 tbs) cold water
	pinch salt

Sift flour and salt together in mixing bowl. Make a well in middle of flour and add shortening. Incorporate, using pastry cutter, until mixture crumbles.

Add water and rapidly form ball.

Wrap dough in clean cloth or wax paper. Refrigerate 1 hour.

Roll dough and line quiche plate.

Technique : Frozen Pie Crust

1 Here is a frozen 22 cm (9 in) commercial pie crust.

2 Allow pie crust to unthaw several minutes. Carefully place pie crust in microwave quiche plate. Prick dough with fork and microwave 1 minute at HIGH.

3 Brush dough with mixture of egg and soya sauce. Microwave 4 minutes.

Quiche à la provençale

Quiche à la provençale

(serves 4)

Setting:	HIGH and MEDIUM
Cooking time:	27 minutes
Utensil:	22 cm (9 in) quiche plate or pie plate and 2 L round casserole

1	*pie crust*
5 mL	*(1 tsp) bacon fat*
45 mL	*(3 tbs) chopped onion*
1	*garlic clove, smashed and chopped*
1	*small zucchini, unpeeled and diced*
5 mL	*(1 tsp) chopped parsley*
125 mL	*(½ cup) diced mozzarella cheese*
2	*tomatoes, washed, cut in half and thickly sliced*
2	*beaten eggs*
50 mL	*(¼ cup) hot 10% or 15% cream*
50 mL	*(¼ cup) grated Gruyère cheese pinch basil salt and pepper*

Prick pie crust with fork.

Microwave 1 minute at HIGH.

Brush pie crust with mixture of egg and soya sauce.* Continue to microwave 4 minutes; set aside.

Place bacon fat, onion, garlic, zucchini, and parsley in casserole. Season with salt and pepper; cover and microwave 8 minutes at HIGH.

Drain mixture well and place in pie crust. Add mozzarella and tomatoes; season with salt and pepper.

Mix beaten eggs, cream, and basil together. Season and pour over tomatoes; microwave 7 minutes at MEDIUM.

Sprinkle quiche with grated Gruyère and turn a ½ turn. Continue to microwave 7 minutes.

Wait 5 minutes before serving.

* See: Several important points regarding quiche: page 76.

Bacon and Corn Quiche

(serves 4)

Setting:	HIGH and MEDIUM
Cooking time:	25 minutes
Utensil:	22 cm (9 in) quiche plate or pie plate and 2 L round casserole

1	*pie crust*
4	*slices bacon, diced*
45 mL	*(3 tbs) chopped onion*
½	*green pepper, diced*
1	*340 mL (12 oz) can corn kernels, well drained*
5 mL	*(1 tsp) chopped parsley*
2	*beaten eggs*
50 mL	*(¼ cup) hot 10% or 15% cream*
50 mL	*(¼ cup) grated cheddar cheese salt and pepper*

Prick dough with fork.

Microwave 1 minute at HIGH.

Brush pie crust with mixture of egg and soya sauce.* Continue to microwave 4 minutes; set aside.

→

Place bacon, onion, and green pepper in casserole. Cover and microwave 8 minutes at HIGH.

Drain mixture well and place in pie crust. Add corn and press down with hand. Season with salt and pepper; sprinkle with chopped parsley.

Mix beaten eggs with cream; pour over corn. Microwave 6 minutes at MEDIUM.

Sprinkle quiche with grated cheese. Turn a ½ turn and continue to microwave 6 minutes.

Wait 5 minutes before serving.

* See: Several important points regarding quiche: page 76.

Prick pie crust with fork.

Microwave 1 minute at HIGH.

Brush pie crust with mixture of egg and soya sauce.* Continue to microwave 4 minutes; set aside.

Place butter, mushrooms, parsley, lemon juice, and curry powder in casserole. Season with salt and pepper; cover and microwave 3 minutes at HIGH.

Sprinkle bottom of pie crust with half of grated cheese. Add crab meat and drained mushroom mixture.

Mix beaten eggs with cream; pour over mushroom mixture.

Sprinkle in remaining cheese. Microwave 5 minutes at MEDIUM.

Turn a ½ turn and continue to microwave 5 minutes.

Turn a ½ turn and continue to microwave 1 minute.

Wait 5 minutes before serving.

* See: Several important points regarding quiche: page 76.

Crab Quiche

(serves 4)

Setting:	HIGH and MEDIUM
Cooking time:	19 minutes
Utensil:	22 cm (9 in) quiche plate or pie plate and 2 L round casserole

1	*pie crust*
5 mL	*(1 tsp) butter*
250 mL	*(1 cup) mushrooms, diced*
15 mL	*(1 tbs) chopped parsley*
5 mL	*(1 tsp) curry powder*
125 mL	*(½ cup) grated cheddar cheese*
1	*142 g (5 oz) can crab meat, well drained*
3	*beaten eggs*
175 mL	*(¾ cup) hot 10% or 15% cream several drops lemon juice salt and pepper*

Tomato and Broccoli Quiche

(serves 4)

Setting:	HIGH and MEDIUM
Cooking time:	28 minutes
Utensil:	22 cm (9 in) quiche plate or pie plate and 2 L round casserole

1	*pie crust*
5 mL	*(1 tsp) oil*
30 mL	*(2 tbs) chopped onion*
1	*garlic clove, smashed and chopped*
1	*large tomato, peeled and diced*
1	*small broccoli, washed and cut in flowerets*
125 mL	*(½ cup) grated Gruyère cheese*
3	*beaten eggs*
125 mL	*(½ cup) hot 10% or 15% cream pinch oregano salt and pepper*

Prick pie crust with fork.

Microwave 1 minute at HIGH.

Brush pie crust with mixture of egg and soya sauce.* Continue to microwave 4 minutes; set aside.

Place oil, onion, garlic, and tomato in casserole. Season with salt and pepper; cover and microwave 8 minutes at HIGH.

Add broccoli and oregano; cover and continue to microwave 3 minutes.

Place half of grated cheese in bottom of pie crust. Drain vegetable mixture and place in pie crust.

Mix beaten eggs with cream; pour over vegetables. Sprinkle with remaining cheese.

Microwave 6 minutes at MEDIUM.

Turn quiche a ½ turn; continue to microwave 6 minutes.

Wait 5 minutes before serving.

* See: Several important points regarding quiche: page 76.

Chicken Quiche

(serves 4)

Setting:	HIGH and MEDIUM
Cooking time:	23 minutes
Utensil:	22 cm (9 in) quiche plate or pie plate and 2 L round casserole

1	*pie crust*
5 mL	*(1 tsp) butter*
1	*green pepper, cut in fine strips*
1	*large chicken breast, skinned, deboned, and diced*
1	*marinated red pepper, cut in strips*
5 mL	*(1 tsp) chopped parsley*
125 mL	*(½ cup) grated mozzarella cheese*
3	*beaten eggs*
125 mL	*(½ cup) hot 10% or 15% cream pinch nutmeg salt and pepper*

→

Prick pie crust with fork.

Microwave 1 minute at HIGH.

Brush pie crust with mixture of egg and soya sauce.* Continue to microwave 4 minutes; set aside.

Place butter and green pepper in casserole. Cover and microwave 4 minutes at HIGH.

Add chicken and marinated pepper; season with salt and pepper. Sprinkle with chopped parsley; cover and microwave 3 minutes at HIGH.

Sprinkle half of cheese in bottom of pie crust.

Drain chicken mixture well and place in pie crust.

Mix beaten eggs with cream and nutmeg; pour over chicken mixture. Sprinkle with remaining cheese.

Microwave 5 minutes at MEDIUM.

Turn quiche a ½ turn and continue to microwave 6 minutes.

Wait 5 minutes before serving.

* See: Several important points regarding quiche: page 76.

Technique

1 The pie crust after 5 minutes in microwave.

2 Sprinkle with grated cheese.

3 Add drained chicken and vegetable mixture.

Asparagus Quiche

(serves 4)

Setting:	HIGH and MEDIUM
Cooking time:	17 to 18 minutes
Utensil:	22 cm (9 in) quiche plate or pie plate

1	*pie crust*
125 mL	*(½ cup) grated Gruyère cheese*
1	*341 mL (12 oz) can green asparagus, well drained*
3	*beaten eggs*
250 mL	*(1 cup) hot 10% or 15% cream*
	pinch nutmeg
	salt and pepper

Prick pie crust with fork.

Microwave 1 minute at HIGH.

Brush pie crust with mixture of egg and soya sauce.* Continue to microwave 4 minutes.

Sprinkle bottom of pie crust with half of cheese. Add asparagus; season with salt and pepper. Add remaining cheese.

Mix beaten eggs with cream and nutmeg; pour over asparagus. Microwave 6 minutes at MEDIUM.

Turn quiche a ½ turn; continue to microwave 6 to 7 minutes.

Wait 5 minutes before serving.

* See: Several important points regarding quiche: page 76.

Technique

1 Brush pie crust with mixture of egg and soya sauce.

2 Place grated cheese and asparagus in pie crust.

Mushroom Quiche

Mushroom Quiche

(serves 4)

Setting:	HIGH and MEDIUM
Cooking time:	20 minutes
Utensil:	22 cm (9 in) quiche plate or pie plate and 2 L round casserole

1	*pie crust*
5 mL	*(1 tsp) butter*
10	*large mushrooms, sliced*
1	*shallot, chopped*
5 mL	*(1 tsp) chopped parsley*
175 mL	*(¾ cup) grated cheddar cheese*
3	*eggs*
250 mL	*(1 cup) hot 10% or 15% cream*
	pinch nutmeg
	salt and pepper

Prick pie crust with fork.

Microwave 1 minute at HIGH.

Brush pie crust with mixture of egg and soya sauce.* Continue to microwave 4 minutes; set aside.

Place butter, mushrooms, shallot, and parsley in casserole. Cover and microwave 3 minutes at HIGH.

Sprinkle 125 mL (½ cup) cheese in pie crust. Add drained mushroom mixture.

Beat eggs; incorporate cream and nutmeg. Mix well with whisk and season with salt and pepper. Pour over mushrooms.

Sprinkle remaining cheese. Microwave 6 minutes at MEDIUM.

Turn quiche a ½ turn and continue to microwave 6 minutes.

Wait 5 minutes before serving.

* See: Several important points regarding quiche: page 76.

Technique

Place grated cheese and mushroom mixture in pie crust.

Farmer's Quiche

Farmer's Quiche

(serves 4)

Setting:	HIGH and MEDIUM
Cooking time:	17 minutes in microwave
Utensil:	22 cm (9 in) quiche plate or pie plate

1	*pie crust*
5 mL	*(1 tsp) bacon fat*
2	*pork sausages, thickly sliced*
30 mL	*(2 tbs) chopped onion*
2	*cooking apples, peeled and thinly sliced*
15 mL	*(1 tbs) chopped parsley*
125 mL	*(½ cup) grated cheddar cheese*
3	*beaten eggs*
250 mL	*(1 cup) hot 10% or 15% cream*
	pinch cinnamon
	salt and pepper

Prick pie crust with fork; set aside.

Melt bacon fat in sauté pan on stove top. Add sausages and onion; cook 3 to 4 minutes over medium heat.

Add apples and sprinkle with parsley and cinnamon. Season with salt and pepper; continue cooking 2 to 3 minutes.

Microwave pie crust 1 minute at HIGH.

Brush pie crust with mixture of egg and soya sauce.* Continue to microwave 4 minutes.

Using slotted spoon, place sausage mixture in pie crust. Sprinkle with cheese.

Mix eggs with cream; season with salt and pepper. Pour over sausages.

Microwave 6 minutes at MEDIUM.

Turn quiche a ½ turn; continue to microwave 6 minutes.

Wait 5 minutes before serving.

* See: Several important points regarding quiche: page 76.

Technique

1 Place sausage and apple mixture in pie crust.

2 Sprinkle with grated cheese.

Asparagus Omelet

(serves 2)

Setting: HIGH
Cooking time: 5 minutes
Utensil: 1.5 L pie plate

5 mL	(1 tsp) butter
6	cooked asparagus, diced
1	shallot, chopped
2 mL	(½ tsp) curry powder
22 mL	(1½ tbs) butter
4	eggs
30 mL	(2 tbs) milk
	salt and pepper

Place 5 mL (1 tsp) butter in pie plate. Add asparagus, shallot, and curry powder.

Cover with sheet of plastic wrap; microwave 1 minute.

Transfer mixture to bowl and set aside.

Melt remaining butter in pie plate. Place eggs and milk in mixing bowl; season with salt and pepper. Beat with fork.

Pour eggs into melted butter in pie plate. Microwave, uncovered, 2 minutes.

Gently stir middle of omelet. Add asparagus mixture and microwave 1½ minutes.

Using spatula, carefully fold omelet. (Omelet centre will remain moist).

Microwave 30 seconds.

Using spatula, slide omelet onto plate. Serve.

Cheddar Cheese Omelet

(serves 2)

Setting: HIGH
Cooking time: 4 minutes
Utensil: 1.5 L pie plate

22 mL	(1½ tbs) butter
4	eggs
30 mL	(2 tbs) milk
45 mL	(3 tbs) grated cheddar cheese
	salt and pepper

Melt butter in pie plate.

Place eggs and milk in mixing bowl; season with salt and pepper. Beat with fork.

Pour eggs into pie plate. Microwave, uncovered, 2 minutes.

Gently stir middle of omelet. Add 30 mL (2 tbs) cheese; microwave 1½ minutes.

Using spatula, carefully fold omelet. (Omelet centre will remain moist).

Sprinkle with remaining cheese; microwave 30 seconds.

Using spatula, slide omelet onto plate. Serve.

Tomato and Cheese Omelet

(serves 2)

Setting:	HIGH
Cooking time:	11 minutes
Utensil:	1.5 L pie plate

5 mL	*(1 tsp) butter*
15 mL	*(1 tbs) chopped onion*
1	*tomato, chopped*
½	*garlic clove, smashed and chopped*
5 mL	*(1 tsp) tomato paste*
30 mL	*(2 tbs) grated mozzarella cheese*
4	*beaten eggs*
	salt and pepper

Place butter and onion in pie plate. Cover with sheet of plastic wrap; microwave 2 minutes.

Add tomato, garlic, and tomato paste; season with salt and pepper. Cover and microwave 4 minutes.

Mix well with whisk until incorporated.

Sprinkle with 15 mL (1 tbs) cheese. Microwave, uncovered, 1 minute.

Pour beaten eggs over tomatoes; microwave 3 minutes.

Sprinkle with remaining cheese; microwave 1 minute.

Serve.

Note: This omelet is served flat and not folded.

Shrimp Omelet

(serves 2)

Setting:	HIGH
Cooking time:	12 minutes
Utensil:	1.5 L pie plate

15 mL	*(1 tbs) butter*
1	*shallot, chopped*
7	*fresh mushrooms, washed and sliced*
8	*shrimps, deveined (keep whole)*
2 mL	*(½ tsp) flour*
45 mL	*(3 tbs) 35% cream*
4	*beaten eggs*
	several drops lemon juice
	salt and pepper

Place butter, shallot, mushrooms, and shrimps in pie plate. Season with salt and pepper; sprinkle with lemon juice.

Cover with sheet of plastic wrap; microwave 2 minutes.

Sprinkle with flour and mix well.

Add cream; microwave, uncovered, 2 minutes.

Pour in beaten eggs, mix, and continue to microwave 4 minutes.

Gently stir and continue to microwave 2½ minutes.

Carefully fold omelet; microwave 50 seconds. Serve.

Pepper and Mushroom Omelet

(serves 2)

Melt 5 mL (1 tsp) butter in pie plate.

Add vegetables and lemon juice; season with salt and pepper.

Cover with sheet of plastic wrap; microwave 4 minutes.

Transfer mixture to small bowl; set aside.

Melt remaining butter in pie plate.

Place eggs and milk in small bowl; season with salt and pepper. Beat with fork.

Pour eggs into melted butter; microwave, uncovered, 2 minutes.

Gently stir middle of omelet. Add vegetables and microwave 1½ minutes.

Using spatula, carefully fold omelet. (Omelet centre will remain moist)

Microwave 30 seconds.

Using spatula, slide omelet onto plate. Serve.

Setting:	HIGH
Cooking time:	8 minutes
Utensil:	1.5 L pie plate

5 mL	(1 tsp) butter
½	banana pepper, sliced
8	mushrooms, sliced
1	green onion, sliced
22 mL	(1½ tbs) butter
4	eggs
30 mL	(2 tbs) milk
	several drops lemon juice
	salt and pepper

3   Place eggs and milk in bowl; beat with fork.

Technique : Pepper and Mushroom Omelet

1 Place butter and vegetables in pie plate; sprinkle with lemon juice.

2 Cover with sheet of plastic wrap.

4 Pour eggs into melted butter.

5 After 2 minutes in microwave, gently stir.

$\longrightarrow$

Technique : Pepper and Mushroom Omelet (continued)

6   Add vegetables.

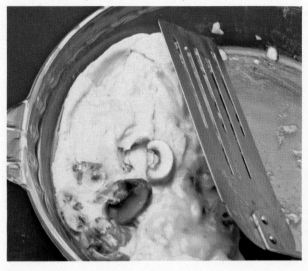

7   Using spatula, carefully fold omelet.

Potato and Green Onion Omelet

(serves 2)

Setting :	**HIGH**
Cooking time :	**7 minutes**
Utensil :	**1.5 L pie plate**

1	*green onion, diced*
1	*slice bacon, diced*
1	*small potato, diced small*
22 mL	*(1½ tbs) butter*
4	*eggs*
30 mL	*(2 tbs) milk*
	salt and pepper

Place onion, bacon, and potato in pie plate; season with pepper.

Cover with sheet of plastic wrap; microwave 2½ minutes.

Transfer to bowl and set aside.

Melt butter in pie plate.

Place eggs and milk in bowl; season with salt and pepper. Beat with fork.

Pour eggs into melted butter; microwave, uncovered, 2 minutes.

Gently stir middle of omelet. Add potato mixture and microwave 1½ minutes.

Using spatula, carefully fold omelet. (Omelet centre will remain moist)

Microwave 30 seconds.

Using spatula, slide omelet onto plate. Serve.

Potato Omelet

(serves 2)

Setting: HIGH
Cooking time: 6 minutes
Utensil: 1.5 L pie plate

5 mL	*(1 tsp) butter*
15 mL	*(1 tbs) chopped red onion*
5 mL	*(1 tsp) chopped parsley*
2	*cooked small potatoes, diced with skin*
2	*slices cooked bacon, diced**
22 mL	*(1½ tbs) butter*
4	*eggs*
30 mL	*(2 tbs) milk*
	salt and pepper

Place 5 mL (1 tsp) butter in pie plate; add onion and parsley. Season with pepper.

Cover with sheet of plastic wrap; microwave 1 minute.

Add potatoes and bacon; continue to microwave 1 minute.

Transfer mixture to bowl; set aside.

Melt remaining butter in pie plate.

Place eggs and milk in bowl; season with salt and pepper. Beat with fork.

Pour eggs into melted butter. Microwave, uncovered, 2 minutes.

Gently stir middle of omelet. Add potato mixture; microwave 1½ minutes.

Using spatula, carefully fold omelet. (Omelet centre will remain moist)

Microwave 30 seconds.

Using spatula, slide onto plate. Serve.

* See cooking bacon; page 173.

Eggplant Omelet

(serves 2)

Setting: HIGH
Cooking time: 12 minutes
Utensil: 1.5 L pie plate

15 mL	*(1 tbs) chopped red onion*
5 mL	*(1 tsp) oil*
¼	*eggplant, peeled and diced*
1	*garlic clove, smashed and chopped*
½	*tomato, diced*
4	*eggs*
30 mL	*(2 tbs) water*
	pinch basil
	salt and pepper

Place onion and oil in pie plate. Cover with sheet of plastic wrap; microwave 2 minutes.

Incorporate eggplant, garlic, and tomato; season with salt, pepper, and basil.

Cover and microwave 4 minutes.

Mix well and microwave, uncovered, 2 minutes.

Place eggs and water in bowl; season with salt and pepper. Beat with fork.

Pour eggs over vegetables and mix.

Microwave, uncovered, 4 minutes. Serve.

Note: This omelet is served flat and not folded.

Poached Eggs Duchesse

Poached Eggs Duchesse

(serves 4)

Preparation of mushroom sauce

Setting: HIGH
Cooking time: 5 minutes
Utensil: 2 L casserole

2	*shallots, chopped*
5 mL	*(1 tsp) butter*
114 g	*(¼ lb) fresh mushrooms, washed and diced*
15 mL	*(1 tbs) chopped parsley*
375 mL	*(1½ cups) hot, commercial brown sauce*
5 mL	*(1 tsp) tomato paste*
	salt and pepper

Place shallots, butter, mushrooms, and parsley in casserole. Season with salt and pepper; cover and microwave 3 minutes.

Add brown sauce and tomato paste; stir and continue to microwave, uncovered, 2 minutes.

Preparation of duchesse potatoes

6	*potatoes, peeled*
30 mL	*(2 tbs) fresh butter*
1	*egg yolk*
50 mL	*(¼ cup) hot 35% cream*
	pinch nutmeg
	salt and white pepper

Cook potatoes in salted boiling water on stove top.

Once cooked, drain and pass through food mill.

Season with salt and pepper. Add butter, nutmeg, egg yolk, and cream. Incorporate ingredients well.

Presentation of poached eggs duchesse

1	*recipe mashed potatoes*
4	*poached eggs* *
1	*recipe mushroom sauce*

Place mashed potatoes in pastry bag fitted with star nozzel. Form nests of potato on service platter.

Place poached eggs over potato and top with mushroom sauce. Serve.

* See cooking poached eggs below.

Poached Eggs Chasseur

(serves 4)

Preparation of poached eggs

Setting: HIGH
Cooking time: 5 minutes
Utensil: 2 L casserole

1.5 L	*(6 cups) boiling water*
15 mL	*(1 tbs) white vinegar*
4	*eggs*

Pour water into casserole. Add vinegar and stir. Cover and microwave 1 minute.

Break eggs into boiling water, being careful not to damage yolks. Cover and microwave 4 minutes.

Drain eggs well on paper towel.

→

Poached Eggs Chasseur (continued)

Preparation of sauce

Setting: HIGH
Cooking time: 11 minutes
Utensil: 2 L casserole

5 mL	*(1 tsp) oil*
30 mL	*(2 tbs) chopped onion*
1	*garlic clove, smashed and chopped*
15 mL	*(1 tbs) chopped parsley*
375 mL	*(1½ cups) diced fresh mushrooms*
375 mL	*(1½ cups) commercial brown sauce*
15 mL	*(1 tbs) tomato paste*
1 mL	*(¼ tsp) tarragon*
	salt and pepper

Place oil, onion, garlic, and parsley in casserole. Cover and microwave 2 minutes.

Add mushrooms and season with salt and pepper; cover and microwave 4 minutes.

Add brown sauce, tomato paste, and tarragon. Microwave, uncovered, 5 minutes.

Presentation of poached eggs chasseur

4	*poached eggs*
1	*recipe of sauce chasseur*
4	*toasted rounds of bread*

Place poached eggs on toasted bread and top with sauce. Serve.

Poached Eggs with Spinach

(serves 4)

Preparation of white cheese sauce

Setting: HIGH
Cooking time: 7 minutes 30 seconds
Utensil: 2 L casserole

45 mL	*(3 tbs) butter*
15 mL	*(1 tbs) chopped shallot*
15 mL	*(1 tbs) chopped parsley*
52 mL	*(3½ tbs) flour*
500 mL	*(2 cups) milk*
50 mL	*(¾ cup) grated Gruyère cheese*
	pinch nutmeg
	pinch paprika
	salt and white pepper

Place butter, shallot, and parsley in casserole. Cover and microwave 1 minute.

Add flour and mix well with whisk.

Incorporate milk slowly, mixing with whisk. Sprinkle with nutmeg and paprika; season with salt and pepper.

Microwave, uncovered, 6 minutes. Stir every minute.

Add cheese; microwave, uncovered, 30 seconds. Serve.

Presentation of poached eggs with spinach

4	*toasted rounds of bread*
250 mL	*(1 cup) cooked spinach, squeezed and chopped*
4	*poached eggs**
1	*recipe of white cheese sauce*

On toasted bread, arrange chopped spinach. Place poached eggs on top and add white cheese sauce. Serve.

* See cooking poached eggs; page 95.

Poached Eggs Soubise

(serves 4)

Preparation of onion puree

Setting: **HIGH**
Cooking time: **18 minutes**
Utensil: **2 L casserole**

15 mL	*(1 tbs) butter*
3	*onions, peeled and chopped*
5 mL	*(1 tsp) cornstarch*
125 mL	*(½ cup) hot milk*
	pinch nutmeg
	salt and pepper

Place butter and onions in casserole; season with salt and pepper. Cover and microwave 15 minutes.

Add cornstarch and mix well.

Add nutmeg and milk; stir well and microwave, uncovered, 3 minutes.

Puree mixture in blender; set aside.

Presentation of eggs soubise

4	*toasted rounds of French bread*
4	*poached eggs* *
1	*recipe of onion puree*
1	*recipe of white cheese sauce* **

Place poached eggs on toasted bread. Cover with onion puree.

Top with white cheese sauce. Serve.

  * See cooking poached eggs; page 95.
** See preparation of white cheese sauce; page 96.

Scrambled Eggs and Mushrooms

(serves 2)

Setting: **HIGH**
Cooking time: **7 minutes**
Utensil: **For mushrooms: 1.5 L pie plate**
                For eggs: 1 L round casserole

30 mL	*(2 tbs) butter*
2	*shallots, chopped*
227 g	*(½ lb) fresh mushrooms, washed and diced*
15 mL	*(1 tbs) chopped parsley*
4	*eggs*
	several drops lemon juice
	salt and pepper
	toasted French bread

Place 15 mL (1 tbs) butter in pie plate. Add shallots, mushrooms, and parsley; season with salt and pepper. Sprinkle with lemon juice.

Cover with sheet of plastic wrap; microwave 3 minutes.

Stir mixture, drain, and set aside.

Melt remaining butter in casserole.

Beat eggs and pour into melted butter; microwave 2 minutes.

Mix and continue to microwave 1½ minutes.

Arrange scrambled eggs over toast and garnish with mushroom mixture. Serve.

Coddled Eggs with Asparagus

Coddled Eggs with Asparagus

(serves 4)

Setting: **HIGH and MEDIUM-HIGH**
Cooking time: **20 minutes**
Utensil: **For asparagus: 2 L casserole
For eggs: 4 individual ramequin dishes**

1	*bunch fresh asparagus, peeled, washed, and cut into pieces of 2.5 cm (1 in)*
250 mL	*(1 cup) water*
8	*fresh eggs*
125 mL	*(½ cup) 35% cream salt and pepper*

Place asparagus in casserole and add salt. Pour in water and cover. Microwave 6 minutes at HIGH.

Turn casserole a ½ turn; continue to microwave 4 minutes.

Drain asparagus well and transfer to ramequin dishes.

Break 2 eggs into each ramequin dish. Using a sharp knife, delicately pierce yolks. Season with salt and pepper.

Divide cream between dishes.

Microwave 5 minutes at MEDIUM-HIGH.

Turn dishes a ¼ turn and continue to microwave 3 minutes.

Turn dishes again and microwave 2 minutes. Serve.

Coddled Eggs

(serves 4)

Setting: **MEDIUM-HIGH**
Cooking time: **10 minutes**
Utensil: **4 individual ramequin dishes**

8	*eggs*
175 mL	*(¾ cup) 35% cream salt and pepper paprika*

Break 2 eggs into each ramequin dish. Using sharp knife, delicately pierce yolks. Season with salt and pepper.

Divide cream between dishes.

Microwave 5 minutes.

Turn dishes a ¼ turn and continue to microwave 3 minutes.

Turn dishes again and microwave 2 minutes.

Sprinkle with paprika and serve.

Muffin Eggs

(serves 3)

Setting: **HIGH**
Cooking time: **4 minutes**
Utensil: **Round muffin mold**
For people who like the yolk cooked.

30 mL	*(2 tbs) butter*
6	*large eggs*

Melt a bit of butter in each muffin mold.

Place egg in each muffin mold. Using sharp knife, delicately pierce yolks; microwave 2 minutes.

Turn mold a ½ turn; microwave 1 minute.

Turn mold again and continue to microwave 1 minute.

Dislodge eggs, using sharp knife. Unmold with soup spoon.

Serve with toast, sausages, and bacon.

Scrambled Eggs and Scallops

(serves 4)

Add scallops and sprinkle with lemon juice. Cover and microwave 2 minutes.

Remove casserole, drain well and set mixture aside.

Beat eggs with fork and season with salt and pepper.

Melt remaining butter in casserole for 30 seconds.

Add beaten eggs; microwave, uncovered, 1½ minutes.

Stir well and continue to microwave 2 minutes.

Mix eggs with whisk and add scallops and vegetables. Microwave, uncovered, 2 minutes.

Mix and continue to microwave 1 minute.

Mix again and microwave 1 minute. Serve.

Setting:	HIGH
Cooking time:	12 minutes 30 seconds
Utensil:	2 L casserole

30 mL	*(2 tbs) butter*
1	*garlic clove, smashed and chopped*
114 g	*(¼ lb) fresh mushrooms, washed and sliced*
1	*green pepper, diced*
12	*large scallops, washed and cut in four*
8	*eggs*
	several drops lemon juice
	salt and pepper

Place 15 mL (1 tbs) butter in casserole; melt 30 seconds in microwave.

Add garlic, mushrooms, and green pepper. Season with salt and pepper; cover and microwave 2 minutes.

Cheddar Scrambled Eggs

(serves 2)

Setting:	HIGH
Cooking time:	4 minutes
Utensil:	1 L round casserole

15 mL	*(1 tbs) butter*
4	*large eggs*
30 mL	*(2 tbs) milk*
125 mL	*(½ cup) grated cheddar cheese*
	salt and pepper
	toasted French bread

Melt butter in casserole.

Place eggs and milk in bowl; season with salt and pepper. Beat with fork.

Pour eggs into melted butter; microwave 1½ minutes.

Add grated cheese and mix. Microwave 1 minute.

Stir well and continue to microwave 1 minute.

Serve on toasted French bread.

Scrambled Eggs *

(serves 4)
* *Serve with croutons.*

Setting: **HIGH**
Cooking time: **7 minutes**
Utensil: **2 L casserole**

Preparation of croutons

50 mL	**(¼ cup) peanut oil**
4	**slices French bread, cut in triangles**
60 mL	**(4 tbs) chopped parsley**

Heat oil in frying pan on stove top. Add bread and fry 2 minutes each side.

Sprinkle bread with parsley and set aside.

Preparation of scrambled eggs

30 mL	**(2 tbs) butter**
8	**fresh eggs**
15 mL	**(1 tbs) chopped fresh parsley**
30 mL	**(2 tbs) 35% cream**
	salt and pepper

Place butter in casserole and melt 1 minute.

Place eggs in mixing bowl; season with salt and pepper. Add parsley and cream; mix with fork.

Pour eggs into melted butter; microwave, uncovered, 1½ minutes.

Mix with whisk and continue to microwave 2 minutes.

Mix again; microwave 1 minute.

Mix again; microwave 1 minute.

Mix rapidly; microwave 30 seconds.

Serve eggs with croutons.

Crêpes

Crêpe Batter

TECHNIQUE

250 mL	*(1 cup) all-purpose flour*
3	*large whole eggs*
375 mL	*(1½ cups) liquid, half milk and half water*
30 mL	*(2 tbs) vegetable oil pinch salt*

Sift flour and salt together in bowl.

Add eggs and half of liquid; mix well with whisk.

Add remaining liquid and oil; mix again.

Pass batter through sieve and refrigerate 1 hour.

In a buttered pan on stove top, pour a small amount of batter. Cook 1 minute each side over medium heat.

Technique

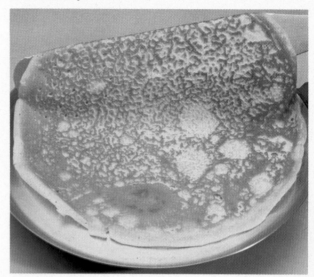

1 Cook crêpe on both sides.

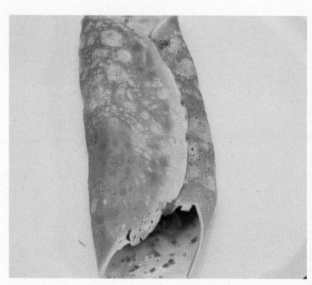

4 Fold other side of crêpe.

2 Arrange filling in centre of crêpe.

3 Fold one side of crêpe over filling.

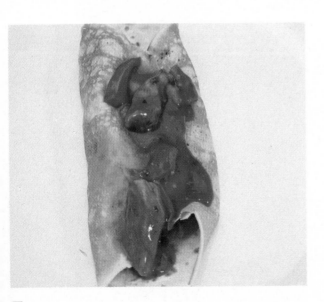

5 Top crêpe with a bit of filling.

6 Sprinkle with grated cheese. Microwave, uncovered, 1 minute at HIGH. Serve.

Eggplant Crêpes

Eggplant Crêpes

(serves 4)

Setting: HIGH
Cooking time: 23 minutes
Utensil: 2 L casserole

Preparation of crêpe batter

250 mL	*(1 cup) flour*
4	*eggs*
300 mL	*(1¼ cups) liquid, half milk and half water*
30 mL	*(2 tbs) vegetable oil*
	salt

Sift flour and salt together in bowl. Add eggs and mix until combined, with whisk.

Add half of liquid; mix well.

Add remaining liquid and oil; mix and pass through sieve.

Refrigerate 1 hour before using. (if possible)

Ligthly butter crêpe pan and heat on stove top.

Pour a bit of batter in pan and rotate pan so batter covers surface. Pour excess batter back into bowl.

Cook crêpes 1 to 2 minutes each side.

Preparation of eggplant filling

1	*eggplant, peeled and sliced*
1	*onion, peeled and sliced*
2	*green peppers, sliced*
1	*zucchini, sliced*
1	*garlic clove, smashed and chopped*
45 mL	*(3 tbs) tomato paste*
125 mL	*(½ cup) grated Gruyère cheese*
	salt and pepper

Place all vegetables in casserole. Add garlic, salt, and pepper.

Cover with sheet of plastic wrap; microwave 15 minutes.

Mix ingredients well. Add tomato paste and season to taste; mix well.

Stuff crêpes.

Roll crêpes and arrange in casserole. Sprinkle with grated cheese.

Cover and microwave 8 minutes. Serve.

Technique

1 The consistency of the crêpe batter should not be too thick nor too thin.

→

Technique : Eggplant Crêpes (continued)

2 Here is the mixture of cooked eggplant.

3 Stuff the crêpes.

4 Sprinkle with grated cheese.

5 Roll crêpes and arrange in casserole. Cover with sheet of plastic wrap and microwave 8 minutes.

Pork and Pineapple Crêpes

(serves 4)

Setting: MEDIUM-HIGH and HIGH
Cooking time: 12 minutes for filling
Utensil: 2 L casserole

5 mL	*(1 tsp) oil*
1	*garlic clove, smashed and chopped*
1	*pork tenderloin, fat trimmed and sliced*
5 mL	*(1 tsp) soya sauce*
½	*red pepper, cut in strips*
4	*pineapple rings, diced*
375 mL	*(1½ cups) hot, very thick brown sauce **
8	*crêpes*
	salt and pepper

Place oil, garlic, pork, and soya sauce in casserole. Season with pepper. Cover and microwave 5 minutes at MEDIUM-HIGH.

Stir well and continue to microwave 3 minutes.

Remove pork from casserole; set aside.

Place red pepper in casserole. Cover and microwave 3 minutes at HIGH.

Add pineapples and replace pork in casserole.

Add brown sauce, stir well, and correct seasoning. Microwave, uncovered, 1 minute at MEDIUM-HIGH.

Stuff crêpes with filling.**

 * See page 22.
** See: How to stuff crêpes; page 104.

Crab Crêpes

(serves 4)

Setting: HIGH
Cooking time: 11½ minutes for filling
Utensil: 2 L round casserole

5 mL	*(1 tsp) butter*
227 g	*(½ lb) fresh mushrooms, washed and sliced*
5 mL	*(1 tsp) chopped parsley*
75 mL	*(5 tbs) flour*
500 mL	*(2 cups) hot milk*
50 mL	*(¼ cup) grated mozzarella cheese*
1	*142 g (5 oz) can crab meat, drained*
8	*crêpes*
	pinch paprika
	several drops lemon juice
	pinch nutmeg
	pinch fennel
	salt and pepper

Place butter, mushrooms, paprika, and parsley in casserole. Season with salt and pepper; sprinkle with lemon juice. Cover and microwave 4 minutes.

Add flour and mix; microwave, uncovered, 1 minute.

Add nutmeg, fennel, and milk; microwave, uncovered, 3 minutes.

Stir and continue to microwave 3 minutes.

Add grated cheese and stir well.

Add crab meat, mix, and continue to microwave, uncovered, 30 seconds.

Stuff crêpes with filling.*

* See: How to stuff crêpes; page 104.

Technique

1 Place butter, mushrooms, paprika, and parsley in casserole. Season with salt and pepper; sprinkle with lemon juice.

2 Add flour and mix well.

3 The sauce should be thick.

4 Add grated cheese.

5 Add crab meat.

Sole Filet Crêpes

Sole Filet Crêpes

(serves 4)

Setting:	HIGH
Cooking time:	17 minutes
Utensil:	2 L casserole

Preparation of crêpe batter

250 mL	*(1 cup) flour*
4	*eggs*
300 mL	*(1¼ cups) liquid, half of milk and half water*
30 mL	*(2 tbs) vegetable oil*
	salt

Sift flour and salt together into bowl. Incorporate eggs and mix with whisk.

Add half of liquid; mix well.

Add remaining liquid and oil; blend and pass through sieve.

Refrigerate batter 1 hour before using, if possible.

To make crêpes, lightly butter crêpe pan and heat on stove top.

Pour a bit of batter in pan and rotate pan so batter covers surface. Pour excess batter back into bowl.

Cook crêpes 1 to 2 minutes each side.

Preparation of sole stuffing

3	*sole filets, washed and dried*
5 mL	*(1 tsp) butter*
2	*parsley sprigs*
1	*shallot, sliced*
2	*lemon slices*
20	*mushrooms, sliced*
250 mL	*(1 cup) cold water*
250 mL	*(1 cup) hot 18% cream*
15 mL	*(1 tbs) chopped parsley*
30 mL	*(2 tbs) cornstarch*
45 mL	*(3 tbs) cold water*
	paprika
	salt and pepper

Place sole, butter, parsley sprigs, shallots, and lemon slices in casserole.

Add mushrooms and water; season with salt and pepper.

Cover with sheet of plastic wrap; microwave 5 minutes.

Remove sole from casserole; set aside.

Pour hot cream into cooking liquid. Sprinkle with chopped parsley.

Mix cornstarch with water; incorporate to sauce.

Microwave, uncovered, 8 minutes. Stir with whisk every 2 minutes.

Flake sole into large pieces and carefully add to sauce.

Stuff crêpes, roll, and transfer to another microwave casserole. Top with remaining sauce.

Microwave, uncovered, 4 minutes.

Sprinkle with paprika and serve.

Technique

1 Place sole, butter, parsley sprigs, shallots, and lemon slices in casserole.

$\longrightarrow$

Technique : *Sole Filet Crêpes* (continued)

2 Add mushrooms.

3 Add cold water.

5 Add cream and parsley to cooking liquid.

6 Add cornstarch mixture.

Crêpes Stuffed with Lobster and Spinach

(serves 4)

Setting:	HIGH
Cooking time:	7 to 8 minutes
Utensil:	3 L casserole and rectangular dish

30 mL	*(2 tbs) butter*
1 ½	*bunches spinach, washed*
375 mL	*(1 ½ cups) cooked lobster, diced*
625 mL	*(2 ½ cups) hot white sauce**
125 mL	*(½ cup) grated mozzarella cheese*
8	*crêpes*
	pinch nutmeg
	salt and pepper

Place butter in 3 L casserole. Add spinach, cover and microwave 3 minutes.

Remove spinach, squeeze dry, and chop. Discard cooking liquid in casserole and replace spinach. Add lobster and mix well.

Add half of white sauce; sprinkle with nutmeg. Mix and microwave, uncovered, 1 minute.

Add half of cheese and incorporate well.

Stuff crêpes with filling, roll, and place in rectangular dish. Top with remaining white sauce and cheese. Microwave, uncovered, 3 to 4 minutes.

Serve.

* See page 21.

4 Remove sole after 5 minutes in microwave; set aside.

7 Replace pieces of fish.

Eggplant and Chicken Crêpes

(serves 4)

Setting:	HIGH
Cooking time:	21 minutes for filling
Utensil:	2 L round casserole

5 mL	*(1 tsp) oil*
30 mL	*(2 tbs) chopped onion*
1	*garlic clove, smashed and chopped*
1	*eggplant, peeled and diced*
5 mL	*(1 tsp) chopped parsley*
1	*chicken breast, skinned, deboned, and cubed*
375 mL	*(1½ cups) tomatoes, drained and chopped*
15 mL	*(1 tbs) tomato paste*
50 mL	*(¼ cup) grated Gruyère cheese*
8	*crêpes*
	pinch savory
	pinch thyme
	salt and pepper

Place oil, onion, garlic, eggplant, and parsley in casserole. Season with salt and pepper; cover and microwave 8 minutes.

Mix, cover and continue to microwave 8 minutes.

Add chicken and herbs; season with salt and pepper. Cover and microwave 3 minutes.

Add tomatoes, tomato paste, and cheese; mix well. Microwave, uncovered, 2 minutes.

Stuff crêpes with filling.*

* See: How to stuff crêpes; page 104.

Technique

1 Place oil, onion, garlic, eggplant, and parsley in casserole.

4 Add tomato paste.

2 Add chicken and herbs; season with salt and
pepper.

3 Add tomatoes.

5 Add grated cheese.

6 The eggplant and chicken filling should be
quite thick.

Crêpes Stuffed with Ham and Spinach

(serves 4)

Setting: HIGH
Cooking time: 16 minutes for filling
Utensil: 2 L round casserole

1	*large bunch fresh spinach*
125 mL	*(½ cup) water*
75 mL	*(5 tbs) flour*
625 mL	*(2½ cups) hot milk*
375 mL	*(1½ cups) cooked ham, cut in strips*
2	*hard boiled eggs, sliced in rings*
50 mL	*(¼ cup) grated Gruyère cheese*
8	*crêpes*
	pinch paprika
	pinch nutmeg
	salt and pepper

Wash and dry spinach; place in casserole. Season with salt and pepper; add water. Cover and microwave 5 minutes.

Remove spinach from casserole and allow cooking liquid to remain.

Drain spinach and press with back of spoon to remove excess water.

Chop spinach and replace in casserole containing cooking liquid.

Sprinkle with flour and paprika; mix well. Season with salt, pepper, and nutmeg.

Add half of milk; stir well.

Add remaining milk; microwave, uncovered, 5 minutes.

Stir well. Correct seasoning and continue to microwave 3 minutes.

Add ham; stir well.

Add eggs, cheese, and paprika. Microwave, uncovered, 3 minutes.

Stuff crêpes with filling.*

* See: How to stuff crêpes; page 104.

Technique

1 Wash and dry spinach; place in casserole. Season with salt and pepper; add water.

4 Add cooked ham.

2 Replace cooked chopped spinach in casserole. Sprinkle with flour and paprika.

3 Add nutmeg and half of hot milk.

5 Add egg slices.

6 Add grated cheese.

Crêpes with Chopped Veal

(serves 4)

Setting:	**HIGH**
Cooking time:	**16 minutes for filling**
Utensil:	**2 L round casserole**

5 mL	*(1 tsp) butter*
½	*celery stalk, chopped, seeded, and chopped*
½	*cucumber, peeled*
5 mL	*(1 tsp) chopped parsley*
8	*large mushrooms, washed and diced*
227 g	*(½ lb) chopped veal*
1	*796 mL (28 oz) can tomatoes, drained and chopped*
5 mL	*(1 tsp) beef bouillon mix*
125 mL	*(½ cup) grated cheddar cheese*
8	*crêpes*
	pinch celery seed
	pinch thyme
	pinch crushed chillies
	pinch paprika
	salt and pepper

Place butter and celery in casserole; cover and microwave 3 minutes.

Add cucumber and parsley; cover and microwave 1 minute.

Add mushrooms and season with salt and pepper. Add veal, herbs, and spices. Cover and microwave 3 minutes.

Stir and continue to microwave 1 minute.

Add tomatoes and beef bouillon mix; mix well. Microwave, uncovered, 5 minutes.

Add cheese and microwave, uncovered, 3 minutes.

Stuff crêpes with filling.*

* See: How to stuff crêpes; page 104.

Technique

1 In casserole containing celery, add cucumber and chopped parsley.

4 Add tomatoes.

2 Add mushrooms ; season with salt and pepper.

3 Add chopped veal, herbs, and spices.

5 Add beef bouillon mix.

6 Add grated cheese.

Crêpes with Eggs and Tomatoes

(serves 4)

Setting: HIGH
Cooking time: 7 minutes for filling
Utensil: 2 L round casserole

5 mL	*(1 tsp) butter*
30 mL	*(2 tbs) chopped onion*
1	*celery stalk, diced*
250 mL	*(1 cup) tomatoes, drained and chopped*
375 mL	*(1½ cups) spaghetti sauce* *
4	*hard boiled eggs, chopped*
125 mL	*(½ cup) grated mozzarella cheese*
30 mL	*(2 tbs) capers*
8	*crêpes*
	pinch basil
	pinch cinnamon
	pinch paprika
	pinch chopped parsley
	salt and pepper

Place butter, onion, and celery in casserole. Cover and microwave 4 minutes.

Add tomatoes, spaghetti sauce, herbs, and spices; mix together.

Add eggs, cheese, and capers; mix delicately. Microwave, uncovered, 3 minutes.

Stuff crêpes with filling.**

* Use commercial brand or your favourite recipe.
** See: How to stuff crêpes; page 104.

Technique

1 Place butter, onion, and celery in casserole.

4 Add grated cheese.

2 Add tomatoes, spaghetti sauce, herbs, and spices.

3 Add chopped eggs.

5 Add capers.

Salmon Crêpes

(serves 4)

Setting: HIGH
Cooking time: 12 minutes for filling
Utensil: 2 L round casserole

5 mL	*(1 tsp) butter*
227 g	*(½ lb) fresh mushrooms, washed and sliced*
5 mL	*(1 tsp) chopped parsley*
75 mL	*(5 tbs) flour*
500 mL	*(2 cups) hot milk*
50 mL	*(¼ cup) grated Gruyère cheese*
1	*220 g (7.75 oz) can salmon, well drained and washed*
2	*hard boiled eggs, chopped*
8	*crêpes*
	several drops lemon juice
	pinch fennel
	paprika
	salt and pepper

Place butter, mushrooms, paprika, and parsley in casserole. Season with salt and pepper; sprinkle with lemon juice. Cover and microwave 4 minutes.

Add flour and mix well. Microwave, uncovered, 1 minute. Add fennel and hot milk; microwave, uncovered, 3 minutes.

Stir and continue to microwave 3 minutes.

Add cheese and stir well.

Add salmon and eggs; mix and microwave, uncovered, 1 minute.

Stuff crêpes with filling.*

* See: How to stuff crêpes; page 104.

Crêpes with Beef and Pickles

(serves 4)

Setting: MEDIUM-HIGH and HIGH
Cooking time: 9 minutes for filling
Utensil: 2 L round casserole

5 mL	*(1 tsp) oil*
454 g	*(1 lb) beef sirloin, cut in strips of 0.65 cm (¼ in)*
5 mL	*(1 tsp) chopped parsley*
30 mL	*(2 tbs) chopped onion*
1	*yellow pepper, cut into julienne*
1	*796 mL (28 oz) can tomatoes, drained and chopped*
30 mL	*(2 tbs) tomato paste*
2	*large marinated pickles, cut into julienne*
8	*crêpes*
	several drops Worcestershire sauce
	several drops soya sauce
	salt and pepper

Place oil, beef, parsley, Worcestershire sauce, soya sauce, and onion in casserole. Season with salt and pepper; cover and microwave 4 minutes at MEDIUM-HIGH.

Stir well and add yellow pepper. Cover and continue to microwave 4 minutes.

Add tomatoes, tomato paste, and pickles. Stir and microwave 1 minute at HIGH.

Stuff crêpes with filling.*

* See: How to stuff crêpes; page 104.

Crêpes with Mushrooms

(serves 4)

Setting: HIGH
Cooking time: 18 minutes for filling
Utensil: 2 L round casserole

5 mL	(1 tsp) butter
350 g	(¾ lb) fresh mushrooms, washed and sliced
75 mL	(5 tbs) flour
625 mL	(2½ cups) hot milk
250 mL	(1 cup) tomatoes, drained and chopped
5 mL	(1 tsp) chopped parsley
8	crêpes
	several drops lemon juice
	pinch tarragon
	salt and pepper

Place butter, mushrooms, and lemon juice in casserole. Season with salt and pepper; cover and microwave 5 minutes.

Add flour, mix, and continue to microwave 1 minute.

Add hot milk; stir well.

Add tomatoes and herbs; season with salt and pepper. Stir and microwave, uncovered, 8 minutes.

Mix well and continue to microwave 4 minutes. Correct seasoning.

Stuff crêpes with filling.*

* See: How to stuff crêpes; page 104.

Crêpes Stuffed with Salmon and Halibut

(serves 4)

Setting: HIGH
Cooking time: 6½ minutes
Utensil: 2 L casserole and rectangular dish

15 mL	(1 tbs) butter
1	shallot, chopped
125 g	(¼ lb) fresh mushrooms, washed and diced
1	sliced cooked salmon, flaked
1	sliced cooked halibut, flaked
625 mL	(2½ cups) hot thick white sauce *
125 mL	(½ cup) grated Gruyère cheese
	salt and pepper

Place butter and shallots in 2 L casserole. Cover and microwave 1 minute.

Add mushrooms; season with salt and pepper. Cover and microwave 3 minutes.

Add salmon, halibut, and half of white sauce. Stir and microwave, uncovered, 30 seconds.

Place 45 mL (3 tbs) of mixture in centre of each crêpe, roll, and place in rectangular dish.

Top crêpes with remaining sauce and sprinkle with cheese. Microwave, uncovered, 2 minutes. Serve.

* See page 21.

Meats

Irish Shoulder of Lamb

Irish Shoulder of Lamb

(serves 4)

Setting:	HIGH
Cooking time:	75 minutes
Utensil:	2.5 to 3 L casserole

1	1.2 kg (2½ lb) shoulder of lamb, deboned, fat trimmed, and cubed
5	potatoes, peeled and sliced
3	onions, peeled and sliced
750 mL	(3 cups) hot chicken stock *
1	bay leaf
3	parsley sprigs
50 mL	(¼ cup) 35% cream
	pinch thyme
	pinch clove
	salt and pepper

Place lamb in casserole and cover with cold water; season with salt. Cover and microwave 6 minutes.

Discard water from casserole.

Add all ingredients, except cream, to casserole. Season to taste. Cover and microwave 35 minutes.

Mix and continue to microwave, uncovered, 34 minutes. Remove lamb and transfer to service platter.

Mix cream with vegetable sauce and pass through food mill.

Pour sauce over lamb and sprinkle with chopped parsley. Serve.

* See page 55.

Shoulder of Lamb with Curry

(serves 4)

Setting:	HIGH and MEDIUM-HIGH
Cooking time:	58 minutes in microwave
Utensil:	2.5 to 3 L casserole

1	1.2 kg (2½ lb) deboned shoulder of lamb
30 mL	(2 tbs) oil
2	onions, peeled and sliced
30 mL	(2 tbs) curry powder
750 mL	(3 cups) hot chicken stock *
40 mL	(2½ tbs) cornstarch
60 mL	(4 tbs) cold water
1	apple, cored, peeled, and quartered
125 mL	(½ cup) dry raisins
50 mL	(¼ cup) grated coconut
1	banana, peeled and thickly sliced
50 mL	(¼ cup) 35% cream
	chopped parsley
	salt and pepper

Trim fat from lamb and cut into medium size cubes.

Heat 15 mL (1 tbs) oil in frying pan on stove top. Add half of lamb and sear 2 minutes each side. Remove lamb and set aside.

Sear remaining lamb. Season lamb with salt and pepper; set aside.

Pour remaining oil in pan. Add onions and cook 4 to 5 minutes over high heat.

Add curry powder; mix and cook 3 to 4 minutes.

Transfer lamb to casserole. Add onion mixture and pour in chicken stock. Season, cover and microwave 12 minutes at HIGH.

Mix gently, cover, and continue to microwave 13 minutes.

Mix again; continue to microwave 13 minutes.

Mix cornstarch with water; incorporate to mixture. Microwave, uncovered, 20 minutes at MEDIUM-HIGH.

3 minutes before end of cooking, add apples and raisins.

Remove casserole from microwave and add remaining ingredients. Mix and let stand 1 minute.

Serve on a bed of rice.

* See page 55.

Leg of Lamb with Garlic

Leg of Lamb with Garlic

(serves 4)

Setting:	MEDIUM-HIGH
Cooking time:	20 minutes in microwave
Utensil:	2.5 to 3 L casserole

1	*1.4 to 1.6 kg (3 to 3½ lb) butterfly deboned leg of lamb*
3	*garlic cloves, peeled and cut in 2*
50 mL	*(¼ cup) melted butter*
1	*large onion, peeled and cut in large pieces*
½	*celery stalk, diced*
15 mL	*(1 tbs) chopped parsley*
500 mL	*(2 cups) hot light brown sauce**
5 mL	*(1 tsp) tomato paste*
	several drops Tabasco sauce
	salt and pepper

Trim fat and skin from lamb.

Make incisions in lamb and insert garlic pieces; generously season with salt and pepper.

Secure lamb with string and generously brush with melted butter. Place in roasting pan and sear 20 minutes in preheated oven at 200°C (400 F).

Transfer seared lamb to casserole; partially cover. Microwave 20 minutes, then set aside.

Place roasting pan containing cooking juices on stove top. Add onion, celery, and parsley; cook 10 minutes over medium heat. Mix well.

Add brown sauce, tomato paste, and Tabasco sauce; stir well. Simmer several minutes over medium heat.

Pass sauce through food mill and serve with lamb.

* See page 22.

Technique

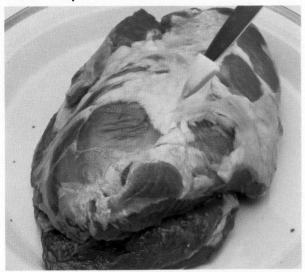

1 Make incisions in lamb and insert garlic pieces.

2 Tie and generously brush lamb with melted butter.

Stuffed Leg of Lamb

Stuffed Leg of Lamb

(serves 4)

Setting:	**MEDIUM-HIGH and HIGH**
Cooking time:	24 minutes in microwave
Utensil:	2.5 L casserole

Preparation of stuffing

1	*onion, peeled and finely chopped*
½	*celery stalk, finely chopped*
2	*garlic cloves, smashed and chopped*
7 to 8	*fresh mushrooms, washed and finely chopped*
15 mL	*(1 tbs) chopped parsley*
175 mL	*(¾ cup) small spicy croutons*
1	*beaten egg*
	pinch thyme
	pinch marjoram
	pinch oregano
	several drops Tabasco sauce
	salt and pepper

Place onion, celery, garlic, mushrooms, and herbs in casserole. Season with salt and pepper; microwave, uncovered, 3 minutes at HIGH.

Add croutons and egg; mix well. Continue to microwave 1 minute. Set aside.

Preparation of lamb

1	*1.4 to 1.6 kg (3 to 3½ lb) butterfly deboned leg of lamb*
1	*stuffing recipe*
	melted butter

Trim fat from lamb. Generously season with salt and pepper.

Stuff lamb and secure with string; brush with melted butter.

Place lamb in ovenproof dish. Sear 20 minutes in preheated oven at 200 C (400 F).

Transfer lamb to casserole; partially cover. Microwave 20 minutes at MEDIUM-HIGH. Set aside.

Preparation of sauce

15 mL	*(1 tbs) butter*
1	*onion, peeled and cut in large pieces*
½	*celery stalk, cut in 3*
1	*garlic clove, smashed and chopped*
15 mL	*(1 tbs) chopped parsley*
500 mL	*(2 cups) brown sauce* *

In roasting pan containing lamb juices, place butter, onion, celery, garlic, and parsley. Mix and cook 10 minutes over medium heat on stove top.

Add brown sauce, stir, and simmer several minutes.

Pass sauce through food mill and serve with lamb.

Lamb can be served with cauliflower and sautéed peppers.

* See page 22.

Technique

1 Here is the butterfly deboned leg of lamb.

Technique : *Stuffed Leg of Lamb* (continued)

2 Place onion, celery, garlic, mushrooms, and herbs in casserole. Season with salt and pepper; microwave, uncovered, 3 minutes.

3 Add spicy croutons and egg; mix well.

4 Stuff lamb.

5 Secure lamb with string.

Lamb Chops with Artichoke Hearts

(serves 4)

Setting:	HIGH
Cooking time:	7 minutes in microwave
Utensil:	3 L casserole

15 mL	*(1 tbs) oil*
8	*lamb chops, fat trimmed*
1	*dry shallot, chopped*
5 mL	*(1 tsp) chopped parsley*
15 mL	*(1 tbs) green peppercorns, smashed*
175 mL	*(¾ cup) brown sauce* *
50 mL	*(¼ cup) 35% cream*
1	*can artichoke hearts, well drained and cut in 2*
	salt and pepper

Heat oil in frying pan on stove top. Add lamb and shallots; cook over high heat 1 minute each side.

Transfer lamb to casserole; season with salt and pepper. Lightly cover and microwave 2 minutes.

Turn chops; cover and microwave 2 minutes.

Remove chops from casserole; set aside.

Add parsley, green peppercorns, brown sauce, cream, and artichoke hearts to casserole. Season with salt and pepper; microwave, uncovered, 3 minutes. Serve.

* See page 22.

Shoulder of Lamb Jardinière

(serves 4)

1	bay leaf
30 mL	(2 tbs) cornstarch
60 mL	(4 tbs) cold water
	pinch thyme
	salt and pepper

Trim fat from lamb and cut into medium size cubes.

Heat oil in frying pan on stove top. Add half of lamb and sear 2 minutes each side.

Remove seared lamb and set aside. Sear remaining lamb.

Transfer lamb to casserole; season with salt, pepper, and parsley.

Add potatoes, carrots, onions, and garlic.

Add eggplant, tomatoes and juice, and tomato paste. Season with salt and pepper; add bay leaf and thyme. Mix well.

Add beef bouillon mix; cover and microwave 13 minutes.

Gently mix, cover and continue to microwave 13 minutes.

Mix again, cover and continue to microwave 13 minutes.

Remove potatoes and carrots from casserole; set aside.

Replace casserole in microwave and microwave, uncovered, 20 minutes.

Mix cornstarch with water; incorporate to mixture.

Replace potatoes and carrots in casserole; microwave, uncovered, 3 minutes. Serve.

Setting:	HIGH
Cooking time:	62 minutes in microwave
Utensil:	3 L casserole

1	1.2 kg (2½ lb) deboned shoulder of lamb
15 mL	(1 tbs) oil
15 mL	(1 tbs) chopped parsley
3	potatoes, peeled and cut in 4
3	carrots, peeled and cut in large pieces
2	onions, peeled and cut in 6
2	garlic cloves, smashed and chopped
¼	eggplant, peeled and diced
1	796 mL (28 oz) can tomatoes, reserve juice
15 mL	(1 tbs) tomato paste
5 mL	(1 tsp) beef bouillon mix

Technique

1 Sear lamb in hot oil. Transfer lamb to casserole and sprinkle with chopped parsley.

2 Add potatoes, carrots, onions, and garlic.

3 Add eggplant, tomatoes, tomato paste, and herbs. Season with salt and pepper.

Braised Lamb Chops

Braised Lamb Chops

(serves 2)

Setting:	**HIGH**
Cooking time:	**20 minutes in microwave**
Utensil:	**2 L casserole**

15 mL	*(1 tbs) vegetable oil*
4	*lamb chops (from shoulder)*
1	*onion, peeled and chopped*
1	*garlic clove, smashed and chopped*
15 mL	*(1 tbs) chopped parsley*
1	*796 mL (28 oz) can tomatoes, drained and coarsely chopped*
1	*celery stalk, sliced*
15 mL	*(1 tbs) beef bouillon mix*
15 mL	*(1 tbs) cornstarch*
30 mL	*(2 tbs) cold water*
	salt and pepper

Heat oil in frying pan on stove top. Add lamb and sear 3 minutes each side.

Transfer lamb to casserole. Add onion, garlic, and parsley; cover and microwave 3 minutes.

Add tomatoes, celery, and beef bouillon mix. Cover and microwave 10 minutes.

Mix cornstarch with water; incorporate to mixture. Microwave, uncovered, 7 minutes.

Serve.

Technique

1 Presentation of lamb.

2 Sear lamb in hot oil 3 minutes each side. Transfer to casserole.

→

Technique : Braised Lamb Chops (continued)

3 Add onion, garlic, and parsley.

4 Add tomatoes and celery.

5 Add beef bouillon mix.

Beef Stroganoff

(serves 4)

Setting: HIGH
Cooking time: 11 to 12 minutes in microwave
Utensil: 2 L casserole

30 mL	*(2 tbs) vegetable oil*
680 g	*(1½ lb) beef sirloin, cut into strips*
15 mL	*(1 tbs) butter*
1½	*onions, peeled and chopped*
227 g	*(½ lb) fresh mushrooms, washed and sliced*
45 mL	*(3 tbs) flour*
250 mL	*(1 cup) hot beef stock*
50 mL	*(¼ cup) dry Madeira wine*
30 mL	*(2 tbs) sour cream*
15 mL	*(1 tbs) chopped fresh parsley paprika salt and pepper*

Heat oil in frying pan on stove top. Add meat in 2 stages and cook 2 minutes on one side, 1 minute on other side. Season with salt and pepper; sprinkle with paprika. Set aside.

Place butter in casserole. Add onions and mushrooms; cover and microwave 4 minutes.

Add flour and mix well. Cover and microwave 2 minutes.

Incorporate beef stock and wine; mix well. Microwave, uncovered, 5 to 6 minutes. Stir once. Remove casserole from microwave.

Add beef and mix. Let stand 2 minutes.

Stir in cream and parsley.

Serve over noodles or rice.

Filet Mignon with Medeira Sauce

(serves 4)

Setting: HIGH
Cooking time: 12 to 13 minutes in microwave
Utensil: 2 L casserole

4	*slices toasted bread*
30 mL	*(2 tbs) vegetable oil*
4	*filet mignons, 227 to 280 g (8 to 10 oz)*
30 mL	*(2 tbs) butter*
2	*shallots, chopped*
227 g	*(½ lb) fresh mushrooms, washed and chopped*
45 mL	*(3 tbs) flour*
250 mL	*(1 cup) hot beef stock*
50 mL	*(¼ cup) dry Madeira wine chopped parsley salt and pepper*

Place toasted bread on service platter; set aside.

Heat oil in frying pan on stove top. Add meat and cook 7 to 8 minutes, depending on thickness. Turn and continue to cook 3 to 4 minutes. Season with salt and pepper.

Place meat on toasted bread; keep hot.

Place butter in casserole. Add shallots, cover and microwave 2 minutes.

Add mushrooms; season with salt and pepper. Cover and microwave 2 minutes.

Stir well and continue to microwave 2 minutes.

Add flour, mix, and microwave, uncovered, 1 minute.

Incorporate beef stock; stir and microwave 4 to 5 minutes. Stir once.

Add wine; stir and microwave 1 minute.

Pour sauce over meat and sprinkle with chopped parsley. Serve.

Beef Bourguignon

Beef Bourguignon

(serves 4)

Setting:	HIGH and MEDIUM-HIGH
Cooking time:	1 hour 10 minutes in microwave
Utensil:	2 L casserole

30 mL	*(2 tbs) peanut oil*
3	*slices bacon, diced*
2	*onions, peeled and chopped*
680 g	*(1½ lb) flank steak, cubed*
2	*garlic cloves, smashed and chopped*
375 mL	*(1½ cups) dry red wine, reduced by ½ on stove top*
250 mL	*(1 cup) tomato sauce*
250 mL	*(1 cup) hot beef stock*
37 mL	*(2½ tbs) cornstarch*
45 mL	*(3 tbs) cold water*
227 g	*(½ lb) mushrooms, washed and cut in 2*
	pinch thyme
	bay leaf
	chopped parsley
	salt and pepper

Heat oil in sauté pan over high heat on stove top.

Add bacon, onions, and half of meat; sear 2 to 3 minutes each side. Season with salt and pepper.

Sear remaining meat.

Place seared meat in casserole; add thyme, garlic, and bay leaf.

Add reduced wine, tomato sauce, and beef stock.

Mix cornstarch with water; incorporate to mixture.

Season with pepper and cover with sheet of plastic wrap. Microwave 70 minutes at MEDIUM-HIGH.

8 minutes before end of cooking, add mushrooms.

Once beef bourguignon is cooked, let stand 8 to 10 minutes in microwave.

Sprinkle with chopped parsley. Serve with croutons and dry red wine.

Technique

1 Place seared meat, onions, and bacon in casserole.

Technique : Beef Bourguignon (continued)

2 Add reduced red wine.

3 Add tomato sauce.

4 Add beef stock.

5 Add cornstarch mixture.

Beef Paupiettes

(serves 4)

Using a wooden mallet, pound each slice of meat between 2 sheets of wax paper. Roll slices and set aside.

Heat oil in frying pan on stove top. Add meat rolls and cook 2 minutes each side.

Transfer meat to casserole. Add onion, celery, and carrot; season with salt and pepper. Add parsley, Tabasco sauce, herbs, and clove.

Add brown sauce and tomato paste; mix gently. Cover and microwave 20 minutes at MEDIUM-HIGH.

Turn meat; cover and continue to microwave 20 minutes at MEDIUM-HIGH.

Add mushrooms; cover and microwave 3 minutes at HIGH.

Serve.

* See page 22.

Setting: **HIGH and MEDIUM-HIGH**
Cooking time: **43 minutes in microwave**
Utensil: **2 L casserole**

4	*slices beef sirloin, 0.65 cm (¼ in) thick and 8 cm (3 in) long*
15 mL	*(1 tbs) oil*
1	*red onion, peeled and sliced*
1	*celery stalk, sliced*
1	*carrot, peeled and sliced*
3	*parsley sprigs*
750 mL	*(3 cups) brown sauce**
15 mL	*(1 tbs) tomato paste*
8	*fresh large mushrooms, washed and sliced*
	several drops Tabasco sauce
	pinch thyme
	pinch clove
	pinch basil
	salt and pepper

Beef Braised with Eggplant

Beef Braised with Eggplant

(serves 4)

Setting:	HIGH and MEDIUM-HIGH
Cooking time:	1 hour 10 minutes
Utensil:	2 L casserole

30 mL	*(2 tbs) peanut oil*
680 g	*(1½ lb) flank steak, cubed*
1	*onion, peeled and diced*
1	*garlic clove, smashed and chopped*
15 mL	*(1 tbs) chopped parsley*
1 mL	*(¼ tsp) thyme*
1	*796 mL (28 oz) can tomatoes, drained*
1	*small ripe eggplant, peeled and sliced thickly*
375 mL	*(1½ cups) hot beef stock*
30 mL	*(2 tbs) cornstarch*
45 mL	*(3 tbs) cold water*
	salt and pepper

Heat oil in frying pan over high heat on stove top.

When hot, add half of beef and all onion. Sear 3 minutes each side; season with salt and pepper.

Sear remaining meat.

Place meat and onion in casserole. Add garlic, parsley, and thyme.

Add tomatoes, eggplant, and beef stock.

Cover with sheet of plastic wrap; microwave 70 minutes at MEDIUM-HIGH.

10 minutes before end of cooking, mix cornstarch with water and incorporate to sauce.

When beef is cooked, let stand 8 to 10 minutes in microwave.

Technique

1 The beef, onion, and eggplant.

2 Place seared meat and onions in casserole.

→

Technique : *Beef Braised with Eggplant (continued)*

3 Add tomatoes.

4 Add eggplant.

5 Add beef stock.

6 Add cornstarch mixture.

Beef Brochettes

(serves 4)

Setting: **HIGH**
Cooking time: **15 minutes**
Utensil: **2 L casserole and large plate**

Preparation of marinade

5 mL	(1 tsp) butter
15 mL	(1 tbs) chopped parsley
1	garlic clove, smashed and chopped
1	shallot, smashed and chopped
5 mL	(1 tsp) soya sauce

Place all ingredients in small saucepan and heat on stove top. Cook several minutes until butter melts completely; set aside.

Preparation of brochettes

½	eggplant, cubed
1	celery stalk, cubed
2	onions, peeled and cut in 4
1	garlic clove, smashed and chopped
15 mL	(1 tbs) soya sauce
680 g	(1½ lb) beef tenderloin, cubed
	salt and pepper

Place eggplant, celery, onion, garlic, and soya sauce in casserole. Season with salt and pepper; cover and microwave 5 minutes.

Mix and cover; continue to microwave 5 minutes.

Remove cover and let stand 2 minutes.

On skewers, alternate eggplant, beef, onion, and celery.

Place skewers in large microwave plate and generously brush with marinade. Cover and microwave 3 minutes.

Turn skewers and baste. Cover and microwave 2 minutes. Serve with buttered noodles.

Roast Beef with Pepper Sauce

Roast Beef with Pepper Sauce

(serves 4)

Setting: MEDIUM
Cooking time: 30 minutes in microwave
Utensil: 2 L square casserole

Preparation of roast beef

30 mL	*(2 tbs) maple syrup*
5 mL	*(1 tsp) soya sauce*
1	*1.4 kg (3 lb) rib-eye roast*
30 mL	*(2 tbs) mustard butter**
	salt and pepper

Mix maple syrup with soya sauce; brush over meat.

Set meat in ovenproof platter and grill (broil), 15 cm (6 in) from top element, for 7 minutes.

Remove meat and place in square casserole; generously pepper.

Cover with sheet of wax paper; microwave 15 minutes at MEDIUM.

Brush meat with mustard butter; season with salt and pepper.

Replace in microwave and turn a ½ turn; continue to microwave 15 minutes.

Remove casserole, cover meat with aluminium foil, and let stand 10 minutes.

* See recipe in book.

Preparation of pepper sauce

Setting: HIGH
Cooking time: 8 minutes
Utensil: 2 L round casserole

1½	*green peppers, sliced*
5 mL	*(1 tsp) butter*
1	*garlic clove, smashed and chopped*
15 mL	*(1 tbs) chopped parsley*
250 mL	*(1 cup) hot beef stock*
30 mL	*(2 tbs) cornstarch*
45 mL	*(3 tbs) cold water*
	cooking juices from roast
	salt and pepper

Place peppers, butter, garlic, and parsley in casserole. Cover with sheet of plastic wrap; microwave 3 minutes.

Add cooking juices and beef stock.

Mix cornstarch with water; incorporate to sauce with whisk.

Correct seasoning; microwave, uncovered, 5 minutes. Stir every 2 minutes.

Serve with roast.

See technique on following page.

Technique : Roast Beef with Pepper Sauce (continued)

1 The rib-eye roast.

2 Brush meat with mixture of maple syrup and soya sauce.

3 The meat was seared in a conventional oven, set at grill (broil) for 7 minutes.

4 After 15 minutes in microwave, brush meat with mustard butter.

Steak, Japanese Style

(serves 4)

Setting:	HIGH
Cooking time:	9 minutes in microwave
Utensil:	3 L casserole

30 mL	(2 tbs) vegetable oil
680 g	(1½ lb) beef sirloin, cut in strips
15 mL	(1 tbs) butter
1	onion, peeled and sliced
½	celery stalk, sliced
114 g	(¼ lb) fresh mushrooms, washed and sliced
125 mL	(½ cup) hot chicken stock *
22 mL	(1½ tbs) cornstarch
45 mL	(3 tbs) cold water
30 mL	(2 tbs) soya sauce
250 mL	(1 cup) canned bamboo shoots, well drained
	pinch sugar
	salt and pepper

Heat oil in frying pan on stove top. Add half of meat and cook 2 minutes over high heat. Turn meat and continue cooking 1 minute. Remove meat and keep hot.

Cook remaining meat, season with salt and pepper, and set aside.

Place butter in casserole. Add onion, celery, and mushrooms. Season with salt and pepper; cover and microwave 5 minutes.

Add chicken stock; stir well. Add sugar.

Mix cornstarch with water; incorporate to mixture. Add half of soya sauce; cover and microwave 3 minutes.

Add meat, remaining soya sauce, and bamboo shoots. Mix and microwave, uncovered, 1 minute. Serve.

* See page 55.

Curried Sliced Beef

(serves 4)

Setting:	HIGH
Cooking time:	12 minutes in microwave
Utensil:	2 L casserole

15 mL	(1 tbs) vegetable oil
680 g	(1½ lb) beef tenderloin, cut in large slices
5 mL	(1 tsp) olive oil
1	onion, peeled and chopped
30 mL	(2 tbs) curry powder
1	celery stalk, sliced
45 mL	(3 tbs) butter
60 mL	(4 tbs) flour
625 mL	(2½ cups) hot chicken stock *
5 mL	(1 tsp) tomato paste
1	apple, peeled, cored, and sliced
50 mL	(¼ cup) dry raisins
	salt and pepper

→

Salted Beef Brisket with Red Cabbage

Heat vegetable oil in frying pan on stove top. Add meat and cook 2 minutes each side. Remove and keep hot.

Place olive oil, onion, and curry powder in casserole. Cover and microwave 2 minutes.

Add celery and mix well.

Add butter, cover, and microwave 2 minutes.

Add flour; mix well. Add chicken stock and incorporate. Season with salt and pepper.

Add tomato paste and stir well. Microwave, uncovered, 6 minutes.

Add apples and raisins; microwave, uncovered, 2 minutes.

Add meat, mix, and serve.

* See page 55.

(serves 4)

Setting:	HIGH and MEDIUM-HIGH
Cooking time:	1 hour 45 minutes
Utensil:	2 L casserole for meat
	2 L casserole for vegetables

1	*650 g (1½ lb) salted beef brisket*
1	*red cabbage, washed and cut in 4*
2	*carrots, peeled and cut in 2*
3	*potatoes, peeled and cut in 2*
3	*parsley sprigs*
1	*bay leaf*
	pinch thyme

Place beef in casserole and cover with cold water. Cover and microwave 10 minutes at HIGH.

Remove beef and discard water.

Replace beef in casserole and cover with water. Cover and microwave 30 seconds at MEDIUM-HIGH.

Turn casserole a ¼ turn; continue to microwave 30 minutes * at MEDIUM-HIGH.

Remove casserole and cover; let beef stand in juices.

Place cabbage, carrots, potatoes, and herbs in other casserole. Add 500 mL (2 cups) cooking juices; cover and microwave 35 minutes at HIGH.

Reheat beef several minutes in microwave.

Serve beef with vegetables and strong mustard.

* Cooking time will vary depending on weight of meat.

Technique

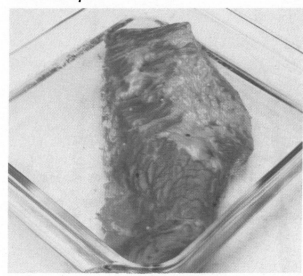

1 Place beef in casserole and cover with cold water. Cover and microwave 10 minutes.

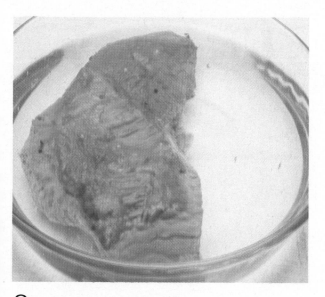

2 Change cooking water.

3 Place cabbage, carrots, potatoes, and herbs in other casserole.

Yankee Style Beef

Yankee Style Beef

(serves 4)

Setting: **MEDIUM-HIGH**
Cooking time: 1 hour 40 minutes in microwave
Utensil: 3 L casserole

1.6 kg	*(3½ lb) rump roast, lined with fat*
2	*garlic cloves, peeled and cut into small sticks*
30 mL	*(2 tbs) bacon fat*
3	*onions, peeled and coarsely diced*
375 mL	*(1½ cups) chopped tomatoes*
250 mL	*(1 cup) brown sauce**
5 mL	*(1 tsp) oregano*
1	*bay leaf*
15 mL	*(1 tbs) chopped parsley*
	salt and pepper

Using small knife, make incisions in meat and insert pieces of garlic.

Heat bacon fat in frying pan on stove top. When very hot, add meat and sear 6 to 7 minutes on all sides.

Transfer meat to casserole; add all remaining ingredients. Season with salt and pepper; cover with sheet of plastic wrap. Microwave 35 minutes.

Turn meat; cover and continue to microwave 30 minutes.

Turn meat again; cover and microwave 35 minutes.

Let meat stand in microwave 7 to 8 minutes. Serve.

* See page 22.

Beef Casserole

(serves 4)

Setting: **MEDIUM-HIGH**
Cooking time: 16 minutes
Utensil: 2 L casserole

5 mL	*(1 tsp) vegetable oil*
454 g	*(1 lb) beef tenderloin, diced*
1	*onion, peeled and chopped*
2	*celery stalks, washed and diced*
2	*potatoes, peeled and coarsely diced*
1	*garlic clove, smashed and chopped*
5 mL	*(1 tsp) chopped parsley*
1 mL	*(¼ tsp) oregano*
1	*796 mL (28 oz) can tomatoes, drained and chopped*
250 mL	*(1 cup) hot brown sauce**
	salt and pepper

Pour oil into casserole. Add meat and season with salt and pepper. Cover and microwave 6 minutes.

Mix well. Add onion, celery, potatoes, and garlic; mix again.

Add herbs, cover, and microwave 6 minutes.

Add tomatoes and brown sauce; microwave, uncovered, 4 minutes.

Serve over buttered noodles.

* See page 22.

Beef Flank with Curry

(serves 4)

Setting: HIGH and MEDIUM-HIGH
Cooking time: 56 minutes
Utensil: 2 L casserole

5 mL	*(1 tsp) oil*
2	*onions, peeled and sliced*
1	*garlic clove, smashed and chopped*
22 mL	*(1½ tbs) curry powder*
1	*454 g (1 lb) beef flank*
15 mL	*(1 tbs) soya sauce*
5 mL	*(1 tsp) maple syrup*
500 mL	*(2 cups) hot chicken stock* *
37 mL	*(2½ tbs) cornstarch*
45 mL	*(3 tbs) cold water*
50 mL	*(¼ cup) grated coconut*
50 mL	*(¼ cup) dry sweet raisins*
30 mL	*(2 tbs) sour cream*
	several drops lemon juice
	salt and pepper

Place oil, onions, and garlic in casserole. Cover with sheet of plastic wrap; microwave 3 minutes at HIGH.

Add curry powder and continue to microwave 2 minutes at HIGH. Mix well.

Roll flank (do not tie) and place in casserole.

Mix soya sauce with maple syrup; brush over flank. Season with salt and pepper.

Add chicken stock. Cover with sheet of plastic wrap; microwave 43 minutes at MEDIUM-HIGH.

Turn meat 2 to 3 times.

Remove flank and set aside.

Mix cornstarch with water; incorporate to sauce and mix well.

Microwave, uncovered, 8 minutes at MEDIUM-HIGH. Stir twice.

1 minute before end of cooking, add coconut, raisins, and lemon juice.

Before serving add sour cream.

* See page 55.

Beef Flank with Vegetables

(serves 4)

Setting: HIGH and MEDIUM-HIGH
Cooking time: 55 minutes
Utensil: 2 L casserole

5 mL	*(1 tsp) butter*
1	*onion, peeled and diced*
1	*454 g (1 lb) beef flank*
15 mL	*(1 tbs) soya sauce*
5 mL	*(1 tsp) maple syrup*
625 mL	*(2½ cups) hot beef stock*
30 mL	*(2 tbs) tomato paste*
1	*small bay leaf*
2	*potatoes, cubed*
1	*turnip, cubed*
2	*carrots, thickly sliced*
45 mL	*(3 tbs) cornstarch*
60 mL	*(4 tbs) cold water*
15 mL	*(1 tbs) chopped parsley*
	pinch thyme
	pinch nutmeg
	salt and pepper

Place butter and onion in casserole. Cover with sheet of plastic wrap; microwave 4 minutes at HIGH.

Roll flank (do not tie) and place in casserole.

Mix soya sauce with maple syrup; brush over meat.

Add beef stock, nutmeg, tomato paste, bay leaf, and thyme. Season with salt and pepper; mix well.

Cover with sheet of plastic wrap; microwave 43 minutes at MEDIUM-HIGH. Turn meat 2 to 3 times.

20 minutes before end of cooking, add vegetables.

At cooking end, mix cornstarch with water and incorporate to sauce. Mix well.

Microwave, uncovered, 8 minutes at MEDIUM-HIGH. Stir 2 times.

Let stand 7 to 8 minutes; sprinkle with chopped parsley. Serve.

Beef Flank
with Mushrooms
and Cucumbers

(serves 4)

Setting:	HIGH and MEDIUM-HIGH
Cooking time:	55 minutes
Utensil:	2 L casserole

1	*large onion, peeled and diced*
1	*garlic clove, smashed and chopped*
5 mL	*(1 tsp) oil*
1	*454 g (1 lb) beef flank*
15 mL	*(1 tbs) soya sauce*
5 mL	*(1 tsp) maple syrup*
500 mL	*(2 cups) brown sauce**
1 mL	*(¼ tsp) thyme*
114 g	*(¼ lb) mushrooms, cut in 2*
1	*cucumber, peeled, hollowed, and cut in slices of 0.62 cm (¼ in) thick*
	several drops lemon juice
	salt and pepper

Place onion, garlic, and oil in casserole. Cover with sheet of plastic wrap; microwave 4 minutes at HIGH.

Roll flank (do not tie) and place in casserole.

Mix soya sauce with maple syrup; brush over flank.

Add brown sauce, thyme, and salt lightly. Season with pepper.

Cover with sheet of plastic wrap; microwave 43 minutes at MEDIUM-HIGH.

Turn meat 2 to 3 times.

At cooking end, add mushrooms and cucumbers. Sprinkle with lemon juice.

Cover with sheet of plastic wrap; microwave 8 minutes at MEDIUM-HIGH.

Let stand 7 to 8 minutes in microwave. Serve.

* See page 22.

1 Place onion, garlic, and oil in casserole.

→

Technique : Beef Flank with Mushrooms and Cucumbers (continued)

2 Brush flank with mixture of soya sauce and maple syrup.

3 Place flank in casserole.

5 Add cucumbers.

6 Add mushrooms.

4 Add brown sauce, cover and microwave.

Beef Flank with Tomatoes

(serves 4)

Setting:	HIGH and MEDIUM-HIGH
Cooking time:	52 minutes in microwave
Utensil:	2 L casserole

5 mL	*(1 tsp) oil*
1	*onion, peeled and chopped*
2	*garlic cloves, smashed and chopped*
1	*454 g (1 lb) beef flank*
15 mL	*(1 tbs) soya sauce*
5 mL	*(1 tsp) maple syrup*
375 mL	*(1½ cups) tomatoes, drained and chopped*
125 mL	*(½ cup) hot chicken stock **
15 mL	*(1 tbs) tomato paste*
	salt and pepper

Place oil, onion, and garlic in casserole. Cover with sheet of plastic wrap; microwave 2 minutes at HIGH.

Roll flank, tie lightly, and place in casserole.

Mix soya sauce with maple syrup; brush over flank. Season with salt and pepper.

Add tomatoes, chicken stock, and tomato paste; mix well. (Or mix the 3 ingredients together before adding.)

Cover with sheet of plastic wrap; microwave 50 minutes at MEDIUM-HIGH.

Turn flank 2 to 3 times.

When flank is cooked, remove and transfer to service platter.

Pour sauce into saucepan and place on stove top. Reduce sauce, 4 to 5 minutes, over high heat.

Season to taste and serve with flank.

* See page 55.

Beef Stew

Beef Stew

(serves 4)

Setting:	HIGH
Cooking time:	1 hour 13 minutes
Utensil:	2 L casserole with cover

680 g	*(1½ lb) beef flank, cubed*
45 mL	*(3 tbs) soya sauce*
1	*onion, peeled and cubed*
5 mL	*(1 tsp) oil*
30 mL	*(2 tbs) tomato paste*
625 mL	*(2½ cups) hot beef stock*
1	*bay leaf*
45 mL	*(3 tbs) cornstarch*
60 mL	*(4 tbs) cold water*
½	*turnip, peeled and cubed*
2	*potatoes, peeled and cubed*
3	*carrots, cubed*
45 mL	*(3 tbs) sour cream*
	pinch thyme
	pinch oregano
	salt and pepper

Place beef in platter and sprinkle with soya sauce; toss well. Season with pepper and marinate 30 minutes or longer.

Place onion, oil, thyme, and oregano in casserole. Cover with sheet of plastic wrap; microwave 3 minutes.

Remove from microwave. Add meat, tomato paste, and beef stock; mix well.

Add bay leaf, salt, and pepper; cover and microwave 50 minutes.

Mix cornstarch with water; incorporate to mixture.

Add vegetables and mix. Cover and continue to microwave 20 minutes.

Let stand 6 to 7 minutes before serving.

Add sour cream, mix, and serve.

Technique

1 Presentation of cubed beef and vegetables.

Technique : Beef Stew (continued)

2 Place onion, oil, and spices in casserole. Season with salt and pepper.

3 Marinate beef in soya sauce.

5 20 minutes before end of cooking, add vegetables.

6 Add sour cream and mix well.

Meatball Onion Stew

(serves 4)

Setting: HIGH
Cooking time: 12 minutes
Utensil: 2 L casserole

45 mL	*(3 tbs) cooked chopped onion*
454 g	*(1 lb) lean ground beef*
1	*whole egg*
1	*onion, peeled and sliced*
2	*celery stalks, sliced*
15 mL	*(1 tbs) soya sauce*
500 mL	*(2 cups) hot beef stock*
45 mL	*(3 tbs) cornstarch*
60 mL	*(4 tbs) cold water*
	pinch thyme
	pinch oregano
	salt and pepper from mill

4 Place meat in casserole containing cooked onions.

→

Place cooked onion, beef, egg, and spices in bowl of blender. Mix until beef adheres to inside of bowl.

Remove mixture and form into meatballs. Lightly oil your hands.

Place sliced onion and celery in casserole. Add meatballs and sprinkle with soya sauce.

Add beef stock.

Mix cornstarch with water; incorporate to mixture.

Cover with sheet of plastic wrap; microwave 12 minutes. Serve.

Technique

1 Mix cooked onion, beef, and egg in bowl. Season with salt and pepper.

4 Place onion and celery in casserole.

5 Add meatballs and sprinkle with soya sauce.

2 To incorporate ingredients well, it is advisable
to use a blender.

3 Form meatballs.

6 Add beef stock.

Parmesan Casserole

(serves 4)

Setting: HIGH
Cooking time: 17 minutes
Utensil: 3 L casserole

15 mL	*(1 tbs) oil*
680 g	*(1½ lb) lean ground beef*
1	*garlic clove, smashed and chopped*
3	*tomatoes, peeled and chopped*
250 mL	*(1 cup) tomato sauce* *
150 mL	*(2/3 cup) grated mozzarella cheese*
45 mL	*(3 tbs) butter*
625 mL	*(2½ cups) cooked buttered noodles*
45 mL	*(3 tbs) grated parmesam cheese salt and pepper*

Pour oil into 2 L casserole; cover and heat 1 minute. Add beef and garlic; season with salt and pepper. Cover and microwave 5 minutes. Stir once.

Add tomatoes, cover and microwave 3 minutes.

Add tomato sauce and mozzarella cheese; cover and microwave 2 minutes. Set aside.

Place butter in 3 L casserole. Cover and heat 1 minute. Add noodles and remaining cheese; stir and microwave 2 minutes.

Add meat mixture. Stir and microwave, uncovered, 3 minutes. Serve.

* See page 25.

Ground Beef and Potato Casserole

(serves 4)

Setting: HIGH
Cooking time: 11 minutes
Utensil: 2 L casserole

15 mL	*(1 tbs) oil*
1	*garlic clove, smashed and chopped*
1	*celery stalk, chopped*
454 g	*(1 lb) lean ground beef*
125 mL	*(½ cup) hot tomato sauce* *
15 mL	*(1 tbs) sour cream*
500 mL	*(2 cups) mashed potatoes*
50 mL	*(¼ cup) grated mozzarella cheese*
15 mL	*(1 tbs) melted butter salt and pepper*

Pour oil in casserole. Add garlic and celery; cover and microwave 2 minutes.

Add beef; season with salt and pepper. Cover and microwave 4 minutes. Add tomato sauce and stir well.

Add sour cream; cover and microwave 2 minutes.

Spread mashed potatoes on top and sprinkle with cheese. Add melted butter. Microwave, uncovered, 3 minutes to melt cheese. Serve.

* See page 25.

Beef and Macaroni Casserole

(serves 4)

Setting:	HIGH
Cooking time:	10 to 12 minutes
Utensil:	3 L casserole

15 mL	(1 tbs) vegetable oil
1	onion, peeled and chopped
1	garlic clove, smashed and chopped
454 g	(1 lb) lean ground beef
227 g	(½ lb) ground veal
30 mL	(2 tbs) tomato paste
375 mL	(1½ cups) hot white sauce *
125 mL	(½ cup) grated Gruyère cheese
500 mL	(2 cups) cooked macaroni
	several drops Tabasco sauce
	salt and pepper

Pour oil into casserole. Cover and heat 1 minute.

Add onion and garlic; cover and microwave 2 minutes.

Add beef and veal; season with salt and pepper. Cover and microwave 4 to 5 minutes. Stir once and season to taste.

Add tomato paste and stir well. Add white sauce, cheese, and macaroni; blend well. Cover and microwave 3 to 4 minutes. Serve.

* See page 21.

Hamburger Soubise

(serves 4)

Setting:	HIGH
Cooking time:	10 to 12 minutes in microwave
Utensil:	2 L casserole

908 g	(2 lb) lean ground beef
½	beaten egg
30 mL	(2 tbs) vegetable oil
3	large onions, peeled and sliced
375 mL	(1½ cups) hot tomato sauce *
50 mL	(¼ cup) grated parmesan cheese
	several drops Worcestershire sauce
	salt and pepper

Place meat in mixing bowl. Add Worcestershire sauce and egg; season to taste. Mix well and form ball.

Form 4 hamburger steaks; set aside.

Pour half of oil in casserole. Add onions; season with salt and pepper. Cover and microwave 5 to 6 minutes.

Add tomato sauce and cheese; stir well and microwave, uncovered, 2 to 3 minutes. Set aside.

Heat remaining oil in frying pan on stove top. Add hamburger steaks and sear 2 minutes each side, over very high heat. Transfer to microwave service platter.

Pour sauce over steaks; microwave 3 minutes. Serve with buttered noddles.

* See page 25.

Beef Tacos

(serves 4)

Place oil, onion, and green pepper in casserole. Cover and microwave 2 minutes.

Add tomato and beef; season with salt and pepper. Add all spices, cover and microwave 3 minutes.

Stir well. Add bean sprouts and tomato paste; cover and microwave 4 minutes.

Add cheese, mix and microwave, uncovered, 1 minute.

Fill taco shells and serve.

Setting: **HIGH**
Cooking time: **10 minutes**
Utensil: **2 L casserole**

5 mL	*(1 tsp) oil*
½	*red onion, chopped*
½	*green pepper, chopped*
1	*tomato, chopped*
350 g	*(¾ lb) lean ground beef*
250 mL	*(1 cup) bean sprouts*
30 mL	*(2 tbs) tomato paste*
50 mL	*(¼ cup) grated mozzarella cheese*
8	*commercial taco shells*
	several crushed chillies
	several drops spicy Trinidad sauce or Tabasco sauce
	pinch chili powder
	salt and pepper

Tostadas with Peppers

(serves 4)

Setting:	HIGH
Cooking time:	12 minutes
Utensil:	2 — 2 L casseroles

1	*large celery stalk, cut into julienne*
½	*red pepper, cut into julienne*
1	*green pepper, cut into julienne*
2	*green onions, cut into julienne*
1	*carrot, peeled and cut into julienne*
5 mL	*(1 tsp) oil*
1	*garlic clove, smashed and chopped*
1	*red onion, peeled and chopped*
350 g	*(¾ lb) lean ground beef*
30 mL	*(2 tbs) tomato paste*
125 mL	*(½ cup) tomato juice*
3	*slices mozzarella cheese, diced*
8	*commercial tostadas shells*
	pinch cumin
	pinch chili powder
	several drops Tabasco sauce
	salt and pepper

Place celery, peppers, green onions, and carrot in casserole. Cover and microwave 3 minutes.

Mix, cover and continue to microwave 2 minutes. Remove from microwave and set aside.

In other casserole, place oil, garlic, and onion; cover and microwave 1 minute.

Add beef, spices, tomato paste and juice. Mix well; season with salt and pepper. Cover and microwave 5 minutes.

Mix well to incorporate cooking liquid. Add cheese; microwave, uncovered, 1 minute.

Spread beef mixture over shells and top with vegetables. Serve.

Pork Chops, Bourguignonne Sauce

Pork Chops, Bourguignonne Sauce

(serves 4)

Setting:	HIGH and MEDIUM-HIGH
Cooking time:	28 minutes in microwave
Utensil:	2 L casserole

Preparation of pork chops

5 mL	*(1 tsp) soya sauce*
15 mL	*(1 tbs) maple syrup*
4	*pork chops, 2 cm (¾ in) thick, deboned*
	salt and pepper

Preheat convention oven to grill (broil).

Mix soya sauce with maple syrup; brush over chops.

Place chops in ovenproof dish. Grill (broil) 2 minutes each side in oven.

Transfer to microwave. Season with salt and pepper; cover with sheet of plastic wrap and microwave 8 to 9 minutes at MEDIUM-HIGH. (Cooking time may vary depending on thickness of chops) Serve with bourguignonne sauce.

Preparation of bourguignonne sauce

4	*slices bacon, diced*
1	*onion, peeled and chopped*
15 mL	*(1 tbs) chopped parsley*
1	*garlic clove, smashed and chopped*
20	*mushrooms, diced*
375 mL	*(1½ cups) red wine*
375 mL	*(1½ cups) hot beef stock*
5 mL	*(1 tsp) soya sauce*
45 mL	*(3 tbs) cornstarch*
60 mL	*(4 tbs) cold water*
30 mL	*(2 tbs) sour cream*
	salt and pepper

Place bacon, onion, parsley, garlic, and mushrooms in casserole. Microwave, uncovered, 10 minutes at HIGH.

Remove casserole from microwave and set aside.

Pour wine into small saucepan. Reduce by 2/3 over high heat on stove top.

Add wine to casserole.

Add beef stock and soya sauce.

Mix cornstarch with water; incorporate to sauce. Season to taste.

Microwave, uncovered, 10 minutes at HIGH. Stir sauce 1 to 2 times.

When sauce is cooked, remove from microwave.

Stir in sour cream and serve.

See technique on following page.

Cooking Bacon

To obtain crispy bacon follow the method below.

Setting:	HIGH
Cooking time:	6 minutes
Utensil:	Microwave plate

Place 2 sheets of paper towel on plate.

Place 6 slices of bacon on paper towel; cover with another sheet of paper towel.

Microwave 6 minutes.

When bacon is cooked, remove plate and let stand 1 minute. Serve.

Technique : Pork Chops, Bourguignonne Sauce

1 Presentation of pork chops.

2 Brush chops with mixture of soya sauce and maple syrup.

Technique : Bourguignonne Sauce

1 Microwave bacon, onion, parsley, garlic, and mushrooms. Add red wine.

2 Add beef stock.

Garlic Butter Pork Chops

(serves 4)

Setting: MEDIUM
Cooking time: 12 minutes in microwave
Utensil: 30 × 20 × 5 cm (11¾ × 7½ × 1¾ in) casserole

5 mL	*(1 tsp) oil*
4	*butterfly pork chops, 200 g (7 oz) and 1.2 cm (½ in) thick*
4	*slices garlic butter*
	salt and pepper

Heat oil in frying pan with heavy bottom, over high heat on stove top.

Add 2 chops and cook 1 minute each side.

Remove chops and set aside.

Heat pan again over high heat and add remaining chops; cook 1 minute each side.

Place chops in casserole, with thickest sections towards exterior of dish. Microwave, uncovered, 6 minutes.

Turn chops and continue to microwave, uncovered, 6 minutes.

1 minute before end of cooking, place slice of garlic butter on each chop.

3   Sear chops under grill (broil), then place in microwave dish.

3   Add cornstarch mixture.

Pork Chops à la Flamande

(serves 2)

Setting: MEDIUM and HIGH
Cooking time: 15 minutes in microwave
Utensil: 2 L square casserole

5 mL	*(1 tsp) oil*
2	*pork chops, 2.5 cm (1 in) thick*
1	*onion, peeled and sliced*
3	*potatoes, peeled and sliced*
15 mL	*(1 tbs) chopped parsley*
125 mL	*(½ cup) hot chicken stock* *
15 mL	*(1 tbs) soya sauce*
	salt and pepper

Heat oil in frying pan over high heat on stove top. When oil is very hot, sear pork chops 1 minute each side.

Transfer chops to casserole. Microwave, uncovered, 5 minutes at MEDIUM.

Remove chops and set aside.

Place onion in casserole; cover with potatoes and chopped parsley.

Add chicken stock; season with salt and pepper.

Cover with sheet of plastic wrap; microwave 10 minutes at HIGH.

3 minutes before end of cooking, place chops on potatoes and sprinkle with soya sauce.

Cover and continue to microwave. Serve.

* See page 55.

Technique

1 Place onion in casserole and cover with potatoes and chopped parsley.

2 Place seared chops on cooked potatoes.

Grilled Pork Chops

(serves 2)

Setting:	MEDIUM
Cooking time:	16 minutes in microwave
Utensil:	30 × 20 × 5 cm (11¾ × 7½ × 1¾ in) casserole

5 mL	*(1 tsp) oil*
4	*pork chops, 2.5 cm (1 in) thick*
	salt and pepper

Heat oil in frying pan over high heat on stove top.

Add 2 chops and cook 1 minute each side.

Remove and set aside.

Heat pan over high heat and add remaining chops; cook 1 minute each side.

Place chops in casserole, with thickest section towards exterior of dish. Lightly cover with wax paper; microwave 8 minutes.

Turn chops; cover and continue to microwave 8 minutes. Serve with applesauce.

Preparation of garnish *

5 mL	*(1 tsp) butter*
½	*onion, finely chopped*
2	*potatoes, peeled and diced*
25	*mushrooms, diced*
375 mL	*(1½ cups) brown sauce*
15 mL	*(1 tbs) chopped parsley*
	salt and pepper

Place butter, onion, and potatoes in casserole; season with salt and pepper.

Cover with sheet of plastic wrap; microwave 4 minutes at HIGH.

Remove casserole and add mushrooms, brown sauce, and parsley.

Microwave, uncovered, 9 minutes.

Serve with pork chops.

* It is advisable to prepare garnish before pork chops. To reheat, microwave 2 minutes at HIGH.

Pork Chops with Bonne-femme Garnish

(serves 4)

Setting:	HIGH and MEDIUM
Cooking time:	29 minutes in microwave
Utensil:	meat: 30 × 20 × 5 cm casserole
	garnish: 2 L casserole

Preparation of pork chops

5 mL	*(1 tsp) oil*
4	*pork chops, 2.5 cm (1 in) thick*
	salt and pepper

Heat oil in frying pan with heavy bottom, over high heat on stove top.

Add 2 chops and cook 1 minute each side.

Remove chops and set aside.

Reheat pan over high heat; add remaining chops and cook 1 minute each side.

Place chops in casserole, with thickest section towards exterior of dish.

Cover lightly with wax paper; microwave 8 minutes at MEDIUM.

Turn chops, cover and continue to microwave 8 minutes.

Serve with bonne-femme garnish.

Slices of Pork, Onion and Red Pepper

Slices of Pork, Onion, and Red Pepper

(serves 4)

Setting:	HIGH
Cooking time:	14 minutes
Utensil:	2 L round casserole

5 mL	(1 tsp) butter
1	onion, peeled and sliced
1	red pepper, sliced
1	796 mL (28 oz) can tomatoes, drained and chopped
250 mL	(1 cup) hot chicken stock
22 mL	(1½ tbs) cornstarch
30 mL	(2 tbs) cold water
4	cooked pork chops, sliced slantwise
15 mL	(1 tbs) soya sauce
	pinch oregano
	salt and pepper

Place butter, onion, and red pepper in casserole; season with salt and pepper.

Cover with sheet of plastic wrap; microwave 4 minutes.

Add tomatoes and spices; mix well with wooden spoon.

Microwave, uncovered, 4 minutes.

Mix well and add chicken stock.

Mix cornstarch with water; incorporate to mixture. Mix well.

Add soya sauce and correct seasoning.

Microwave, uncovered, 6 minutes.

2 minutes before end of cooking, add pork.

Pork Tenderloins with Curry

(serves 4)

Setting:	HIGH and MEDIUM
Cooking time:	35 minutes
Utensil:	2 L square casserole

15 mL	(1 tbs) butter
1	onion, peeled and chopped
30 mL	(2 tbs) curry powder
2	pork tenderloins, fat trimmed and cut in 2
15 mL	(1 tbs) soya sauce
15 mL	(1 tbs) maple syrup
375 mL	(1½ cups) hot beef stock
30 mL	(2 tbs) cornstarch
45 mL	(3 tbs) cold water
50 mL	(¼ cup) dry sweet raisins
125 mL	(½ cup) grated coconut
30 mL	(2 tbs) sour cream
	salt and pepper

Place butter, onion, and curry powder in casserole.

Cover with sheet of plastic wrap; microwave 5 minutes at HIGH.

Place pork in casserole, with thickest section towards exterior of dish.

Mix soya sauce with maple syrup; brush over pork.

Add beef stock; season with salt and pepper.

Microwave, uncovered, 15 minutes at MEDIUM.

Remove casserole and set pork aside.

Mix cornstarch with water; incorporate to sauce.

Replace pork in casserole and continue to microwave, uncovered, 15 minutes at MEDIUM.

2 minutes before end of cooking time, add raisins and coconut.

Remove casserole, incorporate sour cream, and serve.

Pork Tenderloins with Onions

Pork Tenderloins
with Onions

(serves 4)

handwritten note:
- 1 tenderloin cut in ½   may10 8
- small corningware
- 10 minutes! let sit
- no tomato paste

Setting:	HIGH and MEDIUM
Cooking time:	35 minutes
Utensil:	2 L square casserole

15 mL	*(1 tbs) butter*
1½	*onions, peeled and sliced*
1	*garlic clove, smashed and chopped*
2	*pork tenderloins, fat trimmed and cut in 2*
15 mL	*(1 tbs) soya sauce*
15 mL	*(1 tbs) maple syrup*
375 mL	*(1½ cups) hot beef stock*
15 mL	*(1 tbs) tomato paste*
30 mL	*(2 tbs) cornstarch*

[...] **s) cold water**
[...] **nd pepper**

[...] nions, and garlic in casserole; *[...]* et of plastic wrap; microwave 5 minutes at HIGH.

Remove casserole and stir onions well.

Place pork in casserole, with thickest section towards exterior of dish.

Mix soya sauce with maple syrup; brush over pork.

Add beef stock; season with salt and pepper.

Microwave, uncovered, 15 minutes at MEDIUM.

Remove casserole and set pork aside.

Add tomato paste to casserole.

Mix cornstarch with water; incorporate to sauce. Mix well.

Replace pork in casserole and continue to microwave, uncovered, 15 minutes at MEDIUM.

Serve with broccoli.

Pork Chops with
Green Pepper Garnish

(serves 4)

Setting:	HIGH and MEDIUM
Cooking time:	23 minutes in microwave
Utensil:	for meat: 30 × 20 × 5 cm casserole
	for garnish: 2 L casserole

Preparation of garnish *

5 mL	*(1 tsp) butter*
3	*green onions, chopped*
1	*green pepper, diced*
1	*celery stalk, finely diced*
20	*mushrooms, diced*
375 mL	*(1½ cups) cooked long grain rice*
15 mL	*(1 tbs) soya sauce*
	salt and pepper

Place butter, onions, green pepper, celery, and mushrooms in casserole. Season with salt and pepper.

Cover with sheet of plastic wrap; microwave 5 minutes at HIGH.

Remove casserole; add rice and mix with fork. Microwave, uncovered, 2 minutes at HIGH.

Add soya sauce and mix well with fork.

Serve with pork chops.

* It is advisable to prepare garnish before pork chops. To reheat, microwave 2 minutes at HIGH.

Preparation of pork chops

5 mL	*(1 tsp) oil*
4	*pork chops, 2.5 cm (1 in) thick*
	salt and pepper

Heat oil in frying pan with heavy bottom, over high heat on stove top.

Add 2 chops and cook 1 minute each side.

Remove chops and set aside.

Reheat pan over high heat and add remaining chops; cook 1 minute each side.

Place chops in casserole, with thickest section towards exterior of dish.

Lightly cover with wax paper and microwave 8 minutes at MEDIUM.

Turn chops; cover and continue to microwave 8 minutes.

Serve with green pepper garnish.

Suffed Pork Tenderloin

Stuffed Pork Tenderloin

(serves 2)

Setting:	HIGH and MEDIUM-HIGH
Cooking time:	37 minutes
Utensil:	2 L casserole

5 mL	*(1 tsp) butter*
30 mL	*(2 tbs) chopped onion*
½	*celery stalk, chopped*
15	*mushrooms, washed and chopped*
30 mL	*(2 tbs) breadcrumbs*
30 mL	*(2 tbs) 35% cream*
1	*pork tenderloin, fat trimmed*
5 mL	*(1 tsp) maple syrup*
15 mL	*(1 tbs) soya sauce*
1	*onion, peeled and diced*
250 mL	*(1 cup) commercial tomato sauce*
250 mL	*(1 cup) hot beef stock*
227 g	*(½ lb) mushrooms, washed and cut in 2*
	chopped parsley
	pinch thyme
	salt and pepper

Place butter, chopped onion, celery, and chopped mushrooms in casserole.

Add thyme; season with salt and pepper.

Cover with sheet of plastic wrap; microwave 4 minutes at HIGH.

Remove casserole and pour mixture into bowl.

Add breadcrumbs and cream; mix until very well incorporated.

Cut tenderloin in 2, lengthwise and place between 2 sheets of wax paper. Using mallet, pound to enlarge.

Season pork with salt and pepper. Spread stuffing over pork and fold shut; lightly secure with string.

Mix maple syrup with soya sauce; brush over pork.

Place diced onion in casserole; cover with sheet of plastic wrap and microwave 3 minutes.

Place pork on onions; pour in tomato sauce and beef stock. Season with pepper.

Cover with sheet of plastic wrap; microwave 30 minutes at MEDIUM-HIGH.

Turn tenderloin once during cooking.

10 minutes before end of cooking, add mushrooms.

Let pork stand in sauce 5 to 6 minutes. Sprinkle with parsley.

Note: If you find sauce too thin, follow this procedure: Pour sauce into saucepan; add 15 mL (1 tbs) cornstarch mixed with 30 mL (2 tbs) cold water. Incorporate well and bring to boil 2 minutes on stove top.

Technique

1 Place butter, chopped onion, celery, and chopped mushrooms in casserole; microwave.

→

Technique : Stuffed Pork Tenderloin (continued)

2 Pour mixture into bowl and add breadcrumbs.

3 Add cream; mix until very well incorporated.

6 Spread filling over tenderloin.

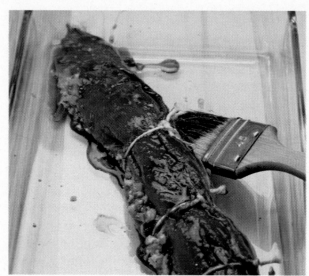

7 Brush tenderloin with mixture of soya sauce and maple syrup.

4 Cut tenderloin in two.

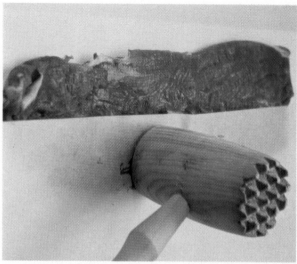

5 Place filet between 2 sheets of wax paper and using mallet, pound.

8 Place pork on cooked onions; pour in tomato sauce and beef stock. Season with pepper.

9 Ten minutes before end of cooking, add mushrooms.

Pork Roast with Applesauce

(serves 4)

Remove pork and transfer to casserole; season generously with pepper.

Cover roast with sheet of wax paper; microwave 20 minutes at MEDIUM.

Remove casserole and baste with horseradish butter; season with salt and pepper.

Replace in microwave and turn a ½ turn. Microwave 20 minutes.

Remove and cover roast with aluminium foil. Let stand 10 minutes.

Serve with applesauce.

* See recipe in book.

Setting:	MEDIUM
Cooking time:	40 minutes in microwave
Utensil:	2 L square casserole

Preparation of roast

1	1.4 kg (3 lb) pork loin
1	garlic clove, peeled and cut in small pieces
30 mL	(2 tbs) maple syrup
5 mL	(1 tsp) soya sauce
30 mL	(2 tbs) horseradish butter *
	salt and pepper

Make incisions in pork and insert pieces of garlic.

Mix maple syrup with soya sauce; brush over pork.

Place pork in ovenproof dish and grill (broil) in conventional oven, 15 cm (6 in) from top element for 7 minutes.

Technique

1 Presentation of pork loin secured with string.

Preparation of applesauce

Setting: HIGH
Cooking time: 6 minutes
Utensil: 2 L round casserole

4	*apples, cored, peeled, and sliced*
30 mL	*(2 tbs) brown sugar*
15 mL	*(1 tbs) lemon juice*
5 mL	*(1 tsp) cinnamon*
1 mL	*(¼ tsp) allspice*

Place all ingredients in casserole. Cover with sheet of plastic wrap; microwave 6 minutes.

Remove casserole from microwave.

Stir applesauce well and serve with pork.

2   Insert pieces of garlic into loin.

Slices of Ham à l'Orange

(serves 2)

Setting: HIGH
Cooking time: 4 minutes
Utensil: 2.5 or 3 L casserole

2	*large slices ham, 0.65 cm (¼ in) thick*
1	*orange, peeled and sliced*
30 mL	*(2 tbs) maple syrup*
	zest ½ lemon, finely sliced

Make several incisions along edge of ham to avoid curling during cooking.

Place ham in casserole and top with orange slices.

Sprinkle with maple syrup.

Add orange zest; cover and microwave 4 minutes.

Serve with garlic rice.

Sliced Pork with Eggplant

Sliced Pork with Eggplant

(serves 4)

Setting:	HIGH
Cooking time:	45 minutes in microwave
Utensil:	3 L casserole

1	*medium size eggplant, cubed with skin*
½	*red onion, chopped*
30 mL	*(2 tbs) chopped banana pepper*
2	*small zucchini, sliced with skin*
1	*796 mL (28 oz) can tomatoes, drained and coarsely chopped*
30 mL	*(2 tbs) tomato paste*
5 mL	*(1 tsp) soya sauce*
15 mL	*(1 tbs) oil*
454 g	*(1 lb) pork loin, sliced*
50 mL	*(¼ cup) grated mozzarella cheese*
	salt and pepper

Place eggplant, onion, banana pepper, and zucchini in casserole. Season with salt and pepper; cover and microwave 8 minutes.

Add tomatoes, tomato paste, and soya sauce; season with salt and pepper. Microwave, uncovered, 15 minutes.

Mix well and continue to microwave 20 minutes.

Heat oil in frying pan on stove top. Add pork; sear 2 minutes each side.

Incorporate pork to eggplant mixture; sprinkle with cheese. Microwave, uncovered, 2 minutes.

Serve.

Technique

1 Place eggplant, onion, banana pepper, and zucchini in casserole.

2 Add tomatoes, tomato paste, and soya sauce.

Marinated Pork Skewers

(serves 4)

Place pork, soya sauce, wine, oil, Tabasco sauce, and garlic in bowl; marinate 1 hour.

Place onions, zucchini, celery, and mushrooms in casserole. Season with salt and pepper; sprinkle with lemon juice. Cover and microwave 3 minutes.

Alternate zucchini, mushrooms, celery, onions, and pork on skewers.

Place skewers on microwave plate; generously season with salt and pepper. Cover and microwave 3 minutes.

Turn skewers and continue to microwave 3 minutes.

Serve with tomato salad.

Setting:	HIGH
Cooking time:	9 minutes
Utensil:	2 L casserole and large microwave plate

680 g	*(1½ lb) pork loin, fat trimmed and cubed*
5 mL	*(1 tsp) soya sauce*
50 mL	*(¼ cup) dry white wine*
30 mL	*(2 tbs) oil*
2	*garlic cloves, smashed and chopped*
2	*onions, peeled and cut in 4*
1	*small zucchini, thickly sliced*
1	*celery stalk, cubed*
12	*fresh large mushrooms, washed and cut in 2*
	several drops Tabasco sauce
	lemon juice
	salt and pepper

Technique

1 Place pork, soya sauce, wine, oil, Tabasco sauce, and garlic in bowl; marinate 1 hour.

Tomato Salad

2	*tomatoes, washed, cut in 2, and sliced*
1	*red onion, peeled and sliced*
15 mL	*(1 tbs) wine vinegar*
45 mL	*(3 tbs) oil*
15 mL	*(1 tbs) chopped parsley*
	several drops Tabasco sauce
	salt and pepper

Place all ingredients in bowl; toss well. Correct seasoning.

2 The vegetables after 3 minutes in microwave.

Chasseur Sliced Pork

(serves 4)

Setting:	HIGH
Cooking time:	6 minutes in microwave
Utensil:	2 L casserole

15 mL	*(1 tbs) butter*
½	*red onion, chopped*
1	*garlic clove, smashed and chopped*
5 mL	*(1 tsp) chopped parsley*
50 mL	*(¼ cup) dry white wine*
1	*796 mL (28 oz) can tomatoes, drained and chopped*
15 mL	*(1 tbs) tomato paste*
15 mL	*(1 tbs) oil*
1½	*pork tenderloin, sliced*
12	*fresh mushrooms, washed and sliced*
	pinch oregano
	salt and pepper

→

Place butter, onion, garlic, and parsley in casserole. Cover and microwave 2 minutes.

Add wine, tomatoes, and oregano; stir well. Season with salt and pepper.

Add tomato paste; microwave, uncovered, 4 minutes.

Heat oil in frying pan on stove top. Add pork; cook 2 minutes each side.

Add mushrooms to pan; season with salt and pepper. Cook 3 minutes.

Incorporate pork and mushrooms to sauce.

Serve on turret noddles.

Technique

1 Place butter, onion, garlic, and parsley in casserole.

2 Add wine, tomatoes, and oregano.

3 Incorporate pork and mushrooms to sauce.

Sliced Pork au Soya

(serves 4)

Setting: HIGH
Cooking time: 6 minutes in microwave
Utensil: 2 L casserole

15 mL	*(1 tbs) oil*
454 g	*(1 lb) pork loin, cut in strips*
1	*red onion, peeled and sliced in rings*
5 mL	*(1 tsp) soya sauce*
1	*red pepper, sliced in rings*
114 g	*(¼ lb) pea pods*
250 mL	*(1 cup) bean sprouts*
250 mL	*(1 cup) brown sauce*
	several drops oil
	salt and pepper

Heat oil in frying pan on stove top. Add pork and sear 2 minutes each side. Set aside.

Place onion and soya sauce in casserole; cover and microwave 2 minutes.

Add red pepper, pea pods, and bean sprouts. Sprinkle with soya sauce and several drops oil. Season with salt and pepper; cover and microwave 3 minutes.

Add brown sauce and pork; microwave, uncovered, 1 minute. Serve.

Pork Tenderloins and Mushrooms

(serves 4)

Setting: HIGH and MEDIUM
Cooking time: 36 minutes
Utensil: 2 L square casserole

15 mL	*(1 tbs) butter*
1	*onion, peeled and chopped*
227 g	*(½ lb) mushrooms, sliced*
15 mL	*(1 tbs) chopped parsley*
2	*pork tenderloins, fat trimmed and cut in 2*
15 mL	*(1 tbs) soya sauce*
15 mL	*(1 tbs) maple syrup*
250 mL	*(1 cup) hot beef stock*
15 mL	*(1 tbs) tomato paste*
45 mL	*(3 tbs) cornstarch*
60 mL	*(4 tbs) cold water*
30 mL	*(2 tbs) sour cream*
	several drops lemon juice
	salt and pepper

Place butter, onion, mushrooms, and parsley in casserole. Season with salt and add several drops lemon juice.

Cover with sheet of plastic wrap; microwave 6 minutes at HIGH.

Remove casserole and mix well.

Place pork in casserole, with thickest section towards exterior of dish.

Mix soya sauce with maple syrup; brush over pork.

Add beef stock; season with salt and pepper.

Microwave, uncovered, 15 minutes at MEDIUM.

Remove casserole and set pork aside.

Add tomato paste to sauce.

Mix cornstarch with water; incorporate to sauce.

Replace pork in casserole; continue to microwave, uncovered, 15 minutes at MEDIUM.

Slice pork, add sour cream to sauce, and serve.

Veal Chops à l'Orange

(serves 2)

Setting: HIGH
Cooking time: 4 minutes in microwave
Utensil: 2 L casserole

2	*large veal chops*
50 mL	*(¼ cup) flour*
30 mL	*(2 tbs) butter*
6	*fresh mushrooms, washed and sliced*
1	*small zucchini, sliced*
5	*cherry tomatoes, cut in 2*
½	*green pepper, sliced*
¼	*can bamboo shoots, sliced*
	zest ½ orange
	juice 1 orange
	salt and pepper

Season veal with salt and pepper; dredge with flour.

Heat butter in frying pan on stove top. Add veal and sear over medium heat, 2 to 3 minutes each side.

Transfer veal to casserole. Add vegetables, orange zest and juice. Cover and microwave 4 minutes. Serve.

Technique

1 Presentation of veal chops and vegetables.

2 Sear chops in frying pan and transfer to casserole.

3 Add vegetables.

Veal Scallops with Eggplant

Veal Scallops with Eggplant

(serves 4)

Setting:	HIGH
Cooking time:	28 minutes in microwave
Utensil:	2 L casserole

4	large veal scallops
125 mL	(½ cup) flour
15 mL	(1 tbs) oil
5 mL	(1 tsp) vegetable oil
1	onion, peeled and chopped
2	garlic cloves, smashed and chopped
½	796 mL (28 oz) can tomatoes, drained, chopped, and smashed
1	eggplant, cubed
5 mL	(1 tsp) chopped parsley
15 mL	(1 tbs) butter
30 mL	(2 tbs) tomato paste
	several drops Tabasco sauce
	pinch oregano
	salt and pepper

Roll veal scallops and dredge with flour.

Heat 15 mL (1 tbs) oil in frying pan on stove top. Add veal and cook 2 minutes each side. Set aside.

Place vegetable oil, onion, garlic, tomatoes, eggplant, parsley, and butter in casserole. Season with salt and pepper; cover and microwave 20 minutes.

Add tomato paste and mix well.

Add Tabasco sauce and oregano; microwave, uncovered, 6 minutes.

Add veal to casserole; microwave, uncovered, 2 minutes. Serve.

Veal Chops with Apples

(serves 2)

Setting:	HIGH
Cooking time:	5 minutes in microwave
Utensil:	2 L casserole

2	large veal chops
125 mL	(½ cup) flour
15 mL	(1 tbs) oil
30 mL	(2 tbs) chopped green onion
1	apple, peeled, cored, and sliced
¼	celery stalk, sliced
5 mL	(1 tsp) butter
	salt and pepper

Dredge veal with flour. Heat oil in frying pan on stove top and sear veal 1 minute each side.

Transfer veal to casserole. Add green onion, apple, celery, and butter. Season with salt and pepper; cover and microwave 4 minutes.

Turn casserole a ¼ turn; continue to microwave 1 minute. Serve.

Veal Liver Lyonnaise

(serves 4)

Setting: **HIGH**
Cooking time: **12 to 14 minutes in microwave**
Utensil: **2 L casserole**

Preparation of sauce

30 mL	*(2 tbs) butter*
3	*onions, peeled and sliced*
5 mL	*(1 tsp) soya sauce*
15 mL	*(1 tbs) wine vinegar*
375 mL	*(1½ cups) brown sauce**
	several drops Worcestershire sauce
	chopped parsley
	salt and pepper

Place butter in casserole; cover and heat 1 minute.

Add onions; season with salt and pepper. Cover and microwave 4 minutes.

Stir onions well. Add soya sauce and vinegar; cover and microwave 4 to 6 minutes.

Add brown sauce and Worcestershire sauce; microwave 3 minutes. Set aside.

* See page 22.

Preparation of veal livers

4	*slices veal liver*
50 mL	*(¼ cup) flour*
45 mL	*(3 tbs) butter*
	salt and pepper

Season liver with salt and pepper; dredge with flour.

Heat butter in frying pan on stove top. Add liver and cook 2 to 3 minutes each side.

Transfer liver to service platter. Top with lyonnaise sauce. Serve with fresh vegetables.

Veal Liver with Tomatoes

(serves 4)

Setting: **HIGH**
Cooking time: **10 to 12 minutes in microwave**
Utensil: **2 L casserole**

15 mL	*(1 tbs) olive oil*
1	*onion, peeled and chopped*
1	*green pepper, thinly sliced*
3	*tomatoes, peeled, seeded, and chopped*
1	*garlic clove, smashed and chopped*
15 mL	*(1 tbs) chopped parsley*
5 mL	*(1 tsp) soya sauce*
4	*slices veal liver, cut in strips*
50 mL	*(¼ cup) flour*
45 mL	*(3 tbs) butter*
	salt and pepper

Place oil in casserole; cover and heat 1 minute.

Add onion, green pepper, tomatoes, garlic, and chopped parsley. Season with salt and pepper; cover and microwave 8 to 10 minutes.

Add soya sauce, mix and set aside.

Season liver with salt and pepper; dredge with flour.

Melt butter in frying pan on stove top. Add half of liver and cook over very high heat 1 minute each side. Remove liver and keep hot.

Sear remaining liver.

Incorporate liver to tomato mixture; mix well and microwave 1 minute.

Serve with noddles or rice.

Blanquette de Veau

(serves 4)

Place veal in casserole and cover with hot water. Cover and microwave 8 minutes at HIGH.

Remove veal and drain well. Discard cooking liquid.

Replace veal in casserole. Add onions, parsley sprig, and bay leaf. Cover with water.

Season with salt and pepper; cover and microwave 30 minutes at MEDIUM-HIGH.

Stir veal, cover and continue to microwave 30 minutes.

Add mushrooms, butter, and chopped parsley; mix well.

Mix cornstarch with water; incorporate to veal mixture. Microwave, uncovered, 3 minutes at HIGH.

Add cream, stir, and microwave, uncovered, 1 minute at HIGH. Serve.

Setting:	HIGH and MEDIUM
Cooking time:	72 minutes
Utensil:	2 to 2.5 L casserole

800 g	(1¾ lb) leg of veal, cubed
3	onions, peeled and cut in 4
1	parsley sprig
1	bay leaf
227 g	(½ lb) fresh mushrooms, washed and cut in 2
15 mL	(1 tbs) butter
5 mL	(1 tsp) chopped parsley
45 mL	(3 tbs) cornstarch
75 mL	(5 tbs) cold water
50 mL	(¼ cup) 35% cream
	salt and pepper

Technique

1 Presentation of cubed veal.

→

Technique : Blanquette de Veau (continued)

2 Cover veal with hot water. Cover and microwave 8 minutes at HIGH.

3 Drain veal and replace in casserole. Add onions, parsley sprig, and bay leaf. Cover with water.

4 Add mushrooms, butter, and chopped parsley.

Veal and Tomato Sauté

(serves 4)

Heat butter in frying pan on stove top. Add veal, onions, and garlic; sear 3 to 4 minutes each side.

Sprinkle with flour; continue to cook 2 minutes.

Transfer veal mixture to casserole. Add tomatoes, chicken stock, tomato paste, and remaining ingredients. Season with salt and pepper.

Cover and microwave 30 minutes.

Mix well; cover and microwave 30 minutes. Serve.

* See page 55.

Setting:	**MEDIUM-HIGH**
Cooking time:	**60 minutes in microwave**
Utensil:	**2 to 2.5 L casserole**

30 mL	*(2 tbs) butter*
800 g	*(1¾ lb) leg of veal, cubed*
2	*onions, peeled and chopped*
2	*garlic cloves, smashed and chopped*
30 mL	*(2 tbs) flour*
1	*796 mL (28 oz) can tomatoes, drained and chopped*
125 mL	*(½ cup) hot chicken stock* *
15 mL	*(1 tbs) tomato paste*
15 mL	*(1 tbs) chopped parsley*
1	*bay leaf*
2 mL	*(½ tsp) oregano*
	salt and pepper

Technique

1 Transfer veal and onions to casserole.

→

Technique : Veal and Tomato Sauté (continued)

2 Add tomatoes, chicken stock, and tomato paste.

3 Add herbs.

Ossi-Buchi

(serves 4)

Setting :	MEDIUM-HIGH
Cooking time :	50 minutes in microwave
Utensil :	2 to 2.5 L casserole

4	veal knuckles, 3 cm (1¼ in) thick
125 mL	(½ cup) flour
15 mL	(1 tbs) oil
2	onions, peeled and chopped
2	garlic cloves, smashed and chopped
2 mL	(½ tsp) oregano
5 mL	(1 tsp) chopped parsley
125 mL	(½ cup) dry white wine
1	796 mL (28 oz) can tomatoes, drained and chopped
	salt and pepper

Season veal with salt and pepper; dredge with flour.

Heat oil in frying pan on stove top. Add veal and cook 4 minutes each side.

Transfer veal to casserole; set aside.

Replace frying pan on stove top. Add onions, garlic, and herbs. Cook 2 minutes over medium heat.

Add wine; cook 3 minutes over very high heat. Pour over veal.

Add tomatoes to casserole. Season with salt and pepper; cover and microwave 25 minutes.

Mix delicately; cover and continue to microwave 25 minutes.

Serve.

Technique

1 Presentation of veal knuckles.

2 Sear veal and transfer to casserole.

3 Add tomato and onion mixture to casserole.

203

Fowl

Turkey Breast Jardinière

Turkey Breast Jardinière

(serves 4)

Setting:	HIGH and MEDIUM-HIGH
Cooking time:	30 minutes
Utensil:	2 L casserole

1	*900 g (2 lb) deboned turkey breast*
15 mL	*(1 tbs) soya sauce*
15 mL	*(1 tbs) honey*
5 mL	*(1 tsp) oil*
3	*carrots, cut in sticks and blanched*
2	*celery stalks, cut in sticks and blanched*
24	*parisienne style potatoes, blanched*
250 mL	*(1 cup) hot brown sauce **
5 mL	*(1 tsp) chopped fresh parsley*
5 mL	*(1 tsp) tomato paste*
	salt and pepper

Place turkey breast in casserole.

Mix soya sauce, honey, and oil together in small bowl; brush over turkey. Season with salt and pepper; microwave, uncovered, 8 minutes at HIGH.

Turn turkey breast and continue to microwave 8 minutes at HIGH.

Turn turkey breast again; continue to microwave, uncovered, 10 minutes at MEDIUM-HIGH.

Remove turkey from casserole; set aside.

Place vegetables in casserole with cooking juices. Add brown sauce, parsley, and tomato paste. Stir well.

Add turkey breast. Microwave, uncovered, 4 minutes at HIGH.

Slice turkey and serve with vegetables and sauce.

* See page 22.

Cornish Hen à l'Italienne

(serves 2)

Setting:	HIGH
Cooking time:	31 minutes
Utensil:	2 L casserole

1	*Cornish hen, unfrozen*
15 mL	*(1 tbs) soya sauce*
15 mL	*(1 tbs) honey*
5 mL	*(1 tsp) oil*
1	*garlic clove, smashed and chopped*
1	*shallot, chopped*
2	*fresh tomatoes, diced*
	pinch oregano
	salt and pepper

Place hen in casserole.

Mix soya sauce, honey, and oil together in small bowl; brush over hen. Season with salt and pepper. Microwave, uncovered, 6 minutes.

→

Cornish Hen à l'Italienne (continued)

Turn hen and continue to microwave, uncovered, 6 minutes.

Turn hen again; microwave 6 minutes.

Remove hen from casserole and split in two. Set aside.

Place garlic in casserole with cooking juice. Add shallot, tomatoes, and oregano. Season with salt and pepper; cover and microwave 9 minutes.

Place hen halves in casserole; microwave, uncovered, 4 minutes.

Serve.

Cornish Hen with Olives and Red Pepper

(serves 2)

Setting:	**HIGH**
Cooking time:	**27 minutes**
Utensil:	**2 L casserole**

1	*Cornish hen, unfrozen*
15 mL	*(1 tbs) soya sauce*
15 mL	*(1 tbs) honey*
5 mL	*(1 tsp) oil*
6	*green onions, bulbs only*
125 mL	*(½ cup) hot brown sauce* *
8	*green olives, pitted*
½	*red pepper, sliced*
15 mL	*(1 tbs) tomato paste*
1	*garlic clove, smashed and chopped*
	salt and pepper

Place hen in casserole.

Mix soya sauce, honey, and oil together in small bowl; brush over hen. Season with salt and pepper; microwave, uncovered, 6 minutes.

Cornish Hen with Olives and Red Pepper (continued)

Turn hen and continue to microwave, uncovered, 6 minutes.

Turn hen again; microwave 6 minutes.

Remove hen from casserole and split in two. Set aside.

Place onions in casserole with cooking juice. Add brown sauce, cover and microwave 5 minutes.

Add olives, red pepper, tomato paste, and garlic. Add hen halves and microwave, uncovered, 4 minutes. Serve.

* See page 22.

Parisienne Chicken Breasts

(serves 4)

Setting:	HIGH and MEDIUM-HIGH
Cooking time:	20 minutes
Utensil:	2.5 to 3 L casserole

15 mL	*(1 tbs) butter*
2	*chicken breasts, split in half, skinned, and deboned*
1	*small onion, peeled and chopped*
227 g	*(½ lb) fresh mushrooms, washed and diced*
500 mL	*(2 cups) white sauce* *
125 mL	*(½ cup) grated Gruyère cheese*
15 mL	*(1 tbs) chopped parsley*
	paprika
	salt and pepper

Place butter in casserole and heat 1 minute at HIGH.

Add chicken breasts; season with salt and pepper. Cover and microwave 3 minutes each side at MEDIUM-HIGH.

Turn breasts; cover and continue to microwave 2 minutes.

Remove breasts from casserole; set aside.

Place onion and mushrooms in casserole. Add white sauce and cheese; mix well and season to taste. Microwave, uncovered, 10 minutes at HIGH.

Replace breasts in casserole; microwave, uncovered, 1 minute at HIGH.

Sprinkle with chopped parsley and paprika. Serve.

* See page 21.

Chicken Breast au Gratin

Chicken Breasts au Gratin

(serves 4)

Setting: **MEDIUM-HIGH and HIGH**
Cooking time: **20 minutes**
Utensil: **2 L casserole**

2	*chicken breasts, split in two, skinned, and deboned*
2	*celery stalks, sliced*
375 mL	*(1½ cups) hot chicken stock* *
15 mL	*(1 tbs) chopped parsley*
1 mL	*(¼ tsp) nutmeg*
37 mL	*(2½ tbs) cornstarch*
60 mL	*(4 tbs) 18% cream*
125 mL	*(½ cup) grated Gruyère cheese*
	paprika
	salt and pepper

Place chicken breasts in casserole; season with salt and pepper.

Add celery, chicken stock, parsley, and nutmeg; mix well.

Cover with sheet of plastic wrap; microwave 11 minutes at MEDIUM-HIGH.

Turn breast once during cooking.

When breasts are cooked, remove from microwave and let stand in casserole 4 to 5 minutes.

Remove breasts and set aside.

Mix cornstarch with cream; incorporate to sauce. Correct seasoning.

Microwave, uncovered, 8 minutes at HIGH. Mix 2 to 3 times with whisk.

Replace breasts in casserole.

Sprinkle with cheese; microwave 1 minute at HIGH to melt cheese.

Sprinkle with paprika and serve.

* See page 55.

Chicken Breasts Indienne

(serves 4)

Setting: **MEDIUM-HIGH and HIGH**
Cooking time: **19 minutes**
Utensil: **2 L casserole**

2	*chicken breasts, split in two, skinned, and deboned*
1	*celery stalk, sliced*
375 mL	*(1½ cups) hot chicken stock* *
1	*onion, peeled and sliced*
22 mL	*(1½ tbs) curry powder*
40 mL	*(2½ tbs) cornstarch*
40 mL	*(2½ tbs) cold water*
	salt and pepper

GARNISH:

50 mL	*(¼ cup) grated coconut*
50 mL	*(¼ cup) golden raisins*
	chutney sauce

Place chicken breasts in casserole; season with salt and pepper. Add celery, chicken stock, onion, and curry powder. Mix well. Cover and microwave 6 minutes at MEDIUM-HIGH.

Turn breasts; cover and continue to microwave 5 minutes at MEDIUM-HIGH.

When breasts are cooked, remove casserole from microwave. Let chicken stand in hot liquid 4 to 5 minutes. Transfer breasts to service platter.

Mix cornstarch with water; incorporate to sauce. Microwave, uncovered, 8 minutes at HIGH. Stir twice during cooking.

Add chicken and garnish to casserole; season to taste. Simmer 3 minutes in hot sauce before serving.

Serve with rice.

* See page 55.

Chicken with Red Wine

(serves 4)

Setting:	HIGH and MEDIUM-HIGH
Cooking time:	41 minutes in microwave
Utensil:	30 × 20 × 5 cm (11¾ × 7½ × 1¾ in) casserole

1	*onion, peeled and diced*
15 mL	*(1 tbs) chopped parsley*
2	*garlic cloves, smashed and chopped*
5	*slices bacon, diced*
1	*1.4 to 1.6 kg (3 to 3½ lb) chicken, cut into 8 pieces*
30 mL	*(2 tbs) peanut oil*
375 mL	*(1½ cups) dry red wine, reduced by half on stove top*
250 mL	*(1 cup) beef stock*
5 mL	*(1 tsp) tomato paste*
25	*mushrooms, washed and cut in 2*
30 mL	*(2 tbs) cornstarch*
45 mL	*(3 tbs) cold water*
	pinch tarragon
	salt and pepper

Technique

1 Place onion, parsley, garlic, and bacon in casserole. Microwave, uncovered, 6 minutes.

Place onion, parsley, garlic, and bacon in casserole; microwave, uncovered, 6 minutes at HIGH.

Remove skin from chicken pieces.

Heat oil in sauté pan over high heat on stove top.

Season chicken with salt and pepper; sear 2 to 3 minutes each side.

Set chicken on onion mixture in casserole. Season.

Add wine, beef stock, tomato paste, and tarragon. Cover with sheet of plastic wrap; microwave 12 minutes at MEDIUM-HIGH.

Turn chicken pieces. Add mushrooms and continue to microwave 5 minutes at MEDIUM-HIGH.

Remove breasts and wings; continue to microwave remaining, 10 minutes at MEDIUM-HIGH.

Place all chicken pieces in service platter and cover with aluminium foil to keep hot.

Mix cornstarch with water; incorporate to sauce.

Microwave, uncovered, 8 minutes at HIGH. Stir sauce 2 to 3 times during cooking. Serve.

2 The cooked onion mixture.

3 Place chicken pieces on cooked onions.

4 Add red wine.

5 Add beef stock.

→

Technique : Chicken with Red Wine (continued)

6 Add spices.

Chicken Breasts à la Bourguignonne

(serves 4)

Preparation of chicken breasts

Setting :	MEDIUM-HIGH and HIGH
Cooking time :	32 minutes
Utensil :	2 L casserole

2	*chicken breasts, deboned, skinned, and split in 2*
375 mL	*(1½ cups) hot chicken stock* *
500 mL	*(2 cups) bourguignonne sauce (following recipe)*
	chopped parsley

Place chicken in casserole; season with salt and pepper. Pour in chicken stock.

Cover with sheet of plastic wrap; microwave 11 minutes at MEDIUM-HIGH.

Remove from microwave and let chicken stand in hot liquid, 10 to 12 minutes.

Preparation of bourguignonne sauce

4	*slices bacon, diced*
15 mL	*(1 tbs) chopped parsley*
1	*onion, peeled and chopped*
1	*garlic clove, smashed and chopped*
20	*mushrooms, washed and diced*
375 mL	*(1½ cups) dry red wine*
375 mL	*(1½ cups) hot beef stock*
45 mL	*(3 tbs) cornstarch*
60 mL	*(4 tbs) cold water*
5 mL	*(1 tsp) soya sauce*
	several drops lemon juice
	salt and pepper

Place bacon, parsley, onion, garlic, and mushrooms in casserole.

Microwave, uncovered, 10 minutes at HIGH.

Pour wine into small saucepan. Bring to boil on stove top and reduce wine by 2/3 over high heat.

Add wine to mushroom mixture; add beef stock and mix well with whisk.

Mix cornstarch with water; incorporate to sauce. Mix well with whisk.

Add soya sauce and season to taste.

Microwave, uncovered, 10 minutes at HIGH. Stir 2 to 3 times.

Place chicken in sauce; microwave 1 minute at HIGH.

Sprinkle with chopped parsley, add lemon juice, and serve.

* See page 55.

Chicken Breasts à la Florentine

(serves 4)

Setting: MEDIUM-HIGH and HIGH
Cooking time: 20 minutes
Utensil: 2 L casserole

2	*chicken breasts, deboned, skinned, and cut in 2*
2	*celery stalks, sliced*
375 mL	*(1½ cups) hot chicken stock* *
15 mL	*(1 tbs) chopped parsley*
1 mL	*(¼ tsp) nutmeg*
37 mL	*(2½ tbs) cornstarch*
60 mL	*(4 tbs) 18% cream*
	salt and pepper

Place chicken in casserole; season with salt and pepper.

Add celery, chicken stock, parsley, and nutmeg; mix well.

Cover with sheet of plastic wrap; microwave 11 minutes at MEDIUM-HIGH.

Turn chicken once during cooking.

When chicken is cooked, remove from microwave and let stand 4 to 5 minutes.

Remove chicken from casserole and set aside.

Mix cornstarch with cream; incorporate to sauce and mix with whisk.

Microwave, uncovered, 8 minutes at HIGH. Stir 3 times during cooking.

Replace chicken in casserole and microwave 1 minute.

Serve with buttered spinach.

* See page 55.

Technique

1 Place chicken in casserole.

→

Technique : Chicken Breasts à la Florentine (continued)

2 Add celery.

3 Add chicken stock. Cover and pierce wrap with small knife, to allow steam to escape during cooking.

4 Remove wrap and let chicken stand 4 to 5 minutes.

5 Add cornstarch mixture to sauce.

Old Fashioned Chicken Breasts

(serves 4)

Setting: HIGH and MEDIUM-HIGH
Cooking time: 22 minutes
Utensil: 2 L casserole

2	*chicken breasts, skinned, deboned, and split in 2*
1	*celery stalk, sliced*
1	*onion, peeled and sliced*
375 mL	*(1½ cups) hot chicken stock* *
40 mL	*(2½ tbs) cornstarch*
45 mL	*(3 tbs) cold water*
250 mL	*(1 cup) fresh mushrooms, washed and diced*
250 mL	*(1 cup) cooked carrots, cut in sticks*
250 mL	*(1 cup) cooked small onions*
125 mL	*(½ cup) 35% cream*
15 mL	*(1 tbs) chopped fresh parsley*
	lemon juice
	salt and pepper

Place chicken in casserole; season with salt and pepper. Add celery, sliced onion, and chicken stock; cover and microwave 6 minutes at MEDIUM-HIGH.

Turn chicken and continue to microwave 5 minutes.

Remove chicken from casserole; set aside.

Mix cornstarch with cold water; incorporate to sauce. Microwave, uncovered, 5 minutes at HIGH.

Stir well and add mushrooms and chicken; microwave 3 minutes.

Remove casserole from microwave. Add carrots, small onions, and cream to sauce. Mix and let simmer 3 to 4 minutes.

Sprinkle with chopped parsley and lemon juice. Serve.

* See page 55.

Lemon Chicken Breasts

(serves 4)

Setting: HIGH and MEDIUM-HIGH
Cooking time: 21 minutes
Utensil: 2 L casserole

15 mL	*(1 tbs) vegetable oil*
2	*chicken breasts, skinned, deboned, and split in 2*
1	*celery stalk, sliced*
375 mL	*(1½ cups) hot chicken stock* *
40 mL	*(2½ tbs) cornstarch*
45 mL	*(3 tbs) cold water*
50 mL	*(¼ cup) 35% cream*
15 mL	*(1 tbs) chopped parsley*
	juice ½ lemon
	salt and pepper

Mix oil with lemon juice.

Place chicken in casserole and pour oil mixture over top. Season with salt and pepper; marinate 30 minutes.

Add celery and chicken stock to casserole; cover and microwave 6 minutes at MEDIUM-HIGH. Turn casserole a ¼ turn during cooking.

Turn chicken; cover and continue to microwave 5 minutes.

Remove chicken from casserole and set aside.

Mix cornstarch with water; incorporate to sauce. Microwave, uncovered, 8 minutes at HIGH. Stir sauce 2 times during cooking.

3 minutes before end of cooking, add cream and parsley.

Replace chicken in casserole; microwave 2 minutes at MEDIUM-HIGH.

Serve with green vegetables.

* See page 55.

Chicken Spiced with Fennel

Chicken Spiced with Fennel

(serves 4)

Setting:	HIGH and MEDIUM-HIGH
Cooking time:	20 minutes
Utensil:	2 L casserole

1	bulb fennel, cut in 4 and cubed
125 mL	(½ cup) cold water
5 mL	(1 tsp) butter
3	chicken breasts halves, deboned, skinned, and cubed
500 mL	(2 cups) hot thick white sauce *
125 mL	(½ cup) grated Gruyère cheese
	salt and pepper

Place fennel cubes in casserole and add water. Season with salt and pepper; cover and microwave 7 minutes at HIGH.

Mix well, cover and continue to microwave 7 minutes.

Drain fennel and set aside.

Leave cooking juice in casserole. Add butter and chicken; season with salt and pepper. Cover and microwave 3 minutes at MEDIUM-HIGH.

Mix, cover and continue to microwave 3 minutes. Remove casserole from microwave and set aside.

Place fennel cubes in buttered gratin dish. Add chicken and white sauce. Sprinkle with cheese.

Melt cheese under grill (broil) in conventional oven for 4 minutes.

Serve.

* See page 21.

Chicken of Arles

(serves 4)

Setting:	HIGH and MEDIUM-HIGH
Cooking time:	31 minutes in microwave
Utensil:	30 × 20 × 5 cm (11¾ × 7½ × 1¾ in) casserole

5 mL	(1 tsp) butter
15 mL	(1 tbs) chopped parsley
1	garlic clove, smashed and chopped
1	onion, peeled and chopped
30 mL	(2 tbs) olive oil
1	1.4 to 1.6 kg (3 to 3½ lb) chicken, cut into 8 pieces
1	796 mL (28 oz) can tomatoes, drained and chopped
½	eggplant, peeled and sliced
125 mL	(½ cup) hot chicken stock *
15 mL	(1 tbs) chopped parsley
	flour
	salt and pepper

Place butter, parsley, garlic, and onion in casserole. Cover with sheet of plastic wrap; microwave 4 minutes at HIGH.

Heat oil in sauté pan over high heat on stove top.

Trim chicken pieces of skin; season with salt and pepper. Dredge with flour.

Sear chicken in hot oil 3 to 4 minutes each side.

Place chicken pieces on cooked onion mixture. Add tomatoes, eggplant, and chicken stock; season with salt and pepper.

Cover and microwave 12 minutes at MEDIUM-HIGH.

Turn chicken pieces, cover and microwave 5 minutes at MEDIUM-HIGH.

Remove chicken wings and breasts. Continue to microwave remaining 10 minutes at MEDIUM-HIGH.

Sprinkle with chopped parsley. Serve.

Note: To obtain a thicker sauce, pour liquid into saucepan and cook 4 to 5 minutes over high heat on stove top.

* See page 55.

Chicken Casserole

(serves 4)

Setting:	MEDIUM-HIGH
Cooking time:	17 minutes
Utensil:	2 L casserole

375 mL	*(1½ cups) diced raw chicken*
2	*celery stalks, cubed*
1	*carrot, cut into sticks*
3	*potatoes, peeled and cut in 4*
500 mL	*(2 cups) hot white sauce* *
1 mL	*(¼ tsp) tarragon*
1	*green pepper, cubed*
125 mL	*(½ cup) grated mozzarella cheese*
	salt and pepper

Place chicken, celery, carrot, and potatoes in casserole. Season with salt and pepper; cover and microwave 7 minutes.

Mix well with wooden spoon. Cover and continue to microwave 7 minutes.

Add white sauce, tarragon, green pepper, and cheese. Mix and microwave, uncovered, 3 minutes. Serve.

* See page 21.

Turkey Casserole

(serves 4)

Setting:	HIGH
Cooking time:	11½ minutes
Utensil:	2 L casserole

50 mL	*(¼ cup) butter*
30 mL	*(2 tbs) chopped onion*
1	*carrot, diced*
½	*celery stalk, diced*
60 mL	*(4 tbs) flour*
250 mL	*(1 cup) hot chicken stock* *
300 mL	*(1¼ cups) 15% cream*
500 mL	*(2 cups) diced cooked turkey*
30 mL	*(2 tbs) finely chopped marinated red pepper*
	chopped parsley
	salt and pepper

Place butter, onion, carrot, and celery in casserole; season with salt and pepper. Cover and microwave 5 minutes.

Mix well. Add flour and stir; microwave, uncovered, 30 seconds.

Add chicken stock and cream; stir well. Microwave, uncovered, 5 minutes. Stir twice during cooking.

Add turkey and red pepper; mix well and microwave 1 minute.

Sprinkle with chopped parsley, correct seasoning, and serve.

* See page 55.

Chicken with Mushrooms

(serves 4)

Setting:	HIGH and MEDIUM-HIGH
Cooking time:	31 minutes in microwave
Utensil:	30 × 20 × 5 cm (11¾ × 7½ × 1¾ in) casserole

5 mL	*(1 tsp) butter*
15 mL	*(1 tbs) chopped parsley*
1	*onion, peeled and chopped*
1	*garlic clove, smashed and chopped*
1	*1.4 to 1.6 kg (3 to 3½ lb) chicken, cut into 8 pieces*
30 mL	*(2 tbs) peanut oil*
375 mL	*(1½ cups) dry white wine, reduced by ½ on stove top*
375 mL	*(1½ cups) hot beef stock*
15 mL	*(1 tbs) tomato paste*
30 mL	*(2 tbs) cornstarch*
45 mL	*(3 tbs) cold water*
15 mL	*(1 tbs) soya sauce*
227 g	*(½ lb) mushrooms, washed and cut in 2*
	chopped parsley
	salt and pepper

Place butter, parsley, onion, and garlic in casserole. Cover with sheet of plastic wrap; microwave 4 minutes at HIGH.

Trim skin from chicken. Season with salt and pepper.

Heat oil in sauté pan over high heat on stove top.

Sear chicken pieces 2 to 3 minutes each side.

Transfer chicken to casserole.

Add wine, beef stock, and tomato paste; season to taste. Mix well.

Mix cornstarch with water; incorporate to sauce.

Add soya sauce; cover with sheet of plastic wrap and microwave 12 minutes at MEDIUM-HIGH.

After 12 minutes in microwave, turn chicken pieces.

Add mushrooms. Cover with sheet of plastic wrap; microwave 5 minutes at MEDIUM-HIGH.

Remove chicken breasts and wings. Continue to microwave remaining 10 minutes at MEDIUM-HIGH. Serve.

See technique on following page.

Technique : Chicken with Mushrooms

1 A chicken cut into 8 pieces.

2 Here are the seared pieces of chicken.

5 Add beef stock.

6 Add tomato paste.

3 Place chicken pieces in casserole.

4 Add reduced white wine.

7 Add mushrooms.

Chicken with Hunter Sauce

Chicken with Hunter Sauce

(serves 4)

Setting:	**HIGH and MEDIUM-HIGH**
Cooking time:	**31 minutes in microwave**
Utensil:	**30 × 20 × 5 cm (11¾ × 7½ × 1¾ in) casserole**

5 mL	*(1 tsp) butter*
15 mL	*(1 tbs) chopped parsley*
1	*onion, peeled and chopped*
1	*garlic clove, smashed and chopped*
1	*1.4 to 1.6 kg (3 to 3½ lb) chicken, cut into 8 pieces*
30 mL	*(2 tbs) peanut oil*
1	*796 mL (28 oz) can tomatoes, drained and chopped*
250 mL	*(1 cup) beef stock*
125 mL	*(½ cup) dry white wine (optional), reduced by ½ on stove top*
15 mL	*(1 tbs) tomato paste*
15 mL	*(1 tbs) cornstarch*
30 mL	*(2 tbs) cold water*
	salt and pepper

Place butter, parsley, onion, and garlic in casserole. Cover and microwave 4 minutes at HIGH.

Trim skin from chicken.

Heat oil in sauté pan over high heat on stove top.

Season chicken with salt and pepper; place in hot oil. Sear 2 to 3 minutes each side.

Place chicken pieces in casserole. Add tomatoes, beef stock, wine and tomato paste.

Cover with sheet of plastic wrap; microwave 12 minutes at MEDIUM-HIGH.

Turn chicken, cover and continue to microwave 5 minutes at MEDIUM-HIGH.

Remove chicken breasts and wings from casserole. Continue to microwave remaining 10 minutes at MEDIUM-HIGH.

Place all chicken pieces in service platter; cover with aluminium foil to keep hot.

Pour sauce into saucepan; season to taste.

Mix cornstarch with water; incorporate to sauce.

Cook 3 to 4 minutes over high heat on stove top.

Pour over chicken and serve.

Technique

1 Place butter, parsley, onion, and garlic in casserole. Cover and microwave 4 minutes. Here are the cooked ingredients.

→

Technique : Chicken with Hunter Sauce (continued)

2 Place seared chicken pieces on onions.

3 Add chopped tomatoes.

5 Add reduced wine and tomato paste.

6 After 12 minutes in microwave, turn chicken pieces.

4 Add beef stock.

Chicken à la Bretonne

(serves 4)

Setting:	HIGH and MEDIUM-HIGH
Cooking time:	31 minutes in microwave
Utensil:	30 × 20 × 5 cm (11¾ × 7½ × 1¾ in) casserole

3	*leeks, white section only, washed and sliced*
1	*onion, peeled and chopped*
5 mL	*(1 tsp) butter*
30 mL	*(2 tbs) peanut oil*
1	*1.4 to 1.6 kg (3 to 3½ lb) chicken, cut into 8 pieces*
125 mL	*(½ cup) hot chicken stock* *
227 g	*(½ lb) mushrooms, cut in 2*
45 mL	*(3 tbs) heavy cream*
	several drops lemon juice
	flour
	salt and pepper

Place leeks, onion, and butter in casserole. Cover with sheet of plastic wrap; microwave 4 minutes at HIGH.

Heat oil in sauté pan over high heat on stove top.

Trim skin from chicken. Season with salt and pepper; dredge with flour.

Place chicken in hot oil; sear 2 to 3 minutes each side.

Transfer chicken to casserole. Add chicken stock; cover and microwave 12 minutes at MEDIUM-HIGH.

Turn chicken pieces, cover and continue to microwave 5 minutes at MEDIUM-HIGH.

Remove chicken breasts and wings from casserole. Add mushrooms to remaining chicken and microwave, uncovered, 7 minutes.

Add cream and microwave, uncovered, 2 minutes. Sprinkle with lemon juice.

Replace breasts and wings in casserole. Simmer in hot liquid 1 minute before serving.

* See page 55.

Chicken Pot Pie

(serves 4)

Setting:	HIGH and MEDIUM-HIGH
Cooking time:	23 minutes
Utensil:	2 L casserole and
	4 large individual microwave bowls

2	*potatoes, peeled and diced*
2	*carrots, peeled and diced*
1	*celery stalk, diced*
250 mL	*(1 cup) hot chicken stock* *
1	*small onion, peeled and cut in 6*
3	*chicken breast halves, deboned, skinned, and diced*
5 mL	*(1 tsp) butter*
1 mL	*(¼ tsp) caraway seeds*
15 mL	*(1 tbs) chopped parsley*
875 mL	*(3½ cups) hot white sauce* *
1	*567 g (20 oz) package commercial flakey dough*
1	*egg yolk*
2 mL	*(½ tsp) soya sauce*
	salt and pepper

Place potatoes, carrots, celery, chicken stock, and onion in 2 L casserole. Season with salt and pepper; cover and microwave 8 minutes at HIGH.

Add chicken and season.

Add butter, caraway seeds, and parsley. Cover and microwave 7 minutes at HIGH.

Remove casserole from microwave. Drain vegetables and chicken well.

Replace drained vegetables and chicken in casserole; add white sauce. Microwave, uncovered, 3 minutes at HIGH.

Fill individual bowls with chicken mixture; set aside.

Roll out dough and cut out 4 large rounds to cover top of bowls.

Mix egg yolk with soya sauce; brush over dough.

Place dough on plate and microwave 4 minutes at MEDIUM-HIGH.

Place dough rounds in bowls, resting on chicken mixture. Microwave, 1 minute at MEDIUM-HIGH. Serve.

 * See page 55.
** See page 21.

Sauteed Chicken Casserole

(serves 4)

Seeting: **HIGH AND MEDIUM-HIGH**
Cooking time: **28 minutes in microwave**
Utensil: **30 × 20 × 5 cm (11¾ × 7½ × 1¾ in) casserole**

1	*onion, peeled and chopeed*
1	*garlic clove, smashed and chopped*
5 mL	*(1 tsp) butter*
30 mL	*(2 tbs) olive oil*
1	*1.4 to 1.6 kg (3 to 3½ lb) chicken, cut into 8 pieces*
375 mL	*(1½ cups) dry white wine, reduced by ½*
375 mL	*(1½ cups) parisienne style potatoes*
4	*carrots, cut into sticks*
20	*small white onions*
	chopped parsley
	lemon juice
	flour
	salt and pepper

Place chopped onion, garlic, and butter in casserole. Cover with sheet of plastic wrap; microwave 4 minutes at HIGH.

Heat oil sauté pan over high heat on stove top.

Trim skin from chicken. Season with salt and pepper; dredge with flour.

Place chicken in hot oil; sear 3 to 4 minutes each side.

Place chicken in casserole on onions.

Add wine; cover and microwave 12 minutes at MEDIUM-HIGH.

Turn chicken; add potatoes, carrots, and small onions. Cover and microwave 5 minutes at MEDIUM-HIGH.

Remove chicken breasts and wings from casserole. Continue to microwave remaining, 7 minutes at MEDIUM-HIGH.

Sprinkle with parsley and lemon juice. Serve.

Chicken Brochettes

(serves 4)

Setting: **HIGH**
Cooking time: **8 minutes**
Utensil: **Large microwave plate**

8	*cherry tomatoes*
3	*chicken breast halves, deboned, skinned, and cubed*
1	*green pepper, cubed*
1	*small onion, quartered*
2	*green onions, cut into sticks*
½	*orange, with skin, sectioned*
¼	*English cucumber, sliced in half lengthwise, and sliced*
30 mL	*(2 tbs) butter*
5 mL	*(1 tsp) chopped parsley*
5 mL	*(1 tsp) soya sauce*
	several drops Tabasco sauce
	pepper from mill

→

Chicken Brochettes (continued)

On wooden skewers, alternate tomato, chicken, green pepper, onion, green onion, orange, and cucumber. Set aside.

Place butter, parsley, pepper, soya sauce, and Tabasco sauce in small saucepan. Simmer over low heat on stove top until butter is completely melted.

Generously brush mixture over skewers. Place skewers in microwave plate; cover and microwave 4 minutes.

Turn skewers and baste; cover and microwave 4 minutes.

Serve with garnish of noodles.

Noodle garnish

500 mL	**(2 cups) cooked, hot turret noddles**
2	**green onions, chopped**
6	**cherry tomatoes, cut in 2**
15 mL	**(1 tbs) butter**

Place all ingredients in large saucepan. Simmer 5 minutes over low heat on stove top. Serve.

Chicken and Tomatoes

(serves 4)

Setting:	**HIGH and MEDIUM-HIGH**
Cooking time:	**29 minutes**
Utensil:	**2 L casserole**

15 mL	**(1 tbs) butter**
2	**chicken breasts, deboned and skinned**
5 mL	**(1 tsp) oil**
1	**small onion, peeled and chopped**
30 mL	**(2 tbs) chopped green banana pepper**
1/3	**celery stalk, diced**
1	**796 mL (28 oz) can tomatoes, drained and chopped**
15 mL	**(1 tbs) chopped parsley**
15 mL	**(1 tbs) cornstarch**
30 mL	**(2 tbs) cold water**
	pinch sage
	pinch basil
	salt and pepper

Place butter in casserole; heat 1 minute at HIGH.

Add chicken; season with salt and pepper. Cover and microwave 3 minutes each side at MEDIUM-HIGH.

Turn chicken; cover and microwave 2 minutes.

Remove chicken from casserole and set aside. Reserve cooking liquid and set aside.

Pour oil into casserole. Add onion, banana pepper, and celery; sprinkle in sage and basil. Cover and microwave 10 minutes at HIGH.

Add tomatoes and reserved cooking liquid. Season with salt and pepper; mix well.

Add parsley; microwave, uncovered, 8 minutes at HIGH.

Mix cornstarch with water; incorporate to mixture.

Replace chicken in casserole. Cover slightly with tomato mixture. Microwave, uncovered, 2 minutes at HIGH.

Serve.

Chicken Sauteed with Olives

(serves 4)

NO

Setting:	HIGH and MEDIUM-HIGH
Cooking time:	28 minutes in microwave
Utensil:	30 × 20 × 5 cm (11¾ × 7½ × 1¾ in) casserole

1	*onion, peeled and chopped*
1	*garlic clove, smashed and chopped*
5 mL	*(1 tsp) butter*
30 mL	*(2 tbs) peanut oil*
1	*1.4 to 1.6 kg (3 to 3½ lb) chicken, cut into 8 pieces*
125 mL	*(½ cup) Madeira wine*
500 mL	*(2 cups) thick brown sauce**
24	*stuffed olives*
	several drops lemon juice
	flour
	salt and pepper

Place onion, garlic, and butter in casserole. Cover with sheet of plastic wrap; microwave 4 minutes at HIGH.

Heat oil in sauté pan over high heat on stove top.

Trim skin from chicken. Season with salt and pepper; dredge with flour.

Sear chicken pieces in hot oil 3 to 4 minutes each side.

Transfer chicken to casserole. Add wine and brown sauce; cover and microwave 12 minutes at MEDIUM-HIGH.

Turn chicken; add olives, cover and microwave 5 minutes.

Remove chicken breasts and wings; continue to microwave remaining 7 minutes at MEDIUM-HIGH.

Sprinkle with lemon juice. Serve.

* See page 22.

Fish and Shellfish

Shrimp Skewers with Pine Nuts

Shrimp Skewers with Pine Nuts

(serves 4)

Setting:	HIGH
Cooking time:	6 minutes in microwave
Utensil:	2 L casserole or large plate

4	*jumbo shrimps, deveined*
½	*red pepper, cubed*
¼	*English cucumber, cubed*
8	*large fresh mushrooms, well washed*
50 mL	*(¼ cup) sweet butter*
1	*garlic clove, smashed and chopped*
5 mL	*(1 tsp) chopped parsley*
15 mL	*(1 tbs) pine nuts*
2 mL	*(½ tsp) soya sauce*
	several drops lemon juice
	pepper

Slice a long incision along the backside of shrimps. Wash well and cut shrimps in two.

On wooden skewers, alternate shrimp, red pepper, cucumber, and mushroom. Repeat procedure.

Place skewers in casserole or plate; set aside.

Place butter in small saucepan. Add garlic, parsley, pine nuts, lemon juice, and soya sauce. Heat over medium heat on stove top to melt butter.

Generously brush mixture over skewers. Microwave, uncovered, 3 minutes.

Turn skewers, baste again, cover and microwave 3 minutes.

Serve skewers on a bed of rice.

Technique

On skewers, alternate shrimp, red pepper, cucumber, and mushroom.

Cooking Shrimps

Setting: HIGH
Cooking time: 4 minutes
Utensil: 2 L casserole

454 g   (1 lb) medium size shrimps
250 mL   (1 cup) hot water
           several drops lemon juice

Place shrimps, water,
and lemon juice in casserole.
Cover with sheet of plastic wrap;
microwave 3 minutes.
Stir very well, moving shrimps
in centre of casserole towards exterior.
Microwave 1 minute.
Cover casserole and let stand
7 to 8 minutes.
Run under cold water; refrigerate.

Newburg Shrimp

(serves 2)

Setting: HIGH
Cooking time: 11 minutes
Utensil: 2 L casserole

30 mL   (2 tbs) butter
114 g   (¼ lb) fresh mushrooms, washed
           and diced
2   shallots, chopped
454 g   (1 lb) medium size cooked
           shrimps, deveined
30 mL   (2 tbs) sherry
5 mL   (1 tsp) paprika
30 mL   (2 tbs) flour
375 mL   (1½ cups) hot 15% cream
1   egg yolk
15 mL   (1 tbs) 35% cream
125 mL   (½ cup) diced cooked lobster
           several drops lemon juice
           salt and pepper

Place 15 mL (1 tbs) butter in casserole. Add mushrooms and shallots; season with salt and pepper. Sprinkle with lemon juice.

Cover with sheet of plastic wrap; microwave 2 minutes.

Add remaining butter, shrimps, sherry, and paprika. Season with salt and pepper.

Microwave, uncovered, 2 minutes; mix well.

Remove shrimps from casserole and set aside.

Add flour, mixing between spoonfuls.

Pour in 15% cream and mix well.

Microwave, uncovered, 4 minutes. Stir every minute.

Mix egg yolk with 35% cream; incorporate to sauce. Microwave, uncovered, 2 minutes.

Add lobster and shrimps; mix and microwave 30 seconds.

Serve in coquille shells or on vol-au-vent pastry.

Shrimps, Chinese Style

(serves 4)

Mix cornstarch with water; incorporate to shrimp mixture. Microwave, uncovered, 2 minutes.

Add bean sprouts and bamboo shoots; microwave, uncovered, 1 minute. Serve.

Note: These Chinese ingredients can easily be found in most Chinese food stores.

Setting:	HIGH
Cooking time:	7 minutes
Utensil:	2 L casserole

400 g	(14 oz) medium size shrimps, deveined and washed
5 mL	(1 tsp) soya sauce
1	398 mL (14 oz) can Chinese mushrooms, well drained
5 mL	(1 tsp) candied ginger
15 mL	(1 tbs) cornstarch
45 mL	(3 tbs) cold water
250 mL	(1 cup) canned bean sprouts
125 mL	(½ cup) bamboo shoots, sliced pepper

Place shrimps in casserole. Add soya sauce and pepper; cover and microwave 2 minutes. Stir well. Add mushrooms and candied ginger; cover and microwave 2 minutes.

Shrimp Skewers

(serves 4)

Setting:	HIGH
Cooking time:	8 minutes
Utensil:	2 L casserole and large microwave plate

1	celery stalk, washed and cubed
½	red pepper, cut in large cubes
1	onion, peeled and cubed
50 mL	(¼ cup) water
8	canned baby corn cobs
16	medium size shrimps, deveined and washed
45 mL	(3 tbs) butter
2 mL	(½ tsp) soya sauce
5 mL	(1 tsp) Dijon mustard
	lemon juice
	salt and pepper

Place celery, red pepper, and onion in casserole; add water. Cover and microwave 3 minutes. Drain vegetables.

→

Shrimp Skewers (continued)

On wooden skewers, alternate corn, shrimp, red pepper, celery, and onion. Repeat procedure and set aside.

Melt butter in saucepan over medium heat on stove top. Remove saucepan from heat and stir in soya sauce, mustard, and lemon juice.

Place skewers on microwave plate; generously brush with butter mixture. Season with salt and pepper; cover and microwave 2 minutes.

Turn skewers and baste again. Cover and microwave 3 minutes. Serve.

Lobster Newburg

(serves 2)

Setting:	HIGH
Cooking time:	11 minutes
Utensil:	2 L casserole

30 mL	*(2 tbs) butter*
114 g	*(¼ lb) fresh mushrooms, washed and diced*
2	*shallots, chopped*
1	*907 g (2 lb) cooked lobster, cut in 2.5 cm (1 in) pieces*
30 mL	*(2 tbs) sherry*
5 mL	*(1 tsp) paprika*
30 mL	*(2 tbs) flour*
375 mL	*(1½ cups) hot 15% cream*
1	*egg yolk*
15 mL	*(1 tbs) 35% cream*
	several drops lemon juice
	salt and pepper

Place 15 mL (1 tbs) butter in casserole; add mushrooms and shallots. Season with salt and pepper; sprinkle with lemon juice.

Cover with sheet of plastic wrap; microwave 2 minutes.

Add remaining butter, lobster, sherry, and paprika. Season with salt and pepper.

Microwave, uncovered, 2 minutes. Mix well.

Remove lobster from casserole and set aside.

Add flour, mixing between spoonfuls.

Add 15% cream and mix well.

Microwave, uncovered, 4 minutes. Stir every minute.

Mix egg yolk with 35% cream; incorporate to sauce. Microwave, uncovered, 2 minutes.

Add lobster, mix and microwave 30 seconds.

Serve in coquille shells or on vol-au-vent pastry.

Shrimps with Beer

(serves 4)

Place shrimps in casserole; season with salt and pepper. Add beer and cover; microwave 2 minutes.

Stir well; cover and continue to microwave 2 minutes.

Remove shrimps from casserole and set aside. Reserve cooking liquid and set aside.

Place celery and onion in casserole. Add soya sauce; cover and microwave 2 minutes.

Add chopped tomato and mushrooms; mix well. Season with salt and pepper; cover and microwave 3 minutes.

Stir well and add reserved cooking liquid.

Mix cornstarch with water; incorporate to sauce. Microwave, uncovered, 3 minutes.

Stir again. Replace shrimps in casserole. Add tomato paste and oregano; generously pepper. Microwave, uncovered, 2 minutes.

Garnish with orange zest. Serve on egg noodles.

Setting:	HIGH
Cooking time:	14 minutes
Utensil:	2 L casserole

454 g	(1 lb) medium size shrimps, deveined
125 mL	(½ cup) beer
1	celery stalk, washed and chopped
1	small onion, peeled and chopped
5 mL	(1 tsp) soya sauce
1	tomato, chopped
227 g	(½ lb) fresh whole mushrooms, washed
30 mL	(2 tbs) cornstarch
45 mL	(3 tbs) cold water
15 mL	(1 tbs) tomato paste
	pinch oregano
	salt and pepper
	zest 1 orange for garnish
	egg noodles for presentation

Maître d'Hôtel Scampi

(serves 4)

Setting: **HIGH**
Cooking time: **7 to 8 minutes**
Utensil: **2 L casserole and small microwave bowl**

24 to 32	*scampi, deveined*
15 mL	*(1 tbs) butter*
125 mL	*(½ cup) butter*
15 mL	*(1 tbs) chopped tarragon*
15 mL	*(1 tbs) chopped parsley*
	juice 1 lemon
	several drops Tabasco sauce
	salt and pepper

Place scampi in casserole. Add 15 mL (1 tbs) butter and lemon juice. Pepper, cover and microwave 3 minutes.

Stir well and continue to microwave 3 to 4 minutes. Remove casserole and set aside.

Mix remaining ingredients in small bowl. Microwave 1 minute to completely melt butter. Arrange scampi on service platter and serve with butter mixture.

Green Peppers Stuffed with Seafood

(serves 4)

Setting: **HIGH**
Cooking time: **14 minutes**
Utensil: **2 L casserole**

2	*large green peppers, washed and cut in half*
125 mL	*(½ cup) water*
1	*garlic clove, smashed and chopped*
1	*dry shallot, chopped*
8	*medium size shrimps, deveined and chopped*
200 g	*(7 oz) crab meat, well drained and chopped*
5 mL	*(1 tsp) soya sauce*
15 mL	*(1 tbs) butter*
250 mL	*(1 cup) tomatoes, drained and chopped*
15 mL	*(1 tbs) tomato paste*
50 mL	*(¼ cup) grated parmesan cheese*
	pinch fennel
	salt and pepper

Place green pepper halves in casserole. Add water and salt; microwave 5 minutes.

Turn casserole a ¼ turn; continue to microwave 2 minutes.

Turn casserole another ¼ turn; continue to microwave 3 minutes.

Drain green peppers and keet hot.

In casserole, place garlic, shallots, shrimps, crab meat, soya sauce, and butter. Season with salt and pepper.

Add fennel; cover and microwave 2 minutes. Mix well.

Add tomatoes, tomato paste, and cheese. Season with salt and pepper; microwave, uncovered, 2 minutes.

Stuff green peppers and serve.

Cut scampi in two, lengthwise and remove black vein.

Place scampi in casserole. Add soya sauce, garlic, and butter. Season with pepper, cover and microwave 2 minutes.

Turn scampi; cover and continue to microwave 2 minutes.

Remove scampi from casserole and set aside.

In casserole containing cooking juice, add shallots, parsley, tomatoes, sugar, herbs, and Tabasco sauce. Season with salt and pepper; microwave, uncovered, 3 minutes.

Add tomato paste and stir well. Microwave, uncovered, 3 minutes.

Replace scampi in sauce; microwave, uncovered, 1 minute.

Serve with saffron rice.

Scampi in Tomato Sauce

(serves 2)

Setting:	HIGH
Cooking time:	11 minutes
Utensil:	2 L casserole

8	*scampi*
15 mL	*(1 tbs) soya sauce*
2	*garlic cloves, smashed and chopped*
5 mL	*(1 tsp) butter*
1	*large dry shallot, chopped*
15 mL	*(1 tbs) coarsely chopped parsley*
1	*796 mL (28 oz) can tomatoes, well drained and chopped*
1 mL	*(¼ tsp) oregano*
30 mL	*(2 tbs) tomato paste*
	pinch sugar
	pinch thyme
	several drops Tabasco sauce
	salt and pepper

Scampi Coquilles au Gratin

(serves 4)

Setting: HIGH
Cooking time: 7 minutes in microwave
Utensil: 2 L casserole

24	scampi, deveined and left whole
15 mL	(1 tbs) butter
30 mL	(2 tbs) chopped shallot
114 g	(¼ lb) fresh mushrooms, washed and cut in 2
15 mL	(1 tbs) brandy
500 mL	(2 cups) hot white sauce *
125 mL	(½ cup) grated Gruyère cheese
	lemon juice
	salt and pepper

Place scampi in casserole. Add butter and shallot; season with pepper. Cover and microwave 7 minutes. Stir 2 times during cooking.

3 minutes before end of cooking, add mushrooms and several drops lemon juice.

Drain scampi mixture and set aside.

Pour cooking liquid into small saucepan. Reduce by half on stove top.

In bowl, mix scampi, mushrooms, cooking liquid, brandy, and white sauce. Arrange mixture in coquille shells; sprinkle with cheese.

Grill (broil) 3 minutes to melt cheese.

* See page 21.

Coquilles Saint-Jacques with Cheese

(serves 4)

Setting: HIGH
Cooking time: 10 minutes
Utensil: 2 L casserole

30 mL	(2 tbs) butter
2	shallots, chopped
15 mL	(1 tbs) chopped parsley
114 g	(¼ lb) fresh mushrooms, washed and sliced
454 g	(1 lb) fresh large scallops
50 mL	(¼ cup) dry white wine
37 mL	(2½ tbs) flour
250 mL	(1 cup) hot milk
50 mL	(¼ cup) hot 18% cream
125 mL	(½ cup) grated Gruyère cheese
	several drops Tabasco sauce
	several drops lemon juice
	salt and pepper

Place 15 mL (1 tbs) butter in casserole. Add shallots, parsley, mushrooms, and scallops; season with salt and pepper. Sprinkle with lemon juice.

Mix ingredients and add white wine. Cover with sheet of plastic wrap; microwave 2 minutes.

Stir and continue to microwave 2 minutes.

Stir again; cover and continue to microwave 1 minute.

Remove scallops from casserole and set aside.

Add remaining butter to casserole; mix and microwave 30 seconds to melt.

Add flour, mixing between spoonfuls.

Incorporate milk and cream; stir with whisk.

Season to taste; microwave, uncovered, 4 minutes. Stir every minute.

Add half of cheese; microwave, uncovered, 30 seconds.

Replace scallops in casserole and mix.

Arrange mixture in coquille shells and sprinkle with remaining cheese.

Grill (broil) 4 minutes in conventional oven.

Serve.

Mussels Marinière

(serves 2)

Setting:	HIGH
Cooking time:	12 minutes
Utensil:	2 L casserole

907 g	*(2 lb) mussels, washed and brushed*
30 mL	*(2 tbs) butter*
30 mL	*(2 tbs) chopped parsley*
30 mL	*(2 tbs) chopped shallot*
30 mL	*(2 tbs) dry white wine*
50 mL	*(¼ cup) fish stock**
15 mL	*(1 tbs) flour*
50 mL	*(¼ cup) 35% cream*
	several drops lemon juice
	salt and pepper from mill

Place mussels in casserole. Add 15 mL (1 tbs) of each: butter, parsley, and shallot. Pour in wine and fish stock.

Sprinkle with lemon juice; season with salt and pepper.

Cover with sheet of plastic wrap; microwave 3 minutes.

Mix mussels well, cover and continue to microwave 3 minutes.

Remove casserole from microwave. Let mussels stand in cooking liquid 3 to 4 minutes. Cover casserole.

Remove mussels from shells; set aside.

Pass cooking liquid through sieve.

Place remaining butter, parsley, and shallots in casserole. Cover with sheet of plastic wrap; microwave 2 minutes.

Add flour and incorporate ingredients well.

Add strained cooking liquid and cream; microwave, uncovered, 2 minutes. Stir every minute.

Continue to microwave 2 minutes.

Stir well and add mussels. Let stand in sauce 1 minute. Serve.

* See page 24.

Sole Filets with Pine Nuts

Sole Filets with Pine Nuts

(serves 4)

Setting: HIGH
Cooking time: 6 minutes
Utensil: 2 L casserole

15 mL	*(1 tbs) butter*
4	*sole filets, washed and dried*
30 mL	*(2 tbs) pine nuts*
5 mL	*(1 tsp) soya sauce*
	several drops lemon juice
	salt and pepper

Butter casserole and place sole in bottom. Season with salt and pepper; sprinkle with pine nuts. Add lemon juice and soya sauce. Cover and microwave 3 minutes.

Remove casserole and turn filets; cover and microwave 3 minutes. Serve.

Technique

Place sole filets in buttered casserole. Season with salt and pepper; sprinkle with pine nuts. Add lemon juice and soya sauce.

Sole Filets Andalusian

(serves 4)

Setting: HIGH
Cooking time: 9 to 10 minutes
Utensil: 2 L casserole

15 mL	*(1 tbs) butter*
4	*sole filets, folded in half*
125 mL	*(½ cup) cold water*
4	*slices tomato*
	juice 1 lemon
	pepper from mill

Sauce

30 mL	*(2 tbs) lemon juice*
30 mL	*(2 tbs) tomato purée*
90 mL	*(6 tbs) olive oil*
5 mL	*(1 tsp) chopped parsley*
4	*anchovy filets*

Place butter and lemon juice in casserole; microwave 1 minute. Add sole and cold water; season with pepper. Cover and microwave 3 minutes.

Turn filets; cover and continue to microwave 3 to 4 minutes.

When sole is cooked, remove and transfer to hot service platter.

Place tomato slices in casserole. Season with pepper and microwave, covered, 2 minutes.

Drain tomato slices and set on filets.

Mix first 4 ingredients of sauce. Spread over sole and tomato slices. Garnish with anchovy filets. Serve.

Sole Filets with Tomatoes

Sole Filets with Tomatoes

(serves 4)

Setting:	**HIGH**
Cooking time:	**13 minutes**
Utensil:	**2 L casserole**

15 mL	*(1 tbs) butter*
30 mL	*(2 tbs) chopped onion*
2 mL	*(½ tsp) tarragon*
1	*796 mL (28 oz) can tomatoes, drained and chopped*
4	*large sole filets*
15 mL	*(1 tbs) chopped parsley*
125 mL	*(½ cup) grated Gruyère cheese*
	pinch oregano
	several drops lemon juice
	salt and pepper

Place butter, onion, and spices in casserole. Cover with sheet of plastic wrap; microwave 3 minutes.

Add tomatoes and season with salt and pepper. Microwave, uncovered, 3 minutes.

Butter a separate microwave casserole and add sole.

Sprinkle sole with lemon juice; season with salt and pepper. Add chopped parsley.

Cover filets with tomato mixture and sprinkle with cheese. Cover and microwave 7 minutes.

Half way through cooking time, turn casserole a ½ turn.

Let casserole stand in microwave 3 to 4 minutes. Serve.

Technique

1 Place butter, onion, and spices in casserole; cover and microwave 3 minutes.

2 Add tomatoes; microwave, uncovered, 3 minutes. Season with salt and pepper.

Technique : Sole Filets with Tomatoes (continued)

3 Place filets in buttered casserole. Add lemon juice and sprinkle with chopped parsley.

4 Cover filets with tomato mixture.

5 Sprinkle with grated cheese; cover and microwave 7 minutes.

Sole Filets with Eggplant

(serves 4)

Setting:	HIGH
Cooking time:	18 to 20 minutes
Utensil:	3 L casserole
	2 L casserole
	Microwave service platter

15 mL	*(1 tbs) olive oil*
30 mL	*(2 tbs) chopped onion*
2	*garlic cloves, smashed and chopped*
1	*large tomato, peeled and chopped*
1	*eggplant, peeled and cubed*
4	*sole filets, washed and folded in half*
50 mL	*(¼ cup) water*
125 mL	*(½ cup) grated mozzarella cheese*
	juice ½ lemon
	salt and pepper

Place oil, onion, and garlic in 3 L casserole. Cover and microwave 2 minutes.

Add tomato and eggplant; season with salt and pepper. Mix well and cover; microwave 4 minutes. Stir well; microwave 3 to 4 minutes. Remove and set aside.

Place sole in 2 L casserole. Add water and lemon juice; cover and microwave 4 minutes. Turn filets and continue to microwave 3 to 4 minutes.

When sole is cooked, transfer to service platter. Top with eggplant mixture and sprinkle with cheese. Microwave, uncovered, 2 minutes. Serve.

Curry Filet of Sole

(serves 4)

Setting:	HIGH
Cooking time:	16 to 17 minutes
Utensil:	30 × 20 × 5 cm (11¾ × 7½ × 1¾ in) casserole

30 mL	*(2 tbs) butter*
4	*large sole filets, folded in half*
2	*shallots, chopped*
375 mL	*(1½ cups) hot fish stock* *
22 mL	*(1½ tbs) curry powder*
45 mL	*(3 tbs) cornstarch*
60 mL	*(4 tbs) cold water*
30 mL	*(2 tbs) tomato paste*
125 mL	*(½ cup) light cream*
	juice ¼ lemon
	salt and pepper

Place butter in casserole and melt 1 minute. Add sole and sprinkle with lemon juice. Add chopped shallots. Pour in fish stock; season with salt, pepper, and curry powder. Cover and microwave 7 to 8 minutes.

Let filets stand in hot liquid 3 minutes. Remove filets and set aside.

Mix cornstarch with water; incorporate to cooking liquid.

Add tomato paste and cream; mix and season sauce to taste. Microwave, uncovered, 8 minutes. Stir once during cooking.

Remove casserole. Replace filets in sauce and let stand 2 minutes. Serve.

* See page 24.

Haddock à la Marseillaise

(serves 4)

Setting: HIGH
Cooking time: 21 minutes
Utensil: 2 L casserole

908 g	*(2 lb) haddock*
1	*fennel sprig*
1	*onion, peeled and sliced*
500 mL	*(2 cups) water*
5 mL	*(1 tsp) oil*
2	*onions, peeled and chopped*
3	*tomatoes, peeled and chopped*
3	*potatoes, peeled and sliced*
50 mL	*(¼ cup) dry white wine*
50 mL	*(¼ cup) coarse breadcrumbs*
50 mL	*(¼ cup) stuffed olives*
	several drops lemon juice
	salt and pepper

Place haddock in casserole. Add lemon juice, fennel, sliced onion, and water. Season with salt and pepper; cover and microwave 4 minutes.

Turn haddock; cover and continue to microwave 4 minutes.

Remove casserole and let fish stand in hot liquid 4 minutes. Drain fish and set aside.

Pour oil into casserole. Add chopped onions, cover and microwave 3 minutes.

Add tomatoes, potatoes, and wine. Season with salt and pepper; microwave, covered, 5 minutes.

Turn casserole a ¼ turn and continue to microwave 5 minutes.

Transfer haddock to ovenproof buttered dish. Cover with potato mixture. Sprinkle with breadcrumbs and olives.

Grill (broil) 4 minutes in conventional oven. Serve.

Halibut Poached with Butter

(serves 2)

Setting: HIGH
Cooking time: 5 minutes
Utensil: 1.5 L pie plate

15 mL	*(1 tbs) butter*
1	*shallot, chopped*
1	*large halibut steak, cut in 2*
5 mL	*(1 tsp) chopped parsley*
50 mL	*(¼ cup) water*
50 mL	*(¼ cup) dry white wine*
	several drops lemon juice
	salt and pepper

Place butter in pie plate. Add shallot, halibut, and chopped parsley. Sprinkle with lemon juice. Season with salt and pepper; add water and wine.

Cover with sheet of plastic wrap; microwave 3 minutes.

Turn fish; cover and continue to microwave 2 minutes. Serve with melted butter.

Halibut and Spinach Casserole

(serves 4)

Setting: **HIGH**
Cooking time: **21 minutes**
Utensil: **3 L casserole**

30 mL	*(2 tbs) butter*
3	*halibut steaks, skinned, deboned, and cut into pieces*
1	*shallot, chopped*
50 mL	*(¼ cup) water*
2	*bunches spinach, washed*
500 mL	*(2 cups) thick white sauce * *
1 mL	*(¼ tsp) nutmeg*
125 mL	*(½ cup) grated cheddar cheese*
	juice ½ lemon
	salt and pepper

Place butter in casserole and heat 1 minute.

Add fish, lemon juice, shallot, and water. Season with salt and pepper; cover and microwave 3 minutes.

Stir well; cover and continue to microwave 3 minutes.

Remove from microwave and pour mixture into bowl; set aside.

Place spinach in casserole. Season with salt; cover and microwave 6 minutes. Mix well; cover and continue to microwave 6 minutes. Drain spinach well and replace in casserole.

Cover spinach with fish mixture. Add white sauce and nutmeg; sprinkle with cheese. Microwave 2 minutes to melt cheese. Serve.

* See page 21.

Halibut Coquilles

(serves 4)

Setting: **HIGH**
Cooking time: **7 minutes**
Utensil: **2 L casserole**

30 mL	*(2 tbs) butter*
2	*shallots, chopped*
114 g	*(¼ lb) fresh mushrooms, washed and diced*
37 mL	*(2½ tbs) flour*
250 mL	*(1 cup) hot milk*
125 mL	*(½ cup) hot 18% cream*
125 mL	*(½ cup) grated mozzarella cheese*
1	*large halibut steak, flaked in large pieces*
	salt and cayenne pepper
	lemon juice

Place 15 mL (1 tbs) butter in casserole. Add shallots and mushrooms; sprinkle with lemon juice.

Cover with sheet of plastic wrap; microwave 2 minutes.

Stir and add remaining butter; mix again.

Add flour, mixing between spoonfuls.

Add milk and cream; incorporate ingredients well.

Microwave, uncovered, 4 minutes. Stir every minute.

Add half of cheese; mix well.

Add fish; season with salt, pepper, and cayenne pepper. Microwave, uncovered, 1 minute.

Arrange mixture in coquille shells; sprinkle with remaining cheese.

Grill (broil) 3 to 4 minutes in conventional oven. Serve.

Cod with Corn

(serves 4)

Setting:	HIGH
Cooking time:	11 minutes in microwave
Utensil:	1.5 or 2 L casserole for vegetables
	2 L casserole for fish

908 g	*(2 lb) cod*
1	*fennel sprig*
1	*onion, peeled and sliced*
500 mL	*(2 cups) water*
15 mL	*(1 tbs) butter*
1	*red pepper, diced*
2	*341 mL (12 oz) cans corn kernels, drained*
30 mL	*(2 tbs) chopped onion*
50 mL	*(¼ cup) grated mozzarella cheese*
500 mL	*(2 cups) hot white sauce**
	several drops lemon juice
	pinch paprika
	salt and white pepper

Place cod in casserole. Add lemon juice, fennel, sliced onion, and water. Season with salt and pepper; cover and microwave 5 minutes.

Turn cod; cover and continue to microwave 4 minutes.

Remove casserole and let cod stand in hot liquid 4 minutes. Drain cod and set aside.

Place butter in casserole. Add red pepper, corn, and chopped onion. Season with salt and pepper; microwave, uncovered, 2 minutes.

Drain vegetables well and place in bottom of casserole. Add cod, cheese, and paprika.

Pour in white sauce and sprinkle with grated cheese. Grill (broil) in conventional oven 4 minutes. Serve.

* See page 21.

Cod with Spinach

(serves 4)

Setting:	HIGH
Cooking time:	14 minutes in microwave
Utensil:	1.5 or 2 L casserole for fish
	1.5 L casserole for spinach

908 g	*(2 lb) cod*
1	*fennel sprig*
1	*onion, peeled and sliced*
500 mL	*(2 cups) water*
15 mL	*(1 tbs) butter*
2	*bunches fresh spinach, well washed*
50 mL	*(¼ cup) grated mozzarella cheese*
500 mL	*(2 cups) hot white sauce**
	several drops lemon juice
	pinch paprika
	salt and pepper

Place cod in casserole. Add lemon juice, fennel, sliced onion, and water. Season with salt and pepper; cover and microwave 5 minutes.

Turn cod; cover and continue to microwave 4 minutes.

Remove casserole and let cod stand in hot liquid 4 minutes.

Drain cod and set aside.

Place butter and spinach in casserole; season with salt. Cover and microwave 3 minutes.

Turn casserole and continue to microwave 2 minutes.

Drain spinach well and press with spoon to remove excess water.

Chop spinach and place in bottom of casserole. Add cod, cheese, and paprika.

Add white sauce and sprinkle with grated cheese.

Grill (broil) 4 minutes in conventional oven.

* See page 21.

Technique

1 Place chopped spinach in bottom of casserole. Add cod.

2 Add cheese and paprika.

3 Add white sauce.

Salmon Coquilles

Salmon Coquilles

(serves 4)

Setting: **HIGH**
Cooking time: **4 minutes in microwave**
Utensil: **1.5 L casserole**

5 mL	*(1 tsp) oil*
1	*dry shallot, chopped or 30 mL (2 tbs) chopped onion*
15 mL	*(1 tbs) chopped parsley*
1	*796 mL (28 oz) can tomatoes, well drained and chopped*
3	*cooked salmon steaks, flaked*
125 mL	*(½ cup) grated parmesan cheese*
	pinch oregano
	pinch basil
	pinch paprika
	salt and pepper from mill

Pour oil into casserole. Add shallot, parsley, tomatoes, herbs, and paprika. Season with salt and pepper; microwave, uncovered, 3 minutes.

Add salmon; mix and microwave, uncovered, 1 minute.

Place mixture in coquille shells. Sprinkle with cheese. Grill (broil) 3 minutes in conventional oven. Serve.

Poached Salmon

(serves 2)

Setting: **HIGH**
Cooking time: **8 minutes in microwave**
Utensil: **1.5 L casserole**

2	*salmon steaks, 1.2 cm (½ in) thick*
15 mL	*(1 tbs) butter*
2	*parsley sprigs*
50 mL	*(¼ cup) water*
1	*shallot, sliced*
2	*slices garlic butter*
	several drops lemon juice
	pepper from mill

Rinse salmon under cold water.

Place butter, parsley, lemon juice, and water in casserole. Add pepper and shallots.

Cover with sheet of plastic wrap; microwave 2 minutes.

Add salmon; cover and microwave 3 minutes.

Turn salmon; continue to microwave 3 minutes.

Turn salmon again; let stand in cooking liquid 3 to 4 minutes. Cover casserole.

Note: If salmon is 1.8 cm (¾ in) thick, finish in microwave at MEDIUM-HIGH for 1 minute.

Place salmon in ovenproof dish. Top with garlic butter.

Grill (broil) 3 to 4 minutes in conventional oven. Sprinkle with lemon juice and serve.

Cod with Potatoes

(serves 4)

Setting: HIGH
Cooking time: 19 minutes in microwave
Utensil: 2 L casserole for potatoes
2 L casserole for fish

908 g	*(2 lb) cod*
1	*fennel sprig*
1	*onion, peeled and sliced*
500 mL	*(2 cups) water*
1	*onion, peeled and chopped*
3	*potatoes, peeled and sliced*
15 mL	*(1 tbs) chopped parsley*
125 mL	*(½ cup) hot chicken stock* *
500 mL	*(2 cups) hot white sauce* **
50 mL	*(¼ cup) grated Gruyère cheese*
	several drops lemon juice
	pinch paprika
	salt and pepper

Place cod in casserole. Add lemon juice, fennel, sliced onion, and water. Season with salt and pepper; cover and microwave 5 minutes.

Turn cod; cover and continue to microwave 4 minutes.

Remove casserole and let cod stand in hot liquid 4 minutes. Drain cod and set aside.

Place chopped onion, potatoes, parsley, and chicken stock in casserole. Cover and microwave 10 minutes.

Drain potatoes well and replace in casserole. Add cod, white sauce, cheese, and paprika.

Grill (broil) 4 minutes in conventional oven. Serve.

 * See page 55.
** See page 21.

Perch Filets with Hollandaise Sauce

(serves 4)

Setting: HIGH
Cooking time: 8 to 9 minutes
Utensil: 30 × 20 × 5 cm (11¾ × 7½ × 1¾ in) casserole

30 mL	*(2 tbs) butter*
2	*shallots, chopped*
15 mL	*(1 tbs) chopped fresh parsley*
4	*large perch filets OR*
8	*small perch filets*
50 mL	*(¼ cup) dry white wine*
50 mL	*(¼ cup) cold water*
125 g	*(¼ lb) fresh mushrooms, washed and sliced*
1	*recipe hollandaise sauce* *
	several drops lemon juice
	salt and pepper

Place butter, shallots, and parsley in casserole; cover and microwave 1 minute.

Place perch in casserole; season with salt and pepper. Add wine and water; sprinkle with lemon juice.

Add mushrooms; cover and microwave 7 to 8 minutes. Turn filets once during cooking.

Let filets stand in cooking liquid 2 to 3 minutes.

Serve with hollandaise sauce.

* See page 29.

Salmon with Curry

(serves 4)

Setting:	HIGH
Cooking time:	11 minutes
Utensil:	2 L casserole

15 mL	*(1 tbs) oil*
1	*onion, peeled and finely chopped*
30 mL	*(2 tbs) curry powder*
1	*green pepper, sliced*
750 mL	*(3 cups) hot white sauce* *
4	*cooked salmon steaks, flaked*
	several drops lemon juice
	salt and pepper from mill

Pour oil into casserole. Add onion, cover and microwave 2 minutes.

Add curry powder and green pepper; mix, cover and microwave 2 minutes.

Add white sauce and stir well; microwave, uncovered, 5 minutes. Season to taste.

Add salmon, stir, and sprinkle with lemon juice. Microwave, uncovered, 2 minutes.

Serve with steamed white rice.

* See page 21.

Salmon with Shallot and Lemon

(serves 4)

Setting:	HIGH
Cooking time:	8 minutes
Utensil:	1.5 or 2 L casserole

4	*salmon steaks, 1.2 cm (½ in) thick*
15 mL	*(1 tbs) chopped parsley*
1	*large dry shallot, chopped*
1	*fennel sprig*
15 mL	*(1 tbs) butter*
125 mL	*(½ cup) dry white wine*
2	*slices lemon*
	salt and pepper from mill

$\rightarrow$

Salmon with Shallot and Lemon (continued)

Rinse salmon under cold water and place in casserole; season with salt and pepper.

Add parsley, shallot, fennel, and butter.

Add wine and lemon; cover and microwave 3 minutes.

Turn salmon; cover and continue to microwave 5 minutes.

Remove casserole. Let salmon stand in cooking liquid 3 minutes. Serve.

Technique

1 Place salmon steaks in casserole.

2 Add parsley, shallot, fennel, and butter.

3 Add wine and lemon.

Salmon Casserole

(serves 4)

Setting: HIGH
Cooking time: 5 minutes
Utensil: 1.5 or 2 L casserole

15 mL	*(1 tbs) butter*
227 g	*(½ lb) fresh mushrooms, washed and diced*
3	*cooked salmon steaks, flaked*
500 mL	*(2 cups) hot white sauce* *
15 mL	*(1 tbs) chopped parsley*
50 mL	*(¼ cup) grated mozzarella cheese*
	several drops lemon juice
	pinch fennel
	salt and pepper from mill

Place butter in casserole. Add lemon juice and mushrooms; cover and microwave 3 minutes.

Add salmon, white sauce, fennel, parsley, and cheese. Season with salt and pepper; microwave, uncovered, 2 minutes.

Serve casserole with steamed broccoli.

* See page 21.

Celebrity Trout

(serves 1)

Setting: HIGH
Cooking time: 6 minutes in microwave
Utensil: 1.5 or 2 L casserole

1	*350 g (¾ lb) trout, cleaned and washed*
15 mL	*(1 tbs) butter*
1	*slice lemon, cut in 2*
50 mL	*(¼ cup) dry white wine*
5 mL	*(1 tsp) chopped parsley*
1	*small dry shallot, sliced*
	fennel sprig
	salt and pepper

→

Celebrity Trout (continued)

Place trout in casserole. Add butter, lemon, wine, parsley, shallot, and fennel. Season with salt and pepper; cover and microwave 3 minutes.

Turn trout; cover and continue to microwave 3 minutes.

Remove trout from casserole. Delicately cut lengthwise along backside to remove back bone. Replace trout together and set in hot service platter.

Sauce

**15 mL   (1 tbs) melted butter
           lemon juice**

Heat melted butter and lemon juice in small saucepan over medium heat on stove top. Cook 1 minute.

Pour over trout and serve with carrot glazed with maple syrup.

Technique

1 Place trout in casserole. Add butter, lemon, wine, parsley, shallot, and fennel. Season with salt and pepper.

2 Delicately cut lengthwise along backside to remove back bone.

3 Replace trout together and place in hot service platter.

Turbot Filets with Tomatoes

(serves 4)

Setting: HIGH
Cooking time: 7 to 8 minutes
Utensil: 30 × 20 × 5 cm (11¾ × 7½ × 1¾ in)
             casserole

4	*turbot filets*
250 mL	*(1 cup) hot fish stock* *
3	*tomatoes, peeled and diced*
15 mL	*(1 tbs) chopped fresh parsley*
1	*garlic clove, smashed and chopped*
45 mL	*(3 tbs) 35% cream*
30 mL	*(2 tbs) soft butter*
15 mL	*(1 tbs) flour*
	lemon juice
	salt and pepper

Place filets in casserole. Add fish stock, tomatoes, parsley, and garlic. Cover and microwave 4 minutes.

Turn filets; cover and continue to microwave 3 to 4 minutes. Let filets stand in liquid 3 minutes.

Transfer filets to service platter and set aside.

Pour tomato mixture into small saucepan. Cook 2 to 3 minutes over medium heat on stove top.

Add cream; stir and season generously.

Mix butter and flour together; incorporate to sauce. Cook 2 minutes.

Pour sauce over filets. Sprinkle with lemon juice and serve.

* See page 24.

Filet of Turbot, New Cuisine Style

(serves 4)

Setting: HIGH
Cooking time: 14 to 15 minutes
Utensil: 30 × 20 × 5 cm (11¾ × 7½ × 1¾ in)
             casserole
             2 L casserole

4	*turbot filets*
125 mL	*(½ cup) water*
15 mL	*(1 tbs) butter*
½	*zucchini, sliced*
250 mL	*(1 cup) pea pods*
2	*tomatoes, peeled and chopped*
5 mL	*(1 tsp) tarragon*
5 mL	*(1 tsp) chopped parsley*
50 mL	*(¼ cup) pine nuts*
	juice ½ lemon
	salt and pepper

Place filets in rectangular casserole. Sprinkle with lemon juice. Add water; season with salt and pepper. Cover and microwave 4 minutes.

Turn filets; cover and continue to microwave 3 to 4 minutes. Remove casserole and set aside.

Place butter in 2 L casserole. Melt in microwave 1 minute.

Add vegetables, herbs, and pine nuts; microwave 6 minutes. Season to taste.

Place filets on service platter; garnish with vegetables. Serve.

Turbot Filets with Wine

(serves 4)

Setting: **HIGH**
Cooking time: **9 minutes**
Utensil: **2 L casserole**

15 mL	*(1 tbs) butter*
2	*shallots, chopped*
15 mL	*(1 tbs) chopped parsley*
4	*medium size turbot filets*
50 mL	*(¼ cup) dry white wine*
4	*lemon slices*
227 g	*(½ lb) fresh mushrooms, washed and diced*
4	*pineapple slices*
	juice ½ lemon
	salt and pepper

Place butter, shallots, parsley, and lemon juice in casserole.

Add filets; season with salt and pepper.

Add wine, lemon slices, and correct seasoning.

Cover with sheet of plastic wrap; microwave 3 minutes.

Add mushrooms and pineapple slices.

Cover and microwave 6 minutes; turn casserole a ½ turn after 3 minutes.

Serve.

Technique

1 Place butter, shallots, parsley, and lemon juice in casserole.

3 Add mushrooms.

Salmon Steaks and Sour Cream Sauce

(serves 4)

Setting: HIGH
Cooking time: 8 minutes
Utensil: 3 L casserole

375 mL	*(1½ cups) hot water*
125 mL	*(½ cup) dry white wine*
3	*black peppercorns*
15 mL	*(1 tbs) finely chopped shallot*
1	*bay leaf*
5 mL	*(1 tsp) finely chopped fresh tarragon*
3 to 4	*pieces fresh salmon, 1.2 cm (½ in) thick, well rinsed*
125 mL	*(½ cup) sour cream*
15 mL	*(1 tbs) chopped fresh parsley*
2 mL	*(½ tsp) finely chopped fresh tarragon*
	juice ½ lemon
	salt and pepper

Pour water and wine into casserole. Add peppercorns, shallot, bay leaf, and 5 mL (1 tsp) tarragon. Cover with sheet of plastic wrap; microwave 2 minutes.

Place salmon in hot liquid; cover and microwave 3 minutes.

Turn salmon; cover and continue to microwave 3 minutes.

Remove casserole from microwave. Turn salmon again; let stand in cooking liquid 3 to 4 minutes. Cover casserole.

Transfer salmon to hot service platter; set aside.

In small mixing bowl, combine sour cream, parsley, and tarragon.

Top salmon with sauce and sprinkle with few drops lemon juice. Serve.

2 Place filets on shallots; add lemon slices and wine.

4 Add pineapple slices; season with salt and pepper.

Pasta

Fettuccini with Asparagus and Peas

Fettuccini with Asparagus and Peas

(serves 4)

Setting:	HIGH
Cooking time:	9 minutes
Utensil:	2 L casserole

4	*portions fettuccini*
15 mL	*(1 tbs) butter*
1	*can asparagus, washed and cubed*
50 mL	*(¼ cup) hot water*
375 mL	*(1½ cups) frozen peas*
125 mL	*(½ cup) grated parmesam cheese*
4	*fresh eggs, beaten*
	salt and pepper

Cook pasta as directed on package. Drain and set aside.

Place butter and asparagus in casserole; season with salt and pepper. Add water; cover and microwave 3 minutes.

Add frozen peas; cover and microwave 5 minutes.

Add cheese and mix. Add beaten eggs; microwave 1 minute. Pour sauce over hot pasta. Serve.

Technique

1 Place butter and asparagus in casserole. Add water; microwave 3 minutes.

2 Add frozen peas; cover and microwave 5 minutes.

→

Technique : Fettuccini with Asparagus and Peas (continued)

3   Add cheese and mix.

4   Add beaten eggs.

Meat and Pasta Casserole
(serves 4)

Setting:	HIGH
Cooking time:	16 minutes
Utensil:	2 to 2.5 L casserole

1 L	*(4 cups) medium bow pasta*
5 mL	*(1 tsp) oil*
45 mL	*(3 tbs) chopped onion*
350 g	*(¾ lb) lean ground beef*
5 mL	*(1 tsp) Worcestershire sauce*
1½	*796 mL (28 oz) can tomatoes, drained and chopped*
1	*garlic clove, smashed and chopped*
45 mL	*(3 tbs) tomato paste*
1 mL	*(¼ tsp) oregano*
1 mL	*(¼ tsp) basil*
50 mL	*(¼ cup) grated mozzarella cheese*
	salt and pepper

Cook pasta as directed on package. Drain and set aside.

Place oil and onion in casserole. Cover and microwave 3 minutes.

Add meat and Worcestershire sauce. Season with salt and pepper; cover and microwave 5 minutes.

Mix well to flake meat. Add tomatoes, garlic, and tomato paste. Sprinkle with herbs; cover and microwave 5 minutes.

Add pasta and mix thoroughly. Sprinkle top with cheese. Microwave, uncovered, 3 minutes. Serve.

Fettuccini Alfredo

(serves 4)

Setting:	HIGH
Cooking time:	12 minutes
Utensil:	2 L casserole

90 mL	(6 tbs) butter
5 mL	(1 tsp) chopped shallot
5 mL	(1 tsp) chopped fresh parsley
90 mL	(6 tbs) grated parmesan cheese
500 mL	(2 cups) 35% cream
4	portions fettuccini, cooked and drained
	dash crushed chillies
	salt and white pepper

Place butter, shallot, and parsley in casserole. Cover and microwave 2 minutes.

Add cheese and mix well; microwave, uncovered, 2 minutes.

Remove casserole and mix ingredients well. Add spices and cream; season with salt and pepper. Stir well. Microwave, uncovered, 3 minutes.

Stir again; continue to microwave 3 minutes.

Add pasta; thoroughly mix and microwave 2 minutes. Serve.

Macaroni and Cheddar Casserole

(serves 4)

Setting:	HIGH
Cooking time:	15 minutes
Utensil:	2.5 L casserole

500 mL	(2 cups) elbow macaroni
30 mL	(2 tbs) butter
30 mL	(2 tbs) chopped onion
45 mL	(3 tbs) flour
375 mL	(1½ cups) hot milk
125 mL	(½ cup) grated cheddar cheese
	pinch clove
	several drops Tabasco sauce
	salt and pepper

Cook macaroni as directed on package. Drain and set aside.

Place butter and onion in casserole; cover and microwave 3 minutes.

Add flour; mix and microwave, uncovered, 1 minute.

Add milk; season with salt and pepper. Sprinkle with Tabasco sauce and clove. Mix with whisk and microwave, uncovered, 4 minutes.

Mix again and continue to microwave 4 minutes.

Mix well; add macaroni and half of cheese. Mix again.

Sprinkle with remaining cheese; microwave, uncovered, 3 minutes. Serve.

Vegetable Lasagna

(serves 4)

Setting:	HIGH
Cooking time:	23 minutes in microwave
Utensil:	3 L casserole
	30 × 20 × 5 cm (11¾ × 7½ × 1¾ in) casserole

15 mL	*(1 tbs) butter*
½	*onion, finely chopped*
1½	*medium size eggplants, cut in small cubes*
1	*head broccoli, washed and chopped*
3	*tomatoes, seeded and chopped*
2	*garlic cloves, smashed and chopped*
30 mL	*(2 tbs) chopped fresh parsley*
500 mL	*(2 cups) grated mozzarella cheese*
1	*750 g (26 oz) package lasagna, cooked*
1 L	*(4 cups) hot white sauce**
	salt and pepper

Place butter and onion in casserole; cover and microwave 3 minutes.

Add all vegetables, garlic, and parsley. Season with salt and pepper; cover and microwave 20 minutes.

Mix ingredients well and add ¾ of cheese. Mix again.

Arrange several slices lasagna in bottom of rectangular casserole. Add layer of vegetables and top with part of white sauce. Sprinkle with cheese.

Arrange second layer of pasta; cover with layer of vegetables, sauce, and cheese.

Cover with third layer of pasta, a touch of sauce, and grated cheese.

Place in preheated oven at 180 C (350 F). Bake 20 minutes.

Serve with green salad.

* See page 21.

Mexican Macaroni

(serves 4)

Setting: HIGH
Cooking time: 10 minutes
Utensil: 2 to 2.5 L casserole

500 mL	*(2 cups) elbow macaroni*
5 mL	*(1 tsp) oil*
30 mL	*(2 tbs) chopped onion*
1	*long, strong marinated pepper, chopped*
1	*796 mL (28 oz) can tomatoes, drained and chopped*
1	*170 mL (6 oz) can tomato juice*
45 mL	*(3 tbs) tomato paste*
45 mL	*(3 tbs) crushed chillies*
3	*pepperoni sausages, sliced*
	several drops Tabasco sauce
	pinch sugar
	salt and pepper

Cook pasta as directed on package. Drain and set aside.

Pour oil into casserole. Add onion and marinated pepper; cover and microwave 3 minutes.

Add tomatoes, tomato juice, tomato paste, crushed chillies, and sugar. Season with salt and pepper; sprinkle with Tabasco sauce. Microwave, uncovered, 4 minutes.

Add pasta and pepperoni. Mix well and microwave, uncovered, 3 minutes.

Serve.

Macaroni, Cucumbers and Mushrooms

Macaroni, Cucumbers, and Mushrooms

(serves 4)

Setting: **HIGH**
Cooking time: **14 minutes**
Utensil: **2 to 2.5 L casserole**

500 mL	*(2 cups) elbow macaroni*
15 mL	*(1 tbs) butter*
227 g	*(½ lb) fresh mushrooms, washed and diced*
45 mL	*(3 tbs) flour*
375 mL	*(1½ cups) hot chicken stock* *
1	*cucumber, peeled, seeded, and diced*
45 mL	*(3 tbs) grated Gruyère cheese*
5 mL	*(1 tsp) chopped fresh parsley*
	lemon juice
	salt and pepper

Cook pasta as directed on package. Drain and set aside.

Place butter and mushrooms in casserole. Season with salt and pepper; add lemon juice. Cover and microwave 3 minutes.

Add flour; mix and microwave, uncovered, 1 minute.

Add chicken stock; stir and microwave, uncovered, 4 minutes.

Stir again; continue to microwave 4 minutes.

Add hot pasta and cucumbers. Season with salt and pepper; mix thoroughly.

Sprinkle with cheese and microwave, uncovered, 2 minutes.

Sprinkle with parsley. Serve.

* See page 55.

Noodles with Cauliflower

(serves 4)

Setting: **HIGH**
Cooking time: **10 minutes**
Utensil: **2 L casserole**

1	*227 g (½ lb) package spinach egg noodles*
15 mL	*(1 tbs) butter*
1	*small cauliflower, washed and sectioned into flowerets*
1	*small can anchovy filets, drained and chopped*
1	*796 mL (28 oz) can tomatoes, crushed*
125 mL	*(½ cup) cooking liquid from noodles*
	salt and pepper

Cook pasta as directed on package. Drain and reserve 125 mL (½ cup) cooking liquid. Set aside.

Place butter and cauliflower in casserole. Season with salt and pepper; cover and microwave 7 minutes.

Add anchovies, tomatoes, and cooking liquid. Season with salt and pepper; cover and microwave 2 minutes.

Add hot noodles; mix and microwave, uncovered, 1 minute. Serve.

Technique : Noodles with Cauliflower

1 Microwave cauliflower 7 minutes.

2 Add anchovies.

3 Add crushed tomatoes.

4 Add 125 mL (½ cup) cooking liquid from noodles.

Pork Rigatoni

(serves 4)

Place olive oil and onion in casserole. Cover and microwave 2 minutes.

Add mushrooms and parsley; cover and microwave 1 minute.

Add tomato juice, brown sauce, and tomato paste. Season with salt and pepper; stir and microwave, uncovered, 10 minutes.

Heat oil in frying pan on stove top. Add pork and sear 2 minutes each side.

Incorporate pork to sauce. Add cheese and microwave, uncovered, 3 minutes. Serve on rigatoni.

Setting:	HIGH
Cooking time:	16 minutes in microwave
Utensil:	2 L casserole

5 mL	*(1 tsp) olive oil*
1	*onion, peeled and chopped*
227 g	*(½ lb) fresh mushrooms, washed and chopped*
15 mL	*(1 tbs) chopped parsley*
500 mL	*(2 cups) tomato juice*
250 mL	*(1 cup) brown sauce*
30 mL	*(2 tbs) tomato paste*
15 mL	*(1 tbs) oil*
454 g	*(1 lb) pork loin, diced*
125 mL	*(½ cup) grated parmesan cheese*
750 mL	*(3 cups) cooked rigatoni*
	salt and pepper

Technique

1 In casserole containing onion, add mushrooms and parsley.

→

Technique : *Pork Rigatoni* (continued)

2 Add tomato juice.

3 The mixture after 10 minutes in microwave.

4 Add pork.

Ravioli with Zucchini

(serves 4)

Setting: HIGH
Cooking time: 22 minutes
Utensil: 2 to 2.5 L casserole
               30 × 20 × 5 cm (11¾ × 7½ × 1¾ in)
               casserole

1	454 g (1 lb) ravioli (cheese filling)
15 mL	(1 tbs) oil
½	eggplant, washed and diced
1	zucchini, sliced
3	large tomatoes, seeded and chopped
2	170 mL (6 oz) cans tomato juice
1	garlic clove, smashed and chopped
50 mL	(¼ cup) grated parmesan cheese
	pinch caraway seed
	pinch thyme
	pinch sugar
	salt and pepper

Cook pasta as directed on package. Drain and set aside.

Place oil and eggplant in 2 L casserole. Season with salt and pepper; cover and microwave 10 minutes.

Add zucchini, tomatoes, tomato juice, garlic, spices, and sugar. Microwave, uncovered, 10 minutes.

Pass mixture through food mill. Correct seasoning.

Spread hot cooked pasta in bottom of rectangular casserole. Cover with sauce. Microwave, uncovered, 2 minutes.

Sprinkle with cheese before serving.

Spaghetti Carbonara

Spaghetti Carbonara

(serves 4)

Setting:	**HIGH**
Cooking time:	**5 minutes**
Utensil:	**2 L casserole**

4   ***slices bacon, cubed***
30 mL   ***(2 tbs) chopped onion***
125 mL   ***(½ cup) grated parmesan cheese***
15 mL   ***(1 tbs) chopped fresh parsley***
3   ***beaten eggs***
4   ***portions hot cooked spaghetti***
         salt and pepper

Place bacon in casserole; microwave, uncovered, 3 minutes.

Add onion; cover and microwave 1 minute.

Add cheese and parsley; mix well. Add beaten eggs; mix and microwave, uncovered, 30 seconds.

Stir well; continue to microwave 30 seconds. Add hot pasta; mix and serve.

Technique

1   Microwave bacon 3 minutes.

2   Add onion; cover and microwave 1 minute.

→

Technique : *Spaghetti Carbonara (continued)*

3 Add cheese and parsley.

4 Add beaten eggs.

5 Add cooked spaghetti.

Spaghetti with Clams

(serves 4)

Setting: HIGH
Cooking time: 14 minutes
Utensil: 2 L casserole

4	portions spaghetti
15 mL	(1 tbs) butter
30 mL	(2 tbs) chopped onion
1	celery stalk, diced
½	red pepper, diced
30 mL	(2 tbs) flour
1	142 g (5 oz) can small clams, reserve juice
2	tomatoes, seeded and diced
	pinch fennel
	salt and pepper

Cook pasta as directed on package. Drain and set aside.

Place butter, onion, celery, and red pepper in casserole. Season with salt and pepper; cover and microwave 3 minutes.

Add flour; mix and microwave, uncovered, 1 minute.

Add clam juice; stir and microwave, uncovered, 3 minutes.

Stir again; continue to microwave 3 minutes.

Add tomatoes, clams, and fennel. Season with salt and pepper; microwave 4 minutes.

Pour sauce over pasta. Serve.

Spiral Pasta with Vegetables and Garlic

(serves 4)

Setting: HIGH
Cooking time: 13 minutes
Utensil: 2 L casserole

750 mL	(3 cups) spiral pasta
30 mL	(2 tbs) butter
227 g	(½ lb) fresh mushrooms, washed and diced
2	garlic cloves, smashed and chopped
45 mL	(3 tbs) flour
375 mL	(1½ cups) hot light beef stock
15 mL	(1 tbs) tomato paste
1	zucchini, diced
	juice ½ lemon
	chopped parsley
	pinch oregano
	salt and pepper

Cook pasta as directed on package. Drain and set aside.

Place butter in casserole. Add mushrooms, lemon juice, and garlic. Season with salt and pepper; cover and microwave 3 minutes.

Add flour; mix and microwave, uncovered, 1 minute.

Add beef stock and tomato paste; stir well and microwave, uncovered, 3 minutes.

Mix again; continue to microwave 3 minutes.

Add herbs, zucchini, and pasta. Season with salt and pepper; continue to microwave 3 minutes. Serve.

Tortellini with Peas

Tortellini with Peas

(serves 4)

Setting:	HIGH
Cooking time:	8 minutes
Utensil:	2 to 2.5 L casserole

1	454 g (1 lb) package tortellini (meat filling)
750 mL	(3 cups) frozen peas
250 mL	(1 cup) hot water
½	green pepper, sliced
½	yellow pepper, sliced
500 mL	(2 cups) white sauce *
	pinch sugar
	salt and pepper

Cook pasta as directed on package. Drain and set aside.

Place frozen peas, hot water, and sugar in casserole. Season with salt and pepper; cover and microwave 4 minutes.

Add peppers; cover and microwave 1 minute.

Drain vegetables and replace in casserole. Add white sauce and pasta. Season with salt and pepper; cover and microwave 3 minutes. Serve.

* See page 21.

Tortellini with Ham

(serves 4)

Setting:	HIGH
Cooking time:	7 minutes
Utensil:	3 L casserole

1	454 g (1 lb) package tortellini (cheese filling)
15 mL	(1 tbs) sweet butter
30 mL	(2 tbs) chopped onion
¼	green pepper, sliced
½	red pepper, sliced
1	celery stalk, sliced
250 mL	(1 cup) cooked sliced ham
500 mL	(2 cups) hot white sauce *
	paprika
	salt and pepper

Cook pasta as directed on package. Drain and set aside.

Place butter, onion, peppers, and celery in casserole. Cover and microwave 3 minutes.

Add ham and white sauce; stir well. Season with salt, pepper, and paprika. Cover and microwave 3 minutes.

Add pasta; stir and microwave, uncovered, 1 minute. Serve.

* See page 21.

Vegetables,
Salads and Rice

Eggplant au Gratin

Eggplant au Gratin

(serves 2)

Setting:	HIGH
Cooking time:	33 minutes
Utensil:	2 L square casserole

1	large eggplant
30 mL	(2 tbs) oil
1	onion, peeled and chopped
1	zucchini, sliced
2	tomatoes, cut in large cubes
1	garlic clove, smashed and chopped
15 mL	(1 tbs) tomato paste
50 mL	(¼ cup) grated Gruyère cheese
	pinch oregano
	salt and pepper

Cut eggplant in two, lengthwise. Using small knife score flesh.

Brush flesh with oil. Microwave, uncovered, 12 minutes. Set aside.

Pour 15 mL (1 tbs) oil into casserole; add onion. Cover with sheet of plastic wrap; microwave 4 minutes.

Add vegetables, garlic, and oregano.

Remove eggplant flesh carefully not to damage skins. Chop flesh and add to casserole.

Season with salt and pepper; add tomato paste and mix ingredients well.

Cover with sheet of plastic wrap; microwave 15 minutes.

Fill eggplant skins with mixture and top with grated cheese.

Microwave, uncovered, 2 minutes. Serve.

Technique

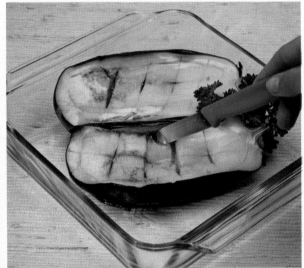

1 Eggplant flesh must be well cooked before attempting to remove it.

2 Place grated cheese on top and continue to microwave. Note that cheese melts but does not brown.

Cooking Asparagus

Setting: HIGH
Cooking time: 12 minutes
Utensil: 2 L rectangular casserole

454 g (1 lb) asparagus
125 mL (½ cup) water
    salt

Peel asparagus and place in casserole; add water and salt.

Cover with sheet of plastic wrap; microwave 6 minutes.

Turn casserole a ½ turn; continue to microwave 6 minutes.

Note: If asparagus are very large, microwave 1½ minutes extra.

Asparagus with Cheese

(serves 2)

Setting: HIGH
Cooking time: 19 minutes
Utensil: 2 L rectangular casserole

454 g (1 lb) asparagus
125 mL (½ cup) water
30 mL (2 tbs) butter
15 mL (1 tbs) chopped onion
15 mL (1 tbs) chopped parsley
37 mL (2½ tbs) flour
375 mL (1½ cups) milk
45 mL (3 tbs) grated mozzarella cheese
    salt and pepper

Peel asparagus and place in casserole; add water and salt. Cover with sheet of plastic wrap; microwave 6 minutes.

Turn casserole a ½ turn; continue to microwave 6 minutes.

Note: If asparagus are very large, microwave 1½ minutes extra.

Place butter, onion, and parsley in microwave bowl. Cover with sheet of plastic wrap; microwave 2 minutes.

Add flour, mixing with whisk between spoonfuls.

Add milk, stir, and season with salt and pepper.

Microwave, uncovered, 4 minutes. Mix every minute.

Add cheese and mix; continue to microwave 30 seconds.

Pour over hot asparagus.

Broccoli with Cheese Sauce

(serves 4)

Preparation of sauce :

Setting :	HIGH and MEDIUM
Cooking time :	7 minutes
Utensil :	2 L round casserole

45 mL	(3 tbs) butter
30 mL	(2 tbs) chopped onion
5 mL	(1 tsp) chopped parsley
52 mL	(3½ tbs) flour
500 mL	(2 cups) hot milk
125 mL	(½ cup) grated Gruyère cheese
	pinch nutmeg
	slivered almonds
	salt and white pepper

Place butter, onion, and parsley in casserole. Cover and microwave 1 minute at HIGH.

Add flour ; mix with wooden spoon.

Add milk, mixing with whisk.

Add nutmeg. Season with salt and pepper ; stir again. Microwave, uncovered, 3 minutes at HIGH.

Stir ingredients well. Add cheese and microwave, uncovered, 3 minutes at MEDIUM. Stir again.

Pour sauce over broccoli, sprinkle with slivered almonds, and serve.

Preparation of brocoli :

Setting :	HIGH
Cooking time :	8 minutes
Utensil :	2 L round casserole

1	large head broccoli, sectioned into flowerets
250 mL	(1 cup) cold water
	salt and pepper

Place broccoli in casserole ; season with salt and pepper.

Add water ; cover and microwave 5 minutes.

Turn casserole a ½ turn ; continue to microwave 3 minutes.

Asparagus with Vinaigrette

(serves 2)

Setting: HIGH
Cooking time: 12 minutes
Utensil: 2 L rectangular casserole

454 g	*(1 lb) asparagus*
125 mL	*(½ cup) water*
15 mL	*(1 tbs) Dijon mustard*
15 mL	*(1 tbs) chopped shallot*
1	*egg yolk*
15 mL	*(1 tbs) chopped parsley*
45 mL	*(3 tbs) wine vinegar*
135 mL	*(9 tbs) oil*
	several drops lemon juice
	salt and pepper

Peel asparagus and place in casserole; add water and salt. Cover with sheet of plastic wrap; microwave 6 minutes.

Turn casserole a ½ turn; continue to microwave 6 minutes.

Note: If asparagus are very large, microwave an extra 1¼ minutes.

Place mustard, shallot, egg yolk, and parsley in mixing bowl. Season with salt and pepper; mix until combined.

Add vinegar; mix again.

Add oil, in thin steady stream while mixing with whisk.

Sprinkle with lemon juice.

Serve vinaigrette over hot or cold asparagus.

Celery Braised with Pork

(serves 4)

Setting: HIGH
Cooking time: 15 minutes in microwave
Utensil: 2 L casserole

2	*head celery, sectioned*
30 mL	*(2 tbs) butter*
15 mL	*(1 tbs) oil*
30 mL	*(2 tbs) chopped onion*
1	*garlic clove, smashed and chopped*
227 g	*(½ lb) lean ground pork*
15 mL	*(1 tbs) chopped fresh chives*
250 mL	*(1 cup) canned crushed tomatoes*
30 mL	*(2 tbs) grated parmesan cheese*
	pinch thyme
	lemon juice
	salt and pepper

Place celery, lemon juice, and butter in casserole. Cover and microwave 10 minutes. Set aside.

Heat oil in sauté pan over medium heat on stove top. Add onion and garlic; cook 2 minutes.

Add pork and mix well. Add herbs; continue cooking 3 minutes.

Add tomatoes; cook 3 to 4 minutes.

Add cheese, mix and cook 1 minute.

Pour pork mixture over celery; cover and continue to microwave 5 minutes. Serve.

Celery Braised with Curry

(serves 4)

Setting:	HIGH
Cooking time:	19 minutes
Utensil:	2 L casserole

6	celery stalks, washed and diced
15 mL	(1 tbs) butter
22 mL	(1½ tbs) curry powder
30 mL	(2 tbs) flour
425 mL	(1¾ cups) hot milk
125 mL	(½ cup) grated coconut
5 mL	(1 tsp) chopped parsley
	salt and pepper

Place celery and butter in casserole. Cover and microwave 10 minutes.

Add curry powder and flour; mix well. Season with salt and pepper; cover and microwave 3 minutes.

Add milk and stir well. Microwave, uncovered, 3 minutes.

Stir again; continue to microwave, uncovered, 3 minutes. Add coconut and parsley; stir and serve.

Corn with Butter

(serves 4)

Setting:	HIGH
Cooking time:	10 minutes
Utensil:	30 × 20 × 5 cm (11¾ × 7½ × 1¾ in) casserole

4	ears corn, husked
250 mL	(1 cup) salted hot water
	fresh butter

Place corn and water in casserole. Cover and microwave 5 minutes.

Turn corn; cover and continue to microwave 5 minutes.

Serve with fresh butter.

Cooking Mushrooms

(serves 4)

Setting: HIGH
Cooking time: 10 minutes
Utensil: 2 L casserole

570 g	*(1½ lb) fresh mushrooms, washed and kept whole*
30 mL	*(2 tbs) butter*
125 mL	*(½ cup) water*
	juice 1 lemon
	salt and pepper

Place all ingredients in casserole. Cover with sheet of plastic wrap; microwave 10 minutes.

After 5 minutes in microwave, stir well and continue to microwave.

Let mushrooms cool in cooking liquid.

Note: The mushrooms will keep in cooking liquid 5 to 6 days refrigerated.

Cabbage Braised with Bacon

(serves 4)

Setting: HIGH
Cooking time: 13 minutes
Utensil: 2 L casserole

1	*green cabbage, washed and cut into 6 pieces*
125 mL	*(½ cup) water*
4	*slices cooked crisp bacon, diced*
	several drops lemon juice
	salt and pepper

Place cabbage in casserole; add water and salt. Cover with sheet of plastic wrap; microwave 13 minutes.

Let cabbage stand; add lemon juice and serve with diced bacon.

Technique

1 Place mushrooms and remaining ingredients in casserole.

2 Here is the finished product.

Technique

1 Place cabbage pieces in casserole.

2 When cabbage is cooked, add lemon juice and diced bacon.

Red Cabbage and Raisins

Red Cabbage and Raisins

(serves 4)

Setting: HIGH
Cooking time: 22 minutes in microwave
Utensil: 2 L casserole

1	*small red cabbage*
50 mL	*(¼ cup) dry red wine*
125 mL	*(½ cup) dry sweet raisins*
4	*slices bacon, chopped*
15 mL	*(1 tbs) chopped fresh parsley*
30 mL	*(2 tbs) chopped onion*
22 mL	*(1½ tbs) flour*
375 mL	*(1½ cups) hot chicken stock* *
	lemon juice
	salt and pepper

Cut cabbage in 4. Remove heart and discard.

Slice cabbage into strips and place in casserole. Add lemon juice, salt, and pepper. Cover and microwave 10 minutes.

Add wine and raisins; stir, cover and microwave 12 minutes. Set aside.

Place bacon, parsley, and onion in sauté pan. Cook 3 to 4 minutes over medium heat on stove top.

Add flour to pan; stir and cook 2 minutes.

Add chicken stock; stir and cook 5 to 6 minutes over high heat.

Pour raisin sauce over cabbage; toss and serve.

* See page 55.

Steamed Green Cabbage

(serves 4)

Setting: HIGH
Cooking time: 45 minutes
Utensil: 2 to 3 L round casserole

1	*green cabbage, cut into 8 pieces*
50 mL	*(¼ cup) dry white wine*
	lemon juice
	salt and pepper

Place all ingredients in casserole. Place thicker section of cabbage towards exterior of dish.

Cover and microwave 45 minutes.

Drain and serve.

Stuffed Cabbage Rolls

Stuffed Cabbage Rolls

(serves 4)

Setting:	HIGH
Cooking time:	26 minutes
Utensil:	2 L casserole
	30 × 20 × 5 cm (11¾ × 7½ × 1¾ in) casserole

1	*medium size green cabbage, washed*
15 mL	*(1 tbs) oil*
45 mL	*(3 tbs) chopped onion*
15 mL	*(1 tbs) chopped fresh parsley*
227 g	*(½ lb) fresh mushrooms, washed and chopped*
1	*garlic clove, smashed and chopped*
15 mL	*(1 tbs) chopped chives*
1	*tomato, seeded and chopped*
50 mL	*(¼ cup) chopped walnuts*
30 mL	*(2 tbs) fine breadcrumbs*
1	*beaten egg*
500 mL	*(2 cups) hot brown sauce **
	several drops soya sauce
	salt and pepper

Remove cabbage heart and discard.

Remove 8 to 12 exterior leaves and place in rectangular casserole. Cover with sheet of plastic wrap; careful not to damage leaves.

Microwave 3 minutes; drain and set aside.

Pour oil into 2 L casserole. Add onion and parsley; cover and microwave 3 minutes.

Add mushrooms, garlic, and chives. Season with salt and pepper; cover and microwave 4 minutes.

Add tomato and nuts; microwave, uncovered, 3 minutes. Stir well, crushing mixture.

Add breadcrumbs and beaten egg; microwave, uncovered, 1 minute.

Stuff cabbage leaves, roll, and set in buttered, rectangular casserole. Top with brown sauce; cover and microwave 8 minutes.

Add several drops soya sauce; cover and continue to microwave 4 minutes. Serve.

* See page 22.

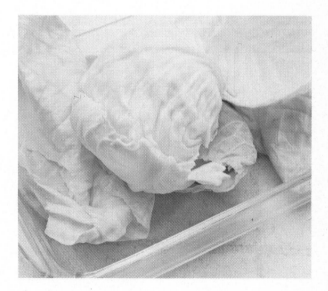

1 Remove 8 to 12 exterior leaves from cabbage.

→

Technique : Stuffed Cabbage Rolls

2 Cover with sheet of plastic wrap ; careful not to damage leaves.

Carrots with Brown Sugar

(serves 4)

Setting: HIGH
Cooking time: 6 minutes
Utensil: 2 L casserole

5	carrots, peeled, and sliced 0.65 cm (¼ in) thick
125 mL	(½ cup) hot chicken stock *
30 mL	(2 tbs) chopped parsley
15 mL	(1 tbs) brown sugar
15 mL	(1 tbs) butter several drops lemon juice salt and pepper

Place carrots in casserole; add chicken stock, parsley, and brown sugar. Season with salt and pepper.

Cover with sheet of plastic wrap; microwave 6 minutes.

Add butter and sprinkle with lemon juice. Serve.

* See page 55.

Buttered Brussels Sprouts and Carrots

(serves 4)

Setting: HIGH
Cooking time : 15 minutes
Utensil: 2 L round casserole

680 g	(1½ lb) Brussels sprouts, washed and drained
5 mL	(1 tsp) butter
3	carrots, peeled and sliced 1.2 cm (½ in) thick
250 mL	(1 cup) hot chicken stock * several drops lemon juice chopped parsley salt and pepper

Using small knife, score base of sprouts in the shape of a cross.

Place butter, sprouts, carrots, and chicken stock in casserole. Season with salt and pepper; cover and microwave 8 minutes.

Stir vegetables; continue to microwave 7 minutes or longer depending on sprout size.

Drain vegetables, sprinkle with lemon juice and parsley. Serve.

* See page 55.

Technique

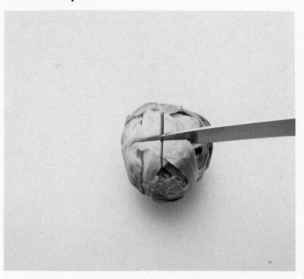

Using small knife, score base of sprouts in the shape of a cross.

Assorted Seasoned Vegetables

(serves 4)

Setting: HIGH
Cooking time: 13 minutes
Utensil: 2 L round casserole

5 mL	*(1 tsp) butter*
1	*green pepper, diced*
1	*celery stalk, sliced*
2	*potatoes, peeled and diced*
1	*large carrot, peeled and diced*
1	*small leek, white section only, sliced*
1	*bay leaf*
50 mL	*(¼ cup) hot chicken stock* *
5 mL	*(1 tsp) fresh butter*
	salt and pepper

Place butter, green pepper, celery, and potatoes in casserole. Season with salt and pepper; cover and microwave 7 minutes.

Mix well. Add carrots and leek; season with salt and pepper. Add bay leaf and chicken stock; stir well.

Cover and microwave 6 minutes.

Before serving, add butter.

Ideal to serve with steak or a roast.

* See page 55.

Stuffed Zucchini

Stuffed Zucchini

(serves 4)

Setting:	HIGH
Cooking time:	20 minutes
Utensil:	28 × 18 cm (12 × 7 in) rectangular casserole
	2 L round casserole

4	*medium size zucchini*
250 mL	*(1 cup) water*
30 mL	*(2 tbs) chopped onion*
5 mL	*(1 tsp) oil*
½	*apple, peeled and finely chopped*
5 mL	*(1 tsp) chopped parsley*
375 g	*(¾ lb) ground veal*
15 mL	*(1 tbs) chopped walnuts*
250 mL	*(1 cup) canned tomatoed, drained and chopped*
175 mL	*(¾ cup) grated mozzarella cheese*
	pinch paprika
	salt and pepper

Trim skin, lengthwise, on one side of zucchini. Using spoon scoop out flesh and chop. Set aside.

Place hollowed zucchini in rectangular casserole; add water. Cover and microwave 7 minutes.

Cool under cold water, drain, and set aside.

In round casserole, place onion, zucchini flesh, oil, apple, and parsley. Season with salt and pepper; cover and microwave 3 minutes.

Add veal and walnuts; season with salt and pepper. Cover and microwave 3 minutes.

Mix well; add tomatoes, half of cheese, and paprika. Microwave, uncovered, 4 minutes.

Dry zucchini shells and stuff with filling; sprinkle with remaining cheese. Microwave, uncovered, 3 minutes. Serve.

Technique

1 Trim skin, lengthwise, on one side of zucchini. Using spoon scoop out flesh.

2 Place hollowed zucchini in casserole; add water.

→

Technique : *Stuffed Zucchini (continued)*

3 Here is the apple and zucchini flesh after 3 minutes in microwave.

4 Add ground veal and walnuts.

5 Add tomatoes.

6 Add grated cheese and paprika.

Beans à la Bretonne

(serves 4)

Setting:	HIGH and MEDIUM
Cooking time:	1 hour 34 minutes
Utensil:	3 L casserole

3	*slices cooked ham, cut in 1.2 cm (½ in) strips*
1	*onion, peeled and chopped*
1	*garlic clove, smashed and chopped*
500 mL	*(2 cups) dry white beans, soaked 12 hours in water and drained*
15 mL	*(1 tbs) chopped parsley*
1	*bay leaf*
30 mL	*(2 tbs) tomato paste*
5 mL	*(1 tsp) soya sauce*
1.5 L	*(6 cups) hot chicken stock**
15 mL	*(1 tbs) Dijon mustard*
	pinch thyme
	salt and pepper

Place ham, onion, and garlic in casserole. Cover and microwave 4 minutes at HIGH.

Add beans, parsley, bay leaf, and thyme; stir well. Add tomato paste, soya sauce, and chicken stock; season with salt and pepper. Stir ingredients again; cover and microwave 15 minutes at HIGH.

Stir; continue to microwave 15 minutes at HIGH.

Stir; continue to microwave 30 minutes at MEDIUM.

Stir well; correct seasoning. Cover and microwave 30 minutes.

Before serving, stir in mustard.

Serve beans with lamb chops, smoked pork chops, etc.

* See page 55.

Spaghetti Squash Garnished with Sour Cream

(serves 4)

Setting:	HIGH
Cooking time:	20 to 25 minutes
Utensil:	2 to 3 L casserole

1	*spaghetti squash*
250 mL	*(1 cup) water*
30 mL	*(2 tbs) fresh butter*
	sour cream
	paprika
	salt and pepper

Peel squash and cut, lengthwise, into 4 sections. Remove seeds and cut sections, widthwise, into two.

Place pieces in casserole; season with salt and pepper. Add water and cover; microwave 15 minutes.

Turn casserole a ½ turn; continue to microwave 5 to 10 minutes.

Drain and flake using fork. Add butter; season with salt and pepper. Sprinkle with paprika. Serve with sour cream.

Braised Endives

Braised Endives

(serves 4)

Setting:	HIGH
Cooking time:	20 minutes in microwave
Utensil:	2 L square casserole

4	*endives*
15 mL	*(1 tbs) butter*
2	*slices lemon*
50 mL	*(¼ cup) hot water*
	garlic croutons
	butter
	salt and white pepper

Place endives in casserole, with thickest section towards exterior of dish.

Add 15 mL (1 tbs) butter, lemon, salt and pepper. Add water; cover and microwave 20 minutes.

Drain endives and place in ovenproof dish. Dot with butter and sprinkle with croutons. Grill (broil) in conventional oven several minutes. Serve.

Technique

1 Place endives in casserole, with thickest section towards exterior of dish. Add butter and lemon.

2 Sprinkle endives with croutons and grill (broil) in conventional oven several minutes.

Buttered Spinach

(serves 4)

Setting: **HIGH**
Cooking time: **5 minutes**
Utensil: **2 L casserole**

4   bunches fresh spinach
30 mL   (2 tbs) butter
**   several drops lemon juice**
**   salt and pepper**

Wash spinach but do not dry. Remove stems.

Place spinach in casserole; season with salt and pepper. Cover with sheet of plastic wrap; microwave 5 minutes.

Remove casserole from microwave; let stand 3 minutes.

Discard cooking liquid. Add butter and several drops lemon juice. Serve.

Note: The spinach can be kept 2 days refrigerated. To do so, squeeze out excess water from spinach and from a ball. Cover with sheet of plastic wrap.

Technique

1 Wash spinach under cold water.

3 When cooked, discard cooking liquid and add butter and lemon juice.

2 Place spinach in casserole and cover with sheet of plastic wrap.

4 To keep spinach in refrigerator, squeeze out excess water and form ball. Cover with sheet of plastic wrap.

Julienne of Vegetables

(serves 4)

Setting:	HIGH
Cooking time:	11 minutes
Utensil:	2 L casserole

5 mL	*(1 tsp) butter*
¼	*eggplant, cut into julienne*
2	*celery stalks, cut into julienne*
½	*red pepper, cut into julienne*
½	*green pepper, cut into julienne*
¼	*English cucumber, cut into julienne*
	pinch tarragon
	pinch thyme
	lemon juice
	salt and pepper

Place butter and eggplant in casserole. Season with salt and pepper; cover and microwave 4 minutes.

Mix well; add celery and microwave 3 minutes.

Add remaining vegetables. Season with salt and pepper; add herbs. Sprinkle with lemon juice; cover and microwave 4 minutes. Serve.

Cooking Beans

(serves 4)

Setting: **HIGH**
Cooking time: **13 minutes**
Utensil: **2 L casserole**

454 g **(1 lb) fresh green beans, washed**
250 mL **(1 cup) water**
15 mL **(1 tbs) butter**
45 mL **(3 tbs) peanut and raisin mix**
salt

Trim beans. Place in casserole;
add water and salt.

Cover with sheet of plastic wrap;
microwave 13 minutes.

Turn beans twice during cooking.

When cooked, drain beans.

Add butter and peanut
and raisin mix. Serve.

Technique

1 Place beans in casserole; add water and salt.
Cover and microwave.

2 Turn beans twice during cooking.

3 Serve with fresh butter and peanut and raisin
mix.

Steamed Vegetables

(serves 4)

Setting:	HIGH
Cooking time:	15 minutes
Utensil:	2 L casserole

4	*carrots, diced*
6	*green onions, remove green section*
½	*turnip, peeled and diced*
250 mL	*(1 cup) cold water*
15 mL	*(1 tbs) butter*
15 mL	*(1 tbs) chopped parsley*
	several drops lemon juice
	salt and pepper

Place vegetables in mixing bowl containing cold water. Let stand 15 minutes.

Transfer vegetables to casserole; add 250 mL (1 cup) water and salt.

Sprinkle with lemon juice.

Cover with sheet of plastic wrap; microwave 15 minutes.

Stir vegetables twice during cooking.

When cooked, remove casserole from microwave and let stand 3 minutes.

Drain vegetables; add butter, parsley, and lemon juice. Serve.

Technique

1 Place vegetables in mixing bowl containing cold water; let stand 15 minutes.

2 Transfer vegetables to casserole; add water and salt. Cover with sheet of plastic wrap and microwave 15 minutes.

$\longrightarrow$

Technique : Steamed Vegetables (continued)

3 Drain cooked vegetables; add butter and parsley. Sprinkle with lemon juice.

Ratatouille

(serves 4)

Setting : **HIGH**
Cooking time : **29 minutes**
Utensil : **2 L casserole**

15 mL	*(1 tbs) oil*
1	*onion, peeled and sliced*
1	*eggplant, peeled and sliced*
1	*large zucchini, sliced*
2	*garlic cloves, smashed and chopped*
2 mL	*(½ tsp) oregano*
15 mL	*(1 tbs) chopped parsley*
1	*796 mL (28 oz) can tomatoes, drained and chopped*
15 mL	*(1 tbs) tomato paste*
	pinch thyme
	dash crushed chillies
	salt and pepper

Pour oil into casserole; add onion. Cover with sheet of plastic wrap; microwave 4 minutes.

Add eggplant, zucchini, garlic, and spices; season with salt and pepper. Mix well with wooden spoon.

Cover and microwave 15 minutes.

Mix well, breaking down vegetables slightly.

Add tomatoes and tomato paste; microwave, uncovered, 10 minutes.

Note : Ratatouille serves well with roasts or can be used to stuff crêpes, peppers, and omelets.

Lentils and Vegetables

(serves 4)

Place carrot, celery, red pepper, onion, lentils, garlic, bay leaf, spices, and thyme in casserole.

Add chicken stock and tomato paste. Stir well; microwave, uncovered, 15 minutes.

Stir again; continue to microwave 15 minutes.

Before serving, sprinkle with bacon.

* See page 55.

Technique

Place ingredients in casserole. Add chicken stock and tomato paste; microwave.

Setting:	HIGH
Cooking time:	30 minutes
Utensil:	2 L round casserole

1	*carrot, peeled and diced*
1	*celery stalk, diced*
½	*red pepper, diced*
1	*small onion, peeled and diced*
250 mL	*(1 cup) lentils, soaked 8 hours in water and well drained*
1	*garlic clove, smashed and chopped*
1	*bay leaf*
500 mL	*(2 cups) hot chicken stock **
15 mL	*(1 tbs) tomato paste*
4	*slices cooked bacon, diced*
	pinch crushed chillies
	pinch thyme
	salt and pepper

Stuffed Onions

Stuffed Onions

(serves 4)

Setting: HIGH
Cooking time: 22 minutes
Utensil: Two — 2 L round casseroles

2	*red onions*
2	*white onions*
250 mL	*(1 cup) water*
5 mL	*(1 tsp) oil*
1	*green pepper, finely chopped*
1	*garlic clove, smashed and chopped*
500 mL	*(2 cups) fresh mushrooms, finely chopped*
5 mL	*(1 tsp) chopped parsley*
250 mL	*(1 cup) canned tomatoes, drained and chopped*
250 mL	*(1 cup) lean ground beef*
30 mL	*(2 tbs) chopped walnuts*
15 mL	*(1 tbs) tomato paste*
175 mL	*(¾ cup) grated mozzarella cheese*

pinch crushed chillies
pinch basil
pinch thyme
salt and pepper

Peel onions, cut ends, and hollow.

Place in casserole; add water and salt. Cover and microwave 6 minutes.

Turn casserole a ½ turn. Cover and continue to microwave 4 minutes. Set aside.

In separate casserole, place oil, green pepper, and garlic. Cover and microwave 2 minutes.

Add mushrooms and parsley; cover and microwave 3 minutes.

Add tomatoes, spices, herbs, beef, walnuts, and tomato paste. Season with salt and pepper; mix well.

Add half of grated cheese; mix again. Cover and microwave 4 minutes.

Drain onions and replace in casserole. Stuff with mixture and top with cheese. Microwave, uncovered, 3 minutes. Serve.

Technique

1 Place hollowed onions in casserole.

2 Here are onions after 10 minutes in microwave.

→

Technique : Stuffed Onions (continued)

3 Place oil, green pepper, and garlic in separate casserole.

4 Add mushrooms and parsley.

5 Add tomatoes and seasoning.

6 Add beef and tomato paste.

Peas à la Française

(serves 2)

Setting: HIGH
Cooking time: 15 minutes
Utensil: 2 L casserole

30 mL	*(2 tbs) butter*
1	*small onion, peeled and diced*
1	*small Boston lettuce, washed and shredded*
227 g	*(½ lb) fresh peas*
2 mL	*(½ tsp) sugar*
125 mL	*(½ cup) hot chicken stock* *
15 mL	*(1 tbs) cornstarch*
15 mL	*(1 tbs) cold water*
	salt and pepper

Place 15 mL (1 tbs) butter in casserole; add onion and season with salt and pepper.

Cover with sheet of plastic wrap; microwave 3 minutes.

Add lettuce, peas, sugar, and chicken stock. Cover and microwave 3 minutes.

Mix well and add remaining butter. Microwave, uncovered, 8 minutes.

Mix cornstarch with water; incorporate to mixture.

Microwave, uncovered, 1 minute. Serve.

* See page 55.

Sweet Potatoes with Sour Cream

(serves 4)

Setting: HIGH
Cooking time: 23 minutes
Utensil: None

4	*large sweet potatoes*
60 mL	*(4 tbs) sour cream*
15 mL	*(1 tbs) chopped parsley*
	salt and pepper

Wash potatoes and prick skins to allow steam to escape during cooking.

Place potatoes in microwave and microwave 8 minutes.

Turn potatoes; continue to microwave 15 minutes.

Slit sweet potato skins. Using fingers press skins open and top with sour cream. Sprinkle with chopped parsley. Serve.

Sweet Potatoes

Sweet Potatoes

(serves 2)

Setting: HIGH
Cooking time: 19 minutes
Utensil: 2 L casserole

2	*sweet potatoes*
4	*small carrots, peeled and cubed*
50 mL	*(¼ cup) water*
30 mL	*(2 tbs) yogurt*
	salt and pepper

Prick sweet potato skins and place in microwave. Microwave 5 minutes.

Turn sweet potatoes; continue to microwave 5 minutes. When cooked, remove from microwave.

Using small, sharp knife and spoon hollow skins. Pass potato pulp through food mill and purée.

Place carrots in casserole; add water and salt. Cover and microwave 5 minutes.

Mix well; cover and continue to microwave 3 minutes. Drain carrots well and purée in food mill.

Incorporate purée sweet potato with carrots; season with salt and pepper. Mix in yogurt.

Place mixture into pastry bag fitted with star nozzle. Stuff hollowed skins.

Microwave, uncovered, 1 minute. Serve.

Technique

Hollow sweet potatoes.

Lyonnaises Potatoes

(serves 4)

Setting: HIGH
Cooking time: 18 minutes
Utensil: 2 L round casserole

15 mL	*(1 tbs) bacon fat*
4	*large potatoes, peeled and sliced*
45 mL	*(3 tbs) chopped onion*
5 mL	*(1 tsp) soya sauce*
125 mL	*(½ cup) hot beef stock* *
	chopped parsley
	salt and pepper

Place bacon fat in casserole. Microwave 1 minute.

Arrange layer of potatoes in casserole; season with salt and pepper. Sprinkle with parsley.

Add layer of onion; sprinkle with soya sauce.

Top with layer of potatoes and onion; sprinkle with soya sauce.

Pour in beef stock; cover and microwave 10 minutes.

Turn casserole a ½ turn; continue to microwave 7 minutes. Serve.

* Your recipe or commercial brand.

Mashed Potatoes

(serves 4)

Setting: HIGH
Cooking time: 15 to 16 minutes
Utensil: Paper towel

5	*medium size potatoes, washed* *
30 mL	*(2 tbs) butter*
175 mL	*(¾ cup) hot milk*
	salt and pepper
	nutmeg

Prick potato skins using small knife.

Place sheet of paper towel in microwave. Place potatoes ** on top; microwave 15 to 16 minutes.

Turn potatoes once during cooking.

When cooked, peel and pass through food mill.

Add butter and milk to purée potatoes. Season with salt, pepper, and nutmeg. Incorporate well and serve.

* It is preferable to use new potatoes.
** For variation, add grated parmesan cheese.

Technique : Mashed Potatoes

1 Prick potato skins, using small knife, to allow steam to escape during cooking.

2 Place cooked potatoes in food mill and purée.

3 Add salt, pepper, and nutmeg. Add butter and hot milk.

Stuffed Peppers

(serves 4)

Setting: HIGH
Cooking time: 21 minutes
Utensil: Two — 2 to 3 L round casseroles

2	*green peppers*
50 mL	*(¼ cup) water*
15 mL	*(1 tbs) oil*
5 mL	*(1 tsp) chopped parsley*
1	*small onion, peeled and chopped*
1	*garlic clove, smashed and chopped*
227 g	*(½ lb) ground veal*
375 mL	*(1½ cups) canned tomatoes, drained and chopped*
15 mL	*(1 tbs) tomato paste*
125 mL	*(½ cup) grated mozzarella cheese*
	pinch clove
	pinch celery seed
	pinch crushed chillies
	salt and pepper

Technique

1 Place peppers in casserole; add water.

Cut peppers in two; remove seeds and white membranes. Place peppers in casserole; add water, cover and microwave 4 minutes.

Turn casserole a ½ turn; continue to microwave 3 minutes.

Plonge peppers under cold water. Let cool and drain; set aside.

Pour oil into separate casserole. Add parsley, onion, and garlic. Cover and microwave 3 minutes.

Add veal; season with salt and pepper. Cover and microwave 3 minutes.

Add tomatoes and seasoning; mix well. Add tomato paste; mix again.

Add half of grated cheese; mix and microwave, uncovered, 3 minutes.

Place drained peppers in casserole and stuff with mixture. Top with remaining cheese.

Microwave, uncovered, 5 minutes. Serve.

2 Pour oil into separate casserole. Add parsley, onion, and garlic.

3 Add veal; season with salt and pepper.

4 Add tomatoes, seasoning, and tomato paste.

5 Stuff peppers and sprinkle with grated cheese.

Braised Fennel Root

Braised Fennel Root

(serves 4)

Setting:	HIGH
Cooking time:	21 minutes
Utensil:	30 × 20 × 5 cm (11¾ × 7½ × 1¾ in) casserole

2	*fennel roots, discard stalks, wash bulbs and cut into sections*
15 mL	*(1 tbs) butter, broken into small pieces*
15 mL	*(1 tbs) chopped fresh parsley*
1	*796 mL (28 oz) can tomatoes, drained and coarsely chopped*
1	*garlic clove, smashed and chopped*
2 mL	*(½ tsp) oregano*
15 mL	*(1 tbs) cornstarch*
30 mL	*(2 tbs) cold water*
125 mL	*(½ cup) grated mozzarella cheese*
	lemon juice
	salt and pepper

Place fennel sections in casserole. Dot with butter and sprinkle with parsley. Season with salt and pepper; add several drops lemon juice.

Cover casserole with sheet of plastic wrap and microwave 10 minutes.

In bowl, mix tomatoes, garlic, and oregano. Pour over fennel; season with salt and pepper. Lightly cover and microwave 5 minutes.

Transfer mixture to separate casserole; set aside. Allow cooking liquid to remain in original casserole.

Mix cornstarch with water; incorporate to cooking liquid. Microwave, uncovered, 3 minutes.

Pour sauce over fennel and tomatoes. Sprinkle with cheese; microwave, uncovered, 3 minutes. Serve.

Technique

1 Presentation of fennel roots.

2 Cut fennel bulbs into sections and place in casserole.

Tomatoes Stuffed with Rice

(serves 4)

Trim off tomato tops. Hollow tomatoes by ¾ and set pulp aside.

Trim tomato bottoms so they sit flat; place in casserole. Season with salt and pepper; add several drops oil inside tomatoes.

Cover casserole; microwave 5 minutes.

Heat oil in sauté pan over medium heat on stove top. Add garlic, onion, and tomato pulp.

Setting:	HIGH
Cooking time:	7 minutes in microwave
Utensil:	2 L round casserole

4	*large tomatoes*
15 mL	*(1 tbs) olive oil*
1	*garlic clove, smashed and chopped*
45 mL	*(3 tbs) chopped onion*
5 mL	*(1 tsp) chopped parsley*
250 mL	*(1 cup) cooked rice*
30 mL	*(2 tbs) grated fresh parmesan cheese*
	salt and pepper

Technique

1 Place hollowed tomatoes in casserole. Season with salt and pepper; add several drops oil.

Sprinkle with chopped parsley; season with salt and pepper. Mix well and cook 3 to 4 minutes.

Add rice to sauté pan; season to taste and mix well.

Add cheese; mix again and remove from stove top.

Stuff tomatoes with mixture; sprinkle with a bit of cheese.

Microwave, uncovered, 2 minutes. Serve.

2 Stuff tomatoes and sprinkle with grated parmesan cheese.

Stewed Tomatoes

(serves 4)

Setting:	HIGH
Cooking time:	11 minutes
Utensil:	2 L round casserole

4	*large tomatoes*
5 mL	*(1 tsp) butter*
1	*small onion, peeled and chopped*
1	*celery stalk, chopped*
5 mL	*(1 tsp) chopped parsley*
2	*garlic cloves, smashed and chopped*
	pinch of each: oregano, thyme, basil, sugar
	salt and pepper

Trim off tomato tops. Plonge tomatoes in boiling water to easily remove skin.

Dice tomatoes.

Place butter, onion, celery, and parsley in casserole. Cover and microwave 3 minutes.

Add tomatoes, herbs, and garlic. Season with salt and pepper.

Add sugar; mix well. Cover and microwave 8 minutes. Serve.

Tomatoes Stuffed with Scrambled Eggs

(serves 4)

Setting:	HIGH
Cooking time:	7 minutes
Utensil:	1.5 L pie plate for tomatoes
	1 L round casserole for eggs

2	*large tomatoes*
15 mL	*(1 tbs) butter*
4	*large eggs*
15 mL	*(1 tbs) 35% cream*
	olive oil
	salt and pepper

Horizontally cut tomatoes in two. Scoop out part of pulp.

Set tomatoes in pie plate; season cavities with salt and pepper. Sprinkle with oil. Cover with sheet of plastic wrap; microwave 4 minutes.

Remove and set aside.

Melt butter in casserole.

Using fork, beat eggs in bowl. Season with salt and pepper.

Pour eggs into melted butter, mix, and micro-wave 2 minutes.

Remove from microwave; mix. Continue to microwave 1 minute.

Mix cream into eggs and stuff tomatoes. Serve.

Gruyère Tomato Halves

(serves 4)

Setting:	HIGH
Cooking time:	4 minutes
Utensil:	2 L round casserole

4	*large tomatoes, cut in half*
45 mL	*(3 tbs) crumbled soda crackers*
15 mL	*(1 tbs) chopped parsley*
1	*garlic clove, smashed and chopped*
125 mL	*(½ cup) grated Gruyère cheese*
3	*slices cooked bacon, chopped*
	salt and pepper

Place tomato halves in casserole; season with salt and pepper.

Microwave, uncovered, 2 minutes.

In bowl, mix soda crackers, parsley, and garlic. Sprinkle over tomatoes.

Top with cheese; cover with sheet of plastic wrap and microwave 2 minutes.

Sprinkle with bacon and serve.

Quick Tomato Sauce

(serves 4)

Setting: **HIGH**
Cooking time: **12 minutes**
Utensil: **2 L casserole**

45 mL	*(3 tbs) chopped onion*
5 mL	*(1 tsp) olive oil*
1	*celery stalk, chopped*
1	*garlic clove, smashed and chopped*
1½	*796 mL (28 oz) cans tomatoes, drained*
1 mL	*(¼ tsp) oregano*
	pinch thyme
	pinch sugar

Place onion, oil, celery, and garlic in casserole. Cover with sheet of plastic wrap and microwave 2 minutes.

Add tomatoes and spices; add sugar and correct seasoning.

Microwave, uncovered, 10 minutes.

Serve with white meat.

Bean Salad

(serves 4)

Here is another way to serve Beans à la Bretonne.

15 mL	*(1 tbs) Dijon mustard*
60 mL	*(4 tbs) wine vinegar*
1	*egg yolk*
15 mL	*(1 tbs) chopped parsley*
125 mL	*(½ cup) olive oil*
1	*recipe Beans à la Bretonne* *
	paprika
	several drops lemon juice
	salt and pepper

Place mustard, paprika, salt, and pepper in mixing bowl. Add vinegar; mix with whisk.

Add egg yolk and parsley; mix again.

Add oil, drop by drop, mixing constantly with whisk.

Add several drops lemon juice.

Pour vinaigrette over beans; toss well. Serve.

* See page 303.

Lentil Salad

(serves 4)

Here is another way to serve
Lentils and Vegetables.

15 mL	**(1 tbs) Dijon mustard**
45 mL	**(3 tbs) wine vinegar**
125 mL	**(½ cup) olive oil**
1	**recipe Lentils and Vegetables ** *
45 mL	**(3 tbs) sour cream**
	paprika
	several drops lemon juice
	salt and pepper

Place mustard, salt, pepper, and vinegar in mixing bowl. Stir well with whisk.

Add oil, drop by drop, mixing constantly with whisk. Add several drops lemon juice.

Pour vinaigrette over lentils; toss to incorporate.

Add sour cream and sprinkle with paprika. Serve.

* See page 311.

Tomato Salad

(serves 4)

Setting :	HIGH
Cooking time :	2 to 3 minutes
Utensil :	2 L casserole

4	**large tomatoes**
125 mL	**(½ cup) water**
45 mL	**(3 tbs) wine vinegar**
90 mL	**(6 tbs) olive oil**
2	**shallots, chopped**
15 mL	**(1 tbs) chopped basil**
	salt and pepper

Place tomatoes and water in casserole. Microwave, uncovered, 2 to 3 minutes.

Peel and cut tomatoes in two. Remove seeds and slice tomatoes; place in salad bowl.

Add remaining ingredients; toss well. Season to taste and marinate 30 minutes before serving.

Russian Style Salad

(serves 4)

Setting: HIGH
Cooking time: 5 to 6 minutes
Utensil: 2 L casserole

1	*envelope gelatine*
50 mL	*(¼ cup) cold water*
125 mL	*(½ cup) diced potato*
125 mL	*(½ cup) diced carrot*
125 mL	*(½ cup) frozen peas*
125 mL	*(½ cup) diced turnip*
50 mL	*(¼ cup) hot water*
15 mL	*(1 tbs) chopped fresh parsley*
125 mL	*(½ cup) curry mayonnaise*
	salt and pepper

Mix gelatine with cold water; set aside.

Place vegetables in casserole; season with salt and pepper. Add gelatine and hot water; cover and microwave 5 to 6 minutes.

Remove casserole and transfer mixture into bowl. Set aside to cool.

Add parsley and mayonnaise to cooled mixture. Season well and transfer to rectangular or round mold. Refrigerate 3 hours.

Unmold and garnish with lettuce leaves, tomato quarters, radishes, and stuffed eggs. Serve.

Ham and Vegetable Salad

(serves 4)

Setting: HIGH
Cooking time: 4 minutes
Utensil: 2 L casserole

1	*celery stalk, cut into julienne*
2	*carrots, peeled and cut into julienne*
2	*green peppers, cut into julienne*
50 mL	*(¼ cup) water*
75 mL	*(1/3 cup) mayonnaise*
15 mL	*(1 tbs) Dijon mustard*
2	*slices cooked ham, cut into julienne*
½	*cucumber, peeled, seeded, and sliced*
	chopped fresh tarragon
	lemon juice
	salt and pepper

Place celery, carrots, and peppers in casserole; season with salt. Add water; cover and microwave 4 minutes.

Cool under cold water; drain and transfer to salad bowl.

Mix mayonnaise with mustard; pour over vegetables. Add remaining ingredients and toss well. Correct seasoning.

Add several drops lemon juice. Serve salad on lettuce leaves. Garnish with sliced hard boiled eggs and quartered tomatoes.

Tomato Rice

Tomato Rice

(serves 4)

Setting: HIGH
Cooking time: 24 minutes
Utensil: 2 L round casserole with cover

5 mL	*(1 tsp) oil*
45 mL	*(3 tbs) chopped onion*
1	*garlic clove, smashed and chopped*
½	*796 mL (28 oz) can tomatoes, drained and chopped*
15 mL	*(1 tbs) chopped parsley*
250 mL	*(1 cup) long grain rice, washed and drained*
375 mL	*(1½ cups) hot chicken stock**
	salt and pepper

Place oil, onion, garlic, and tomatoes in casserole.

Add parsley and season to taste. Cover and microwave 4 minutes.

Add rice and chicken stock; mix well with fork and correct seasoning. Cover and microwave 20 minutes.

After 10 minutes in microwave, mix rice well with fork. Cover and continue to microwave.

When cooked, let rice stand in microwave 7 to 8 minutes.

Mix with fork and serve.

* See page 55.

Technique

1 Place oil, onion, garlic, tomatoes, and parsley in casserole.

→

Technique : Tomato Rice (continued)

2 Cover and microwave 4 minutes.

3 Add rice and mix well with fork.

4 Add hot chicken stock.

Rice Salad
with Curry Vinaigrette

(serves 4)

Setting:	HIGH
Cooking time:	18 or 20 minutes
Utensil:	3 L casserole

550 mL	*(2¼ cups) hot water*
375 mL	*(1½ cups) long grain rice, washed and drained*
5 mL	*(1 tsp) salt*
250 mL	*(1 cup) cooked mushrooms*
125 mL	*(½ cup) cooked peas*
1	*celery stalk, chopped*
2	*canned artichoke bottoms, diced*
175 mL	*(¾ cup) curry vinaigrette pepper from mill*

Place water and rice in casserole; add salt. Cover and microwave 8 minutes.

Stir well; cover and continue to microwave 8 minutes. Stir again; cover and continue to microwave 2 to 4 minutes.

When cooked, drain rice and place in salad bowl. Add vegetables and vinaigrette; toss well. Season to taste, cool, and serve.

Preparation of curry vinaigrette

15 mL	*(1 tbs) Dijon mustard*
15 mL	*(1 tbs) curry powder*
45 mL	*(3 tbs) wine vinegar*
175 mL	*(¾ cup) olive oil*
30 mL	*(2 tbs) yogurt*
15 mL	*(1 tbs) chopped tarragon salt and pepper*

Place mustard, curry powder, and vinegar in mixing bowl; combine well.

Add oil, drop by drop, mixing constantly with whisk. Season with salt and pepper.

Stir in yogurt and tarragon; mix well. Serve.

White Rice

(serves 4)

Setting:	HIGH
Cooking time:	18 minutes
Utensil:	2 L round casserole with cover

250 mL	*(1 cup) long grain rice*
500 mL	*(2 cups) cold water*
½	*bay leaf*
22 mL	*(1½ tbs) butter salt and white pepper*

Wash rice and drain well.

Place in casserole; add water, salt, pepper, and ½ bay leaf. Mix with fork. Cover and microwave 18 minutes.

After 10 minutes in microwave, mix rice with fork. Cover and continue to microwave.

When cooked, let rice stand in microwave 7 to 8 minutes. Remove from microwave; add butter and mix with fork. Serve.

Rice with Curry

(serves 4)

Setting: HIGH
Cooking time: 21 minutes
Utensil: 2 L round casserole with cover

30 mL	*(2 tbs) butter*
45 mL	*(3 tbs) chopped onion*
15 mL	*(1 tbs) curry powder (or to taste)*
250 mL	*(1 cup) long grain rice, washed and drained*
500 mL	*(2 cups) cold water*
½	*bay leaf*
	salt and pepper

Place 15 mL (1 tbs) butter in casserole; add onion and curry powder. Cover and microwave 3 minutes.

Add rice and mix well. Add water, bay leaf, and season with salt and pepper. Cover and microwave 18 minutes.

After 10 minutes in microwave, mix with fork. Cover and continue to microwave.

When cooked, let rice stand in microwave 7 to 8 minutes.

Add remaining butter and mix with fork. Serve.

Rice with Parmesan Cheese

(serves 4)

Setting: HIGH
Cooking time: 18 minutes
Utensil: 2 L round casserole with cover

250 mL	*(1 cup) long grain rice*
500 mL	*(2 cups) cold water*
½	*bay leaf*
125 mL	*(½ cup) grated parmesan cheese*
22 mL	*(1½ tbs) butter*
	salt and white pepper

Wash and drain rice.

Place rice in casserole. Add water, salt, pepper, and bay leaf. Mix with fork. Cover and microwave 18 minutes.

After 10 minutes in microwave, stir with fork. Cover and continue to microwave.

When cooked, add cheese and mix with fork. Cover and let stand in microwave 7 to 8 minutes.

Add butter, mix with fork, and serve.

Vegetable Rice

(serves 4)

Setting:	HIGH
Cooking time:	23 minutes
Utensil:	2 L round casserole

15 mL	*(1 tbs) butter*
45 mL	*(3 tbs) chopped celery*
250 mL	*(1 cup) long grain rice, washed and drained*
500 mL	*(2 cups) hot chicken stock**
½	*red pepper, cubed*
1	*head broccoli, separated into flowerets*
8	*fresh mushrooms, diced*
1	*large tomato, cubed*
1	*garlic clove, smashed and chopped*
	pinch paprika
	pinch basil
	pinch oregano
	salt and pepper

Place butter and celery in casserole. Cover and microwave 3 minutes.

Add rice; season with salt, pepper, and paprika. Mix well with fork.

Pour in chicken stock; cover and microwave 10 minutes. Stir well.

Add red pepper and broccoli; season with salt and pepper. Mix well.

Cover and continue to microwave 5 minutes.

Add mushrooms and tomato; mix carefully.

Add garlic and herbs; mix again. Cover and microwave 5 minutes. Serve.

* See page 55.

Rice Pilaf

(serves 4)

Setting: **HIGH**
Cooking time: **21 minutes**
Utensil: **2 L round casserole with cover**

30 mL	*(2 tbs) butter*
45 mL	*(3 tbs) chopped onion*
250 mL	*(1 cup) long grain rice, washed and drained*
½	*bay leaf*
500 mL	*(2 cups) hot chicken stock**
	salt and pepper

Place 15 mL (1 tbs) butter in casserole; add onion, cover and microwave 3 minutes.

Add rice, bay leaf, and chicken stock; season with salt and pepper. Cover and microwave 18 minutes.

After 10 minutes in microwave, mix rice with fork. Cover and continue to microwave.

When cooked, add remaining butter and mix with fork. Cover and let stand in microwave 7 to 8 minutes. Serve.

* See page 55.

Rice Seasoned with Cinnamon

(serves 4)

Setting: **HIGH**
Cooking time: **21 minutes**
Utensil: **2 L round casserole with cover**

30 mL	*(2 tbs) butter*
2	*shallots, chopped*
2	*apples, cored, peeled, and diced*
15 mL	*(1 tbs) cinnamon*
250 mL	*(1 cup) long grain rice, washed and drained*
500 mL	*(2 cups) hot chicken stock**
½	*bay leaf*
	several drops lemon juice
	salt and pepper

Place 15 mL (1 tbs) butter in casserole; add shallots and apples. Sprinkle with lemon juice and cinnamon.

Cover and microwave 3 minutes. Remove casserole and set aside.

Place rice in casserole; add chicken stock and bay leaf. Season with salt and pepper; cover and microwave 18 minutes.

After 10 minutes in microwave, mix rice with fork.

3 minutes before end of cooking, add apples; mix well with fork. Cover and continue to microwave.

When cooked, let rice stand in microwave 7 to 8 minutes.

Add remaining butter and mix with fork. Serve.

* See page 55.

Rice and Mushrooms

(serves 4)

Setting: **HIGH**
Cooking time: **21 minutes**
Utensil: **2 L round casserole with cover**

30 mL	*(2 tbs) butter*
2	*shallots, chopped*
227 g	*(½ lb) mushrooms, diced*
250 mL	*(1 cup) long grain rice, washed and drained*
500 mL	*(2 cups) hot chicken stock* *
½	*bay leaf*
15 mL	*(1 tbs) chopped parsley*
	several drops lemon juice
	salt and pepper

Place 15 mL (1 tbs) butter in casserole; add shallots and mushrooms. Season with salt and pepper; add lemon juice. Cover and microwave 3 minutes.

Remove casserole; set mushrooms aside.

Place rice in casserole; add chicken stock and bay leaf. Season with salt and pepper; cover and microwave 18 minutes.

After 10 minutes in microwave, mix rice with fork.

3 minutes before end of cooking, add mushrooms. Cover and continue to microwave.

When cooked, let rice stand in microwave 7 to 8 minutes.

Add remaining butter and mix with fork. Garnish with parsley and serve.

* See page 55.

Brown Rice with Peppers

(serves 4)

Setting: **HIGH**
Cooking time: **30 minutes**
Utensil: **3 L casserole**

250 mL	*(1 cup) brown rice, washed and drained*
750 mL	*(3 cups) very hot water*
5 mL	*(1 tsp) salt*
1	*green pepper, diced*
½	*red pepper, diced*
15 mL	*(1 tbs) butter*
	pepper from mill

Place rice in casserole; add water and salt. Cover and microwave 10 minutes.

Stir well; cover and continue to microwave 10 minutes. Stir again; cover and continue to microwave 6 minutes.

Add peppers; mix and microwave 4 minutes.

Stir in butter and serve.

Desserts

Trifle

(serves 4 to 6)

Setting: **HIGH**
Cooking time: **2½ minutes in microwave**
Utensil: **2 L casserole**

Preparation of English cream

15 mL	*(1 tbs) cornstarch*
60 mL	*(4 tbs) sugar*
2	*egg yolks*
1	*whole egg*
15 mL	*(1 tbs) vanilla*
500 mL	*(2 cups) hot milk*

Place cornstarch and sugar in casserole; mix well. Add egg yolks and whole egg; mix again.

Add vanilla and milk; mix. Microwave, uncovered, 1½ minutes.

Using whisk, mix cream well. Microwave, uncovered, 1 minute. Mix and set aside.

Preparation of trifle

1	*white cake* *
1	*recipe English cream*
250 mL	*(1 cup) canned sliced peaches*
250 mL	*(1 cup) canned sliced pears*
2	*bananas, sliced*
250 mL	*(1 cup) thawed strawberries, reserve juice*

Slice cake into 2 layers. Place 1 layer in bottom of large glass bowl.

Add layer of English cream and layer of fruits.

Secure remaining cake over fruits.

Cover with remaining fruits and cream. Refrigerate 1 hour. Serve.

* See page 353.

Technique

1 Place 1 layer of cake in bottom of glass bowl. Add layer of English cream and bananas.

3 Add layer of pears and strawberries.

2 Add layer of peaches.

Bananas with Rum

(serves 4)

Setting: **HIGH**
Cooking time: **4 minutes**
Utensil: **2 L casserole**

45 mL	*(3 tbs) butter*
4	*bananas, peeled and cut in two lengthwise*
125 mL	*(½ cup) brown sugar*
45 mL	*(3 tbs) rum*
	juice 1 lemon

Place butter in casserole and microwave 2 minutes to melt.

Add bananas and sprinkle with brown sugar; add rum and lemon juice.

Microwave, uncovered, 2 minutes. Serve.

4 Secure remaining cake over fruits. Cover with remaining fruits and cream.

Caramel Custard

Caramel Custard

(serves 4)

Setting:	**MEDIUM**
Cooking time:	**12 minutes in microwave**
Utensil:	**Individual custard dishes**

125 mL	*(½ cup) sugar*
50 mL	*(¼ cup) water*
125 mL	*(½ cup) sugar*
500 mL	*(2 cups) hot milk*
15 mL	*(1 tsp) vanilla*
3	*whole eggs*
2	*egg yolks*

Place 125 mL (½ cup) sugar and 45 mL (3 tbs) water in small saucepan.

Bring to boil on stove top. When mixture turns gold in colour, remove from heat and place saucepan in bowl containing cold water. This will stop cooking process.

Add remaining water and replace on stove top over medium heat. Cook until caramel melts with water.*

Pour caramel into custard dishes and set aside.

Heat remaining sugar, milk, and vanilla in saucepan on stove top.

Place whole eggs and yolks in mixing bowl; beat with whisk.

Incorporate hot milk mixture to eggs, mixing with whisk.

Pour custard cream into dishes. Microwave, uncovered, 12 minutes.

After 6 minutes in microwave, turn dishes a ½ turn.

Let stand 3 to 4 minutes before serving.

* Should the caramel be poured into dishes after colouration and without water added, the caramel will stick to dishes rather than unmolding with custard.

Technique

1 Place sugar in saucepan.

2 Add cold water.

Technique : Caramel Custard (continued)

3 Caramelize mixture on stove top. Place sauce-pan in cold water to stop cooking process.

4 Once mixture has cooled, add remaining water. Cook 2 to 3 minutes then pour into custard dishes.

6 Add milk and mix with whisk.

7 Pour custard cream into dishes.

5 Place eggs in mixing bowl and beat with whisk.

Pastry Cream

Setting: **MEDIUM**
Cooking time: 8 minutes
Utensil: 2 L casserole

5	*egg yolks*
125 mL	*(½ cup) sugar*
425 mL	*(1¾ cups) hot milk*
15 mL	*(1 tbs) vanilla*
125 mL	*(½ cup) sifted flour*
30 mL	*(2 tbs) Cointreau*
15 mL	*(1 tbs) unsalted butter*

Place egg yolks in casserole; mix with electric beater.

Add sugar and continue beating until mixture thickens.

Add hot milk; incorporate with whisk.

Add vanilla and mix again.

Incorporate flour using spatula.

Microwave, uncovered, 8 minutes. Stir cream every 2 minutes.

Incorporate Cointreau and butter; cover with sheet of plastic wrap and let cool.

Technique

1 Place egg yolks in casserole; mix well.

→

Technique : Pastry Cream (continued)

2 Add sugar ; mix again.

3 Continue beating mixture until it thickens. Use electric beater if available.

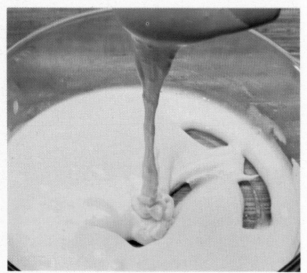

5 The cream should be thick enough to form ribbons when poured.

6 Add vanilla ; mix again.

Banana Crêpes
(serves 4)

Setting: HIGH
Cooking time: 7 minutes in microwave
Utensil: 2 L casserole

Preparation of crêpe batter

250 mL	*(1 cup) flour*
4	*eggs*
300 mL	*(1½ cups) liquid, half water, half milk*
30 mL	*(2 tbs) vegetable oil*
	salt

Sift flour and salt together in bowl. Add eggs and mix with whisk.

Add half of liquid; whisk.

Add remaining liquid and oil; mix and pass through sieve.

If time allows, refrigerate batter 1 hour before preparing crêpes.

To make crêpes: lightly butter crêpe pan and heat on stove top.

Pour a bit of batter in pan and rotate pan so

4 Add hot milk; incorporate with whisk.

7 Incorporate flour using spatula.

batter covers surface. Pour excess batter back into bowl.

Cook crêpes 1 to 2 minutes each side.

See filling and technique following page.

Preparation of banana filling

125 mL	**(½ cup) brown sugar**
30 mL	**(2 tbs) butter**
30 mL	**(2 tbs) Cointreau**
3	**bananas, peeled, and cut in slices of 2.5 cm (1 in) thick**
1	**mango, peeled and sliced**
8	**crêpes**
30 mL	**(2 tbs) icing sugar**
	lemon juice

Place brown sugar, butter, lemon juice, and Cointreau in casserole.

Cover with sheet of plastic wrap; microwave 2 minutes.

Add fruits and mix well.

Cover and microwave 5 minutes. Remove from microwave and let cool.

Drain fruits and stuff crêpes.

Fold crêpes in 4 and arrange on ovenproof service platter.

Technique

1 Place brown sugar, butter, lemon juice, and Cointreau in casserole. Cover with sheet of plastic wrap; microwave 2 minutes.

Sprinkle with icing sugar and cooking juice from fruits.

Grill (broil) 2 minutes in conventional oven.

4 Add mango.

5 Here are the fruits after cooking.

2 Add bananas and mix.

3 Here is a mango cut in two.

6 Drain fruits and stuff crêpes.

7 Sprinkle crêpes with icing sugar and sauce.

Crêpes Stuffed with Apples

(serves 4)

Place apples, cinnamon, and Cointreau in casserole; mix well.

Add brown sugar and lemon juice; mix again.

Cover with sheet of plastic wrap; microwave 10 minutes.

Remove casserole and pour contents into sieve.

Stuff crêpes with apple mixture and fold in 4.

Place crêpes in ovenproof platter.

Pour sauce from apples into small saucepan.

Mix cornstarch with water; incorporate to sauce. Bring to boil on stove top 2 minutes.

Sprinkle crêpes with sugar and grill (broil) in conventional oven 3 minutes.

Serve with sauce.

Setting:	HIGH
Cooking time:	10 minutes in microwave
Utensil:	2 L casserole

4	*apples, cored, peeled, and sliced*
22 mL	*(1½ tbs) cinnamon*
30 mL	*(2 tbs) Cointreau*
125 mL	*(½ cup) brown sugar*
4	*large crêpes or 8 small crêpes*
22 mL	*(1½ tbs) cornstarch*
45 mL	*(3 tbs) cold water*
30 mL	*(2 tbs) sugar*
	lemon juice

3 Sprinkle with lemon juice.

Technique

1 Place apples, cinnamon, and Cointreau in casserole; mix well.

2 Add brown sugar; mix again.

4 Here are the apples after cooking.

5 Stuff crêpes and fold in 4.

Cream of Chestnuts

(serves 4)

Setting: **HIGH**
Cooking time: **3 minutes**
Utensil: **2 L casserole**

4	*egg yolks*
50 mL	*(¼ cup) corn syrup*
50 mL	*(¼ cup) sugar*
250 mL	*(1 cup) purée chestnuts*
500 mL	*(2 cups) 35% cream, whipped*
4	*egg whites, beaten stiff*
50 mL	*(¼ cup) chopped walnuts*

Place egg yolks and corn syrup in casserole; mix well.

Add sugar and mix again; microwave 2 minutes. Stir and continue to microwave 1 minute.

Incorporate chestnut purée and mix with electric beater.

Incorporate whipped cream and egg whites using spatula. Sprinkle with walnuts. Serve.

Technique

1 Place egg yolks and corn syrup in casserole; mix well.

3 Incorporate whipped cream.

White Cake

(serves 4 to 6)

Setting: **HIGH**
Cooking time: **10 minutes in microwave**
Utensil: **2 L mold**

425 mL	*(1¾ cups) all-purpose flour*
45 mL	*(3 tbs) baking powder*
250 mL	*(1 cup) sugar*
175 mL	*(¾ cup) soft butter*
175 mL	*(¾ cup) milk*
15 mL	*(1 tbs) vanilla*
4	*whole eggs*
1	*egg white, beaten*
	pinch salt
	lemon zest

2 Add sugar; microwave. Add chestnut purée; mix with electric beater.

4 Incorporate stiff egg whites. Sprinkle with chopped walnuts.

In mixing bowl, combine flour, baking powder, sugar, and salt. Sift into separate bowl.

Add butter and incorporate with spatula.

Add milk, vanilla, and lemon zest; mix with electric beater at slow speed.

Add whole eggs; mix 2 to 3 minutes with electric beater at medium speed.

Incorporate egg white with spatula.

Pour batter into microwave mold. Microwave, uncovered, 5 minutes.

Turn mold a ¼ turn; continue to microwave 5 minutes.

Let cake stand 12 minutes to finish cooking process. Serve.

Chocolate Cake

Chocolate Cake

(serves 4 to 6)

Setting:	HIGH
Cooking time:	10 minutes in microwave
Utensil:	2 L mold

45 mL	*(3 tbs) baking powder*
375 mL	*(1½ cups) flour*
125 mL	*(½ cup) pure cocoa*
250 mL	*(1 cup) sugar*
250 mL	*(1 cup) soft butter*
250 mL	*(1 cup) milk*
4	*eggs*
	pinch salt

In bowl, combine baker powder, flour, cocoa, sugar, and salt. Sift into separate bowl.

Add butter and incorporate with spatula.

Pour in milk; mix with electric beater at slow speed.

Add eggs; mix with electric beater 2 to 3 minutes at medium speed.

Pour mixture into microwave mold. Microwave, uncovered, 5 minutes.

Turn mold a ¼ turn; continue to microwave 5 minutes.

Let cake stand 12 minutes to finish cooking process.

Before icing cake, slice off fine layer from bottom to even surface.

Icing

120 mL	*(8 tbs) soft butter*
625 mL	*(2½ cups) icing sugar*
10 mL	*(2 tsp) pure cocoa*
10 mL	*(2 tsp) vanilla*

Incorporate butter and sugar together. Mix with spatula 2 minutes.

Add cocoa and vanilla; blend well until creamy.

Technique

Before icing cake, slice off fine layer from bottom to even surface.

All-purpose Cake

(serves 4 to 6)

Setting:	HIGH
Cooking time:	10 minutes in microwave
Utensil:	2 L mold

425 mL	*(1¾ cups) all-purpose flour*
175 mL	*(¾ cup) sugar*
45 mL	*(3 tbs) baking powder*
175 mL	*(¾ cup) soft butter*
175 mL	*(¾ cup) milk*
15 mL	*(1 tbs) vanilla*
4	*eggs*
	pinch salt

In bowl, combine flour, sugar, baking powder, and salt. Sift into separate bowl.

Add butter and incorporate with spatula.

→

All-purpose Cake (continued)

Add milk; mix with electric beater at slow speed.

Add vanilla and eggs; mix with electric beater 2 to 3 minutes at medium speed.

Pour batter into microwave mold. Microwave, uncovered, 5 minutes.

Turn mold a ¼ turn; continue to microwave 5 minutes.

Let cake stand 10 minutes to finish cooking process.

Serve.

Apple Cake

(serves 4 to 6)

Setting:	HIGH
Cooking time:	11 minutes in microwave
Utensil:	2 L mold

375 mL	*(1½ cups) all-purpose flour*
175 mL	*(¾ cup) brown sugar*
45 mL	*(3 tbs) baking powder*
5 mL	*(1 tsp) cinnamon*
175 mL	*(¾ cup) soft butter*
175 mL	*(¾ cup) milk*
3	*eggs*
3	*large apples, peeled, cored, and chopped*
	pinch salt

In bowl, combine flour, brown sugar, baking powder, salt, and cinnamon. Sift into separate bowl.

Technique

1 Place dry ingredients in bowl; sift.

2 Add butter and incorporate with spatula.

Add butter and incorporate with spatula.

Add milk; mix with electric beater at slow speed.

Add eggs; mix with electric beater 2 to 3 minutes at medium speed.

Add apples and incorporate with spatula.

Pour batter into microwave mold. Microwave, uncovered, 6 minutes.

Turn mold a ¼ turn; continue to microwave 5 minutes.

Let cake stand 10 minutes to finish cooking process.

Serve.

3 Add milk and eggs.

Banana Cake

Banana Cake

(serves 6)

Setting:	**MEDIUM**
Cooking time:	**18 minutes in microwave**
Utensil:	**23 × 8 cm (9½ × 3¼ in) bundt pan**

125 mL	*(½ cup) oil*
250 mL	*(1 cup) sugar*
2	*whole eggs*
3	*bananas, purée*
400 mL	*(1⅔ cups) flour*
15 mL	*(1 tbs) baking powder*
30 mL	*(2 tbs) rum*
125 mL	*(½ cup) seedless golden raisins*
2	*egg whites, beaten firm*
	pinch salt

Place oil and sugar in large bowl. Add eggs, one at a time, mixing between additions with electric beater at medium speed.

Incorporate banana purée with spatula.

Sift flour, baking powder, and salt together. Incorporate to banana mixture with spatula; mix several minutes.

Add rum and raisins.

Incorporate egg whites with spatula.

Pour batter into microwave bundt pan. Microwave 18 minutes.

IMPORTANT: Turn mold a ¼ turn from time to time during cooking.

Technique

1 Place oil and sugar in large bowl.

2 Add eggs, one at a time, mixing between additions.

→

Technique : Banana Cake (continued)

3 Incorporate banana purée with spatula.

4 Add sifted flour.

5 Add rum and raisins.

6 Incorporate beaten egg whites. Pour batter into microwave mold.

Coconut Cake

(serves 6)

Setting:	MEDIUM
Cooking time:	18 minutes
Utensil:	2 L casserole

400 mL	(1 ⅔ cups) all-purpose flour
5 mL	(1 tsp) baking soda
250 mL	(1 cup) sugar
2	whole eggs
125 mL	(½ cup) oil
175 mL	(¾ cup) milk
30 mL	(2 tbs) rum
15 mL	(1 tbs) vanilla
250 mL	(1 cup) grated coconut
125 mL	(½ cup) slivered almonds
2	egg whites, beaten
	pinch salt

Sift flour, baking soda, sugar, and salt together in bowl. Mix well with wooden spoon.

Add whole eggs, oil, milk, rum, and vanilla; mix with wooden spoon. Beat with electric beater 2 minutes at high speed.

Add coconut and almonds; mix with spoon.

Incorporate beaten egg whites. Pour batter into casserole and microwave 18 minutes.

IMPORTANT: Turn casserole a ¼ turn every 4 minutes during cooking.

When cooked, let cake stand 3 to 4 minutes. Unmold and cool on wire rack.

Frost with your favourite icing.

Almond Cake

(serves 6)

Setting:	MEDIUM
Cooking time:	18 minutes
Utensil:	2 L casserole

5 mL	(1 tsp) baking soda
400 mL	(1 ⅔ cups) all-purpose flour
250 mL	(1 cup) sugar
50 mL	(¼ cup) powdered almonds
1	whole egg
250 mL	(1 cup) milk
125 mL	(½ cup) vegetable oil
15 mL	(1 tbs) vanilla
50 mL	(¼ cup) slivered almonds
	pinch salt

Sift baking soda, flour, sugar, powdered almonds, and salt together in bowl; mix with wooden spoon.

Add egg, milk, oil, and vanilla; mix again. Beat with electric beater 2 minutes at high speed.

Add slivered almonds and mix with wooden spoon.

Pour batter into casserole and microwave 18 minutes.

IMPORTANT: Turn casserole a ¼ turn every 4 minutes during cooking.

When cooked, let cake stand 3 to 4 minutes. Unmold and let cool on wire rack.

Frost with your favourite icing.

Semi-sweet Chocolate Cake

Semi-sweet Chocolate Cake

(serves 6)

Setting:	HIGH and MEDIUM
Cooking time:	20 minutes
Utensil:	2 L casserole

114 g	*(4 oz) or 4 squares semi-sweet chocolate*
50 mL	*(¼ cup) cold water*
125 mL	*(½ cup) soft butter*
250 mL	*(1 cup) sugar*
3	*eggs*
375 mL	*(1½ cups) flour*
15 mL	*(1 tbs) baking powder*
125 mL	*(½ cup) light cream*
	pinch salt
	whipped cream for topping

Place chocolate and water in casserole; microwave 2 minutes at HIGH. Let mixture cool and mix with spatula to obtain a cream.

Mix butter and sugar together in bowl. Add eggs, one at a time, mixing with electric beater between additions.

Add melted chocolate; incorporate well.

Sift flour, salt, and baking powder together; incorporate to batter.

Add cream; mix well and pour into casserole. Microwave 18 minutes at MEDIUM.

IMPORTANT: Turn casserole a ¼ turn every 5 minutes during cooking.

Let cake cool and top with whipped cream. Serve.

Technique

1 Place chocolate and water in casserole; microwave 2 minutes. Let cool and mix well.

2 Place butter and sugar in bowl; mix well with spatula.

→

Technique : *Semi-sweet Chocolate Cake (continued)*

3 Add eggs, one at a time, mixing between additions.

4 Add melted chocolate ; incorporate well.

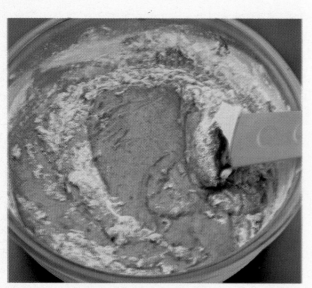

5 Sift flour, salt, and baking powder together ; incorporate to batter.

6 Pour batter into casserole.

Devil Cake

(serves 6)

Setting: **MEDIUM**
Cooking time: **18 minutes**
Utensil: **2 L casserole**

400 mL	*(1⅔ cups) all-purpose flour*
5 mL	*(1 tsp) baking soda*
250 mL	*(1 cup) sugar*
125 mL	*(½ cup) pure cocoa*
2	*whole eggs*
125 mL	*(½ cup) vegetable oil*
175 mL	*(¾ cup) milk*
15 mL	*(1 tbs) vanilla*
125 mL	*(½ cup) chocolate chips*
2	*egg whites, beaten*
	pinch salt

Sift flour, baking soda, sugar, cocoa, and salt together in bowl. Mix with wooden spoon.

Add whole eggs, oil, milk, and vanilla; mix well with wooden spoon. Beat with electric beater 2 minutes at high speed.

Add chocolate chips; mix with spoon.

Incorporate egg whites with whisk.

Pour batter into casserole and microwave 18 minutes.

IMPORTANT: Turn casserole a ¼ turn every 4 minutes during cooking.

When cooked, let cake stand 3 to 4 minutes. Unmold and cool on wire rack.

Serve.

Carrot Cake

(serves 6)

Setting: **MEDIUM**
Cooking time: **18 minutes**
Utensil: **2 L casserole**

400 mL	*(1⅔ cups) all-purpose flour*
5 mL	*(1 tsp) baking soda*
250 mL	*(1 cup) sugar*
5 mL	*(1 tsp) cinnamon*
2	*whole eggs*
125 mL	*(½ cup) oil*
175 mL	*(¾ cup) milk*
15 mL	*(1 tbs) vanilla*
300 mL	*(1¼ cups) grated carrots*
125 mL	*(½ cup) seedless golden raisins*
2	*egg whites, beaten*
	pinch salt

Sift flour, baking soda, sugar, cinnamon, and salt together in bowl. Mix with wooden spoon.

Add whole eggs, oil, milk, and vanilla; mix with wooden spoon. Beat with electric beater 2 minutes at high speed.

Add carrots and raisins; mix with spoon.

Incorporate egg whites with whisk.

Pour batter into casserole and microwave 18 minutes.

IMPORTANT: Turn casserole a ¼ turn every 4 minutes during cooking.

When cooked, let cake stand 3 to 4 minutes. Unmold and cool on wire rack.

Frost with your favourite icing.

Walnut Cake

Walnut Cake

(serves 6)

Setting:	MEDIUM
Cooking time:	18 minutes
Utensil:	2 L casserole

400 mL	*(1 ⅔ cups) all-purpose flour*
5 mL	*(1 tsp) baking soda*
125 mL	*(½ cup) sugar*
125 mL	*(½ cup) brown sugar*
15 mL	*(1 tbs) cinnamon*
2	*whole eggs*
125 mL	*(½ cup) vegetable oil*
175 mL	*(¾ cup) milk*
15 mL	*(1 tbs) vanilla*
125 mL	*(½ cup) maraschino cherries, chopped*
175 mL	*(¾ cup) chopped walnuts*
	pinch salt

Sift flour, baking soda, sugar, brown sugar, cinnamon, and salt together in bowl; mix with wooden spoon.

Add eggs, oil, milk, and vanilla; mix well with wooden spoon. Beat with electric beater 2 minutes at high speed.

Add cherries and walnuts; incorporate with spoon. Pour batter into casserole and microwave 18 minutes.

IMPORTANT: Turn casserole a ¼ turn every 4 minutes during cooking.

When cooked, let cake stand 3 to 4 minutes. Unmold and cool on wire rack. Serve.

Technique

1 Sift flour, baking soda, sugar, brown sugar, cinnamon, and salt together in bowl; mix well.

→

Technique : Walnut Cake (continued)

2 Add eggs.

3 Add oil.

4 Add milk and vanilla; mix well. Add cherries and walnuts.

Chocolate Icing

Setting: **HIGH**
Cooking time: **2 minutes**
Utensil: **2 L casserole**

250 mL   *(1 cup) sugar*
90 g   *(3 oz) cream cheese*
30 mL   *(2 tbs) pure cocoa*
45 mL   *(3 tbs) butter*
5 mL   *(1 tsp) vanilla*
       pinch cinnamon

Place sugar, cinnamon, and cheese in casserole. Add cocoa and butter; cover and microwave 2 minutes.
Add vanilla; mix 1 minute with electric beater.

Technique

1   Place sugar, cinnamon, and cheese in casserole.

2   Add cocoa and butter; cover and microwave. Add vanilla; mix with electric beater.

3   Here is the finished product.

Cheese Icing

Setting: HIGH
Cooking time: 2 minutes
Utensil: 2 L casserole

250 mL   (1 cup) sugar
45 mL   (3 tbs) butter
114 g   (4 oz) cream cheese
5 mL   (1 tsp) vanilla

Place sugar, butter, and cheese in casserole; cover and microwave 2 minutes.

Mix well and add vanilla. Mix 1 minute with electric beater.

Cool.

Technique

1 Place sugar, butter, and cheese in casserole; cover and microwave 2 minutes. Add vanilla; mix with electric beater.

2 Here is the finished product.

Strawberries and Yogurt

(serves 4)

Setting:	HIGH
Cooking time:	5 minutes
Utensil:	2 L casserole

2	*pint boxes strawberries, washed and hulled*
175 mL	*(¾ cup) sugar*
15 mL	*(1 tbs) chopped lemon zest*
30 mL	*(2 tbs) Cointreau*
500 mL	*(2 cups) plain yogurt*
	several drops lemon juice
	lady fingers

Place strawberries in casserole; add sugar, lemon zest, lemon juice, and Cointreau.

Cover with sheet of plastic wrap; microwave 5 minutes. Let strawberries cool in cooking juice.

Place 45 mL (3 tbs) strawberries in bottom of dessert glass. Sprinkle with cooking juice.

Add yogurt but do not mix.

Repeat procedure for remaining glasses.

Decorate with strawberries and serve with lady fingers.

Technique

1 Place strawberries, sugar, lemon zest, and juice in casserole. Add Cointreau ; cover and microwave 5 minutes.

2 Let strawberries cool in cooking juice.

Apple Mousse

Apple Mousse

(serves 4)

Setting: **HIGH**
Cooking time: **8 minutes**
Utensil: **2 L casserole**

4 to 5	*cooking apples, peeled, cored, and sliced*
60 mL	*(4 tbs) water*
15 mL	*(1 tbs) cinnamon*
125 mL	*(½ cup) brown sugar*
30 mL	*(2 tbs) Cointreau*
3	*egg whites, beaten*
30 mL	*(2 tbs) chopped walnuts*
	several drops lemon juice

Place apples, water, lemon juice, cinnamon, brown sugar, and Cointreau in casserole. Cover and microwave 8 minutes.

Remove casserole and cool.

Incorporate egg whites. Pour mousse into dessert dishes and refrigerate. Before serving, sprinkle with walnuts.

Place apples, water, lemon juice, cinnamon, brown sugar, and Cointreau in casserole.

Strawberry Parfait

(serves 4)

Setting: **HIGH**
Cooking time: **9 minutes**
Utensil: **2 L casserole**

2	*pint boxes strawberries, washed and hulled*
30 mL	*(2 tbs) Cointreau*
75 mL	*(5 tbs) sugar*
30 mL	*(2 tbs) cornstarch*
60 mL	*(4 tbs) water*
4	*large scoops ice cream*
4	*whole strawberries for garnish*
	several drops lemon juice

Place pints of strawberries in casserole. Sprinkle with Cointreau and sugar.

Add lemon juice.

Cover with sheet of plastic wrap; microwave 4½ minutes.

Purée strawberries in food processor or blender.

Replace puréed strawberries in casserole.

Mix cornstarch with water; incorporate to strawberries.

Microwave, uncovered, 4 minutes. Stir each minute.

Cool mixture in refrigerator.

Spoon 45 mL (3 tbs) strawberry mixture in each dessert dish.

Add ice cream scoop.

Top with strawberry mixture.

Garnish with whole strawberry. Serve.

Raspberry and Strawberry Parfait

Raspberry and Strawberry Parfait

(serves 4)

Technique

Setting:	HIGH and LOW
Cooking time:	6 minutes
Utensil:	2 L casserole

1	*envelope gelatine*
50 mL	*(¼ cup) cold water*
750 mL	*(3 cups) mixed raspberries and strawberries, washed*
125 mL	*(½ cup) sugar*
175 mL	*(¾ cup) whipped cream*
3	*egg whites, beaten firm*

Sprinkle gelatine over cold water; set aside.

Place fruits in casserole. Add gelatine and sugar; cover and microwave 3 minutes at HIGH.

Mix and continue to microwave 3 minutes at LOW. Let cool.

Incorporate whipped cream and beaten egg whites using spatula. Arrange in dessert dishes. Refrigerate 3 hours.

Garnish with whipped cream. Serve.

1 Place raspberries and strawberries in casserole.

2 Add gelatine and sugar; microwave.

3 Add whipped cream and beaten egg whites. Arrange in dessert dishes. Refrigerate.

Peaches with Brown Sugar

(serves 4)

Technique

Setting: **HIGH**
Cooking time: **6 minutes**
Utensil: **30 × 20 × 5 cm (11¾ × 7½ × 1¾ in) casserole**

6	*fresh peaches, peeled and halved*
125 mL	*(½ cup) brown sugar*
15 mL	*(1 tbs) grated lemon zest*
250 mL	*(1 cup) sour cream*

Place peaches in casserole; cover and microwave 3 minutes.

Turn casserole and continue to microwave 3 minutes.

Mix remaining ingredients together; pour over peaches. Serve.

1 Plunge peaches in boiling water for 30 seconds and then peel.

3 Here are the peaches just removed from microwave.

4 Mix brown sugar, lemon zest, and sour cream together.

Syrupy Pears

(serves 4)

2 Halve peaches and remove pit. Place peaches in casserole, cover, and microwave.

5 Pour mixture over peaches.

Setting:	HIGH
Cooking time:	8 minutes
Utensil:	2 L casserole

6	*pears, peeled, hollowed, and halved*
125 mL	*(½ cup) sugar*
45 mL	*(3 tbs) maple syrup*
125 mL	*(½ cup) cold water*
30 mL	*(2 tbs) slivered orange zest*
50 mL	*(¼ cup) chopped walnuts*

Place pears, sugar, maple syrup, and water in casserole. Cover and microwave 4 minutes.

Add orange zest; cover and continue to microwave 4 minutes.

Let cool.

Serve pears in dessert dishes and top with chopped walnuts.

Baked Apples

Baked Apples

(serves 4)

Setting: HIGH
Cooking time: 10 minutes
Utensil: 2 L casserole

4	*apples, cored*
30 mL	*(2 tbs) butter*
125 mL	*(½ cup) raisins*
60 mL	*(4 tbs) brown sugar*
15 mL	*(1 tbs) maple syrup*
15 mL	*(1 tbs) cinnamon*
	zest 1 lemon, chopped
	juice 1 lemon

Using small knife, score middle of apple skin in circle.

Combine butter and raisins together using spatula. Fill apple cavities.

Place remaining ingredients over apples in casserole. Cover with sheet of plastic wrap and microwave 5 minutes.

Turn casserole a ¼ turn; cover and continue to microwave 5 minutes.

Remove from microwave and let stand 5 to 6 minutes.

Serve with heavy cream.

Grandmother's Favourite Apples

Setting: HIGH
Cooking time: 11 minutes
Utensil: 2 L casserole
4 individual microwave dishes

125 mL	*(½ cup) raisins*
125 mL	*(½ cup) chopped dried apricots*
50 mL	*(¼ cup) rum*
5	*apples, peeled, cored, and sliced*
125 mL	*(½ cup) brown sugar*
45 mL	*(3 tbs) butter*
30 mL	*(2 tbs) cinnamon*
	zest 1 lemon, chopped
	juice 1 lemon
	raisin or date cereal

Place raisins and apricots in bowl. Pour in rum and marinate 2 hours.

Place apples, brown sugar, butter, cinnamon, lemon zest and juice in casserole. Add raisins, apricots, and marinade. Cover and microwave 4 minutes.

→

Grandmother's Favourite Apples (continued)

Stir; well cover and continue to microwave 4 minutes.

Remove casserole from microwave and mix well.

Pour mixture into individual microwave dishes. Sprinkle with choice of cereal and dot with butter.

Microwave, uncovered, 3 minutes.

Peach and Nectarine Mix

(serves 4)

Setting:	MEDIUM
Cooking time:	16 minutes
Utensil:	2 L casserole

4	*peaches, peeled and sliced*
4	*nectarines, peeled and sliced*
30 mL	*(2 tbs) slivered almonds*
125 mL	*(½ cup) brown sugar*
	juice 1½ oranges
	juice 1 lemon
	zest 1 lemon, slivered

Place all ingredients in casserole. Cover and microwave 8 minutes.

Mix; cover and continue to microwave 8 minutes.

Serve in dessert dishes.

Technique

Place all ingredients in casserole.

Creamy Vanilla Pears

(serves 4)

Setting: HIGH
Cooking time: 10 minutes 30 seconds
Utensil: 2 — 2 L casseroles

Preparation of sauce

15 mL	*(1 tbs) cornstarch*
60 mL	*(4 tbs) sugar*
2	*egg yolks*
1	*whole egg*
15 mL	*(1 tbs) vanilla*
500 mL	*(2 cups) hot milk*
125 mL	*(½ cup) 35% cream, whipped*

Place cornstarch and sugar in casserole; mix well.

Add egg yolks and whole egg; incorporate well.

Add vanilla and hot milk; mix well. Microwave, uncovered, 1½ minutes.

Mix sauce well using whisk. Continue to microwave 1 minute.

Mix well again; let stand several minutes. When sauce is cool, incorporate whipped cream. Set aside.

Preparation of pears

4	*pears, cored and peeled*
125 mL	*(½ cup) sugar*
250 mL	*(1 cup) water*
1	*recipe sauce*
30 mL	*(2 tbs) candied apricots*
	zest 1 lemon

Place pears, sugar, and water in casserole. Cover and microwave 8 minutes. Let cool.

Drain pears and transfer to deep service platter. Pour sauce over pears and garnish with apricots and lemon zest. Serve.

Peach Pudding

Peach Pudding

(serves 4)

Setting:	HIGH
Cooking time:	5 minutes 30 seconds
Utensil:	2 — 2 L casserole

125 mL	*(½ cup) sugar*
30 mL	*(2 tbs) cornstarch*
3	*egg yolks*
500 mL	*(2 cups) hot milk*
5 mL	*(1 tsp) vanilla*
1	*796 mL (28 oz) can sliced peaches, well drained*
30 mL	*(2 tbs) brown sugar*

Place sugar, cornstarch, and egg yolks in casserole; mix together with spatula. Microwave, uncovered, 30 seconds.

Add hot milk and vanilla; mix well and microwave, uncovered, 2 minutes.

Mix again and let stand 5 to 6 minutes.

Place peaches in separate casserole and sprinkle with brown sugar. Microwave, uncovered, 1 minute.

Pour pudding over peaches. Microwave, uncovered, 2 minutes. Serve.

Technique

1 Place peaches in casserole and sprinkle with brown sugar. Microwave 1 minute.

2 Pour pudding over peaches; microwave 2 minutes.

Vanilla Pudding

(serves 4)

Remove casserole from microwave and let stand 5 to 6 minutes.

Beat egg whites with electric beater until they peak.

Incorporate egg whites to pudding.

* Cook lemon zest 2 minutes in boiling water.

Decorate pudding with lemon zest. Serve.

Setting:	HIGH
Cooking time:	4 minutes
Utensil:	2 L casserole

125 mL	*(½ cup) sugar*
30 mL	*(2 tbs) cornstarch*
3	*egg yolks*
500 mL	*(2 cups) hot milk*
15 mL	*(1 tbs) vanilla*
3	*egg whites*
	zest 1 lemon, cooked *

Place sugar, cornstarch, and egg yolks in casserole. Microwave, uncovered, 30 seconds.

Add hot milk and vanilla; mix well. Microwave, uncovered, 2 minutes.

Mix with whisk. Microwave, uncovered, 1 minute 30 seconds.

Apple Pudding

(serves 4)

Setting:	HIGH
Cooking time:	10 minutes in microwave
Utensil:	2 L casserole

5	*cooking apples, cored, peeled, and sliced*
125 mL	*(½ cup) brown sugar*
125 mL	*(½ cup) golden raisins*
15 mL	*(1 tbs) cinnamon*
3	*egg yolks*
125 mL	*(½ cup) 35% cream*
	zest 1 lemon
	juice 1 lemon

Place apples, brown sugar, raisins, cinnamon, lemon zest and juice in casserole. Cover and microwave 5 minutes.

Mix together well. Cover and continue to microwave 5 minutes.

Mix egg yolks with cream. Pour over hot apples; incorporate.

Let pudding stand 5 minutes before serving.

Fluffy Chocolate Pudding

(serves 4)

Place chocolate, butter, and 75 mL (5 tbs) sugar in casserole. Microwave, uncovered, 2 minutes.

Mix in egg yolks; microwave, uncovered, 30 seconds.

Beat egg whites with electric beater until they peak. Add remaining sugar; continue to beat 1 minute.

Using spatula, fold egg whites into chocolate to obtain a marbled mixture.

Spoon pudding into dessert dishes and serve.

Setting: **HIGH**
Cooking time: **2 minutes 30 seconds**
Utensil: **2 L casserole**

114 g	*(4 oz) semi-sweet chocolate*
60 mL	*(4 tbs) soft butter*
135 mL	*(9 tbs) sugar*
5	*egg yolks*
5	*egg whites*

Technique

1 Here is chocolate mixture after 2 minutes in microwave.

→

Technique : Fluffy Chocolate Pudding (continued)

2 Add egg yolks.

3 Fold egg whites into chocolate mixture.

Pineapple Pudding

(serves 4)

Setting: HIGH
Cooking time: 8 to 9 minutes
Utensil: 2 L casserole

6	pineapple rings, chopped
300 mL	(1¼ cups) all-purpose flour
175 mL	(¾ cup) sugar
50 mL	(¼ cup) brown sugar
2 mL	(½ tsp) baking soda
125 mL	(½ cup) soft butter
50 mL	(¼ cup) light cream
2	eggs
50 mL	(¼ cup) slivered almonds
	pinch salt

Place pineapples in casserole.

In bowl, sift together flour, sugar, brown sugar, baking soda, and salt.

Add butter to bowl and mix well. Add cream and incorporate with electric beater.

Add eggs, one at a time, mixing between additions.

Mix in almonds and pour pudding over pineapples. Microwave 8 to 9 minutes. Turn casserole a ¼ turn every 3 minutes.

Let cool. Serve with fruit sauce.

Chocolate Cherry Pudding

(serves 4)

Setting: HIGH
Cooking time: 9 minutes
Utensil: 2 L casserole

1	398 mL (14 oz) can cherries, drained
250 mL	(1 cup) all-purpose flour
250 mL	(1 cup) sugar
75 mL	(1/3 cup) pure cocoa
2 mL	(½ tsp) baking soda
125 mL	(½ cup) margarine
50 mL	(¼ cup) milk
2	eggs
175 mL	(¾ cup) mixed nuts, chopped
	pinch salt

Place cherries in casserole.

In bowl, sift together flour, sugar, cocoa, baking soda, and salt. Add margarine and blend.

Using electric beater mix in milk.

Add eggs, one at a time, mixing between additions.

Add nuts and incorporate.

Pour mixture over cherries. Microwave 9 minutes. Turn casserole a ¼ turn every 3 minutes.

Let cool. Serve with ice cream.

Cold Sabayon with Cocoa

Cold Sabayon with Cocoa

(serves 4)

Setting:	**MEDIUM**
Cooking time:	**5 minutes**
Utensil:	**2 L casserole**

5	*egg yolks*
125 mL	*(½ cup) sugar*
150 mL	*(2/3 cup) dry white wine*
150 mL	*(2/3 cup) pure cocoa*
500 mL	*(2 cups) 35% cream, whipped*
2	*egg whites, beaten stiff*

Place egg yolks and sugar in casserole. Add wine and mix well. Microwave 3 minutes; mix twice during cooking.

Stir and continue to microwave 1 minute.

Stir again; continue to microwave 1 minute.

Add cocoa; mix well.

Incorporate whipped cream and beaten egg whites. Serve in dessert dishes.

Technique

1 Place egg yolks and sugar in casserole.

2 Add white wine.

→

Technique : Cold Sabayon with Cocoa (continued)

3 Here is mixture after 3 minutes in microwave.

4 Add cocoa.

5 Incorporate whipped cream and beaten egg whites.

Blueberry Sauce

Setting: HIGH
Cooking time: 7 minutes
Utensil: 2 L casserole

30 mL   *(2 tbs) cornstarch*
125 mL   *(½ cup) orange juice*
500 mL   *(2 cups) blueberries, washed*
250 mL   *(1 cup) apple jelly*

Mix cornstarch with orange juice; pour into casserole.

Add remaining ingredients and mix. Cover and microwave 3 minutes.

Stir well. Continue to microwave, uncovered, 4 minutes.

Technique

1   Pour cornstarch mixture into casserole. Add blueberries.

2   Add apple jelly and mix. Cover and microwave 3 minutes.

3   Stir well. Continue to microwave, uncovered, 4 minutes.

Strawberry Sauce

Ideal for cheesecakes.

Setting: HIGH
Cooking time: 9 minutes
Utensil: 2 L casserole

30 mL	*(2 tbs) cornstarch*
50 mL	*(¼ cup) water*
454 g	*(1 lb) strawberries, washed and hulled*
250 mL	*(1 cup) sugar*
	pinch nutmeg
	zest 1 lemon

Mix cornstarch with water; pour into casserole.

Add strawberries, sugar, nutmeg, and lemon zest. Microwave 5 minutes.

Mix and continue to microwave 4 minutes.

Technique

1 Pour cornstarch mixture into casserole. Add strawberries.

2 Add sugar, nutmeg, and lemon zest.

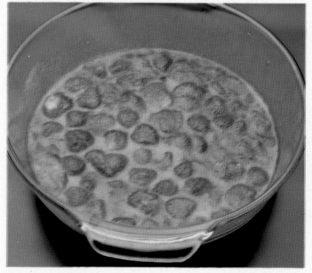

3 Here is the finished sauce.

Applesauce

Setting: HIGH
Cooking time: 11 to 12 minutes
Utensil: 2 L casserole

5	large apples, cored, peeled, and sliced
15 mL	(1 tbs) butter
50 mL	(¼ cup) brown sugar
15 mL	(1 tbs) cinnamon
15 mL	(1 tbs) rum (optional)
	pinch nutmeg

Place apples in casserole. Add butter; cover and microwave 8 to 9 minutes. Stir 2 to 3 times during cooking.

Add remaining ingredients to casserole. Mix and cover; microwave 3 minutes.

Cool and serve.

Cherry Sauce

(serves 4)

Setting: HIGH
Cooking time: 6 to 8 minutes
Utensil: 2 L casserole

1	398 mL (14 oz) can pitted cherries
30 mL	(2 tbs) cornstarch
15 mL	(1 tbs) chopped lemon zest
50 mL	(¼ cup) sugar
	juice 1 lemon

Place all ingredients, including cherry juice, in casserole. Microwave 6 to 8 minutes. Mix twice during cooking.

Let cool and serve over ice cream.

Chocolatey Sauce

Setting: HIGH
Cooking time: 2 minutes
Utensil: 2 L casserole

50 mL	(¼ cup) pure cocoa
175 mL	(¾ cup) sugar
15 mL	(1 tbs) cornstarch
250 mL	(1 cup) very hot water
30 mL	(2 tbs) butter
50 mL	(¼ cup) 35% cream
5 mL	(1 tsp) vanilla

Sift cocoa, sugar, and cornstarch into casserole. Add hot water; mix and microwave 2 minutes. Mix again; add butter, cream, and vanilla. Incorporate well. Serve over ice cream.

Melba Sauce

Setting: HIGH
Cooking time: 4 minutes
Utensil: 2 L casserole

30 mL	(2 tbs) cornstarch
30 mL	(2 tbs) Cointreau or orange liqueur
680 g	(1½ lb) strawberries, washed and hulled
250 mL	(1 cup) apple jelly

Mix cornstarch with Cointreau; set aside.

Place whole strawberries in casserole; pour in cornstarch mixture. Toss until evenly coated.

Add apple jelly and mix. Cover and microwave 4 minutes.

Let sauce cool. Serve with fruits and ice cream.

Quick Chocolate Sauce

Setting: HIGH
Cooking time: 3 minutes
Utensil: 2 L casserole

4	*squares semi-sweet chocolate*
114 g	*(4 oz) caramel chips*
125 mL	*(½ cup) 35% cream*

Place chocolate, caramel chips, and cream in casserole. Microwave 3 minutes.

Serve with cream puffs.

Technique

1 Place chocolate, caramel chips, and cream in casserole; microwave.

2 Here is the finished sauce.

Strawberry Pie

(serves 6)

Setting: HIGH and LOW
Cooking time: 6 minutes
Utensil: 2 L casserole

1	envelope gelatine
125 mL	(½ cup) orange juice
680 g	(1½ lb) strawberries, washed and hulled
175 mL	(¾ cup) sugar
2	egg whites
1	graham-cracker bottom crust, cooked in 22 cm (9 in) pie plate

Place gelatine and orange juice in small bowl; mix and set aside.

Place strawberries and 125 mL (½ cup) sugar in casserole. Add gelatine and mix. Cover and microwave 3 minutes at HIGH.

Mix well; cover and continue to microwave 3 minutes at LOW. Let cool.

Place egg white in stainless steel bowl. Using electric beater, beat until they peak. Add remaining sugar and incorporate strawberries. Pour into cooked pie crust. Refrigerate 6 hours before serving.

Cheesecake

(serves 4 to 6)

Setting: HIGH
Cooking time: 9 minutes in microwave
Utensil: 1.5 L microwave pie plate

Preparation of cake

375 mL	(1½ cups) graham-cracker crumbs
125 mL	(½ cup) sugar
75 mL	(1/3 cup) butter
2	220 g (8 oz) packages cream cheese
125 mL	(½ cup) sugar
125 mL	(½ cup) 35% cream
30 mL	(2 tbs) Tia Maria
15 mL	(1 tbs) chopped lemon zest
15 mL	(1 tbs) chopped orange zest
15 mL	(1 tbs) cornstarch
3	eggs

Place graham-cracker crumbs and 125 mL (½ cup) sugar in mixing bowl. Combine.

→

Cheesecake (continued)

Add butter to bowl and incorporate using pastry cutter.

Place in pie plate and press evenly on bottom only.

Microwave, uncovered, 1¾ minutes. Let cool and set aside.

Place cheese and 125 mL (½ cup) sugar in electric mixer; mix until blended.

Add cream, Tia Maria, lemon and orange zest. Add cornstarch and mix well.

Add eggs, one at a time, mixing between additions.

Pour filling into cooked pie crust. Microwave, uncovered, 7 minutes.

Turn pie plate 1 to 2 times during cooking.

Remove from microwave and set aside.

Preparation of topping

30 mL	*(2 tbs) butter*
30 mL	*(2 tbs) sugar*
125 mL	*(½ cup) pineapple juice*
30 mL	*(2 tbs) Cointreau*
250 mL	*(1 cup) diced pineapples*
1	*pint box strawberries, washed and hulled*
15 mL	*(1 tbs) cornstarch*
30 mL	*(2 tbs) cold water*

Place butter in frying pan. Add sugar and cook several minutes on stove top to brown.

Add pineapple juice and Cointreau; mix well.

Add fruits; mix and cook 2 minutes.

Mix cornstarch with water; incorporate to mixture. Remove frying pan from stove top and let cool.

Pour topping over cheesecake. Refrigerate 2 hours. Serve.

Technique

1 Place graham-cracker crumbs and sugar in stainless steel bowl; combine.

4 Place in pie plate and press evenly. Microwave, uncovered, 1¾ minutes.

2 Add butter.

3 Incorporate using pastry cutter.

5 Pour topping over cooked cheesecake. Refrigerate 2 hours before serving.

Kiwi Pie

Kiwi Pie

(serves 4 to 6)

Setting: HIGH
Cooking time: 1½ minutes in microwave
Utensil: 1.5 L microwave pie plate

375 mL	*(1½ cups) graham-cracker crumbs*
125 mL	*(½ cup) sugar*
75 mL	*(1/3 cup) butter*
3	*kiwis, peeled and sliced in rings*
45 mL	*(3 tbs) sugar*
30 mL	*(2 tbs) Cointreau*
18 to 24	*strawberries, washed and hulled*
250 mL	*(1 cup) pastry cream**

Combine graham-cracker crumbs and 125 mL (½ cup) sugar in mixing bowl.

Add butter to bowl and incorporate using pastry cutter.

Place in pie plate and press evenly on bottom only.

Microwave, uncovered, 1½ minutes. Let cool and set aside.

Place kiwi slices in bowl. Add 30 mL (2 tbs) sugar and 15 mL (1 tbs) Cointreau; marinate 15 minutes.

Place strawberries in separate bowl; add remaining sugar and Cointreau. Marinate 15 minutes.

Spread pastry cream over pie crust. Garnish with marinated kiwis and strawberries.

Refrigerate 30 minutes. Serve.

* See page 345.

Kiwi Pudding

(serves 6)

Setting: HIGH and MEDIUM
Cooking time: 13 minutes
Utensil: 30 × 20 × 5 cm (11¾ × 7½ × 1¾ in) casserole

500 mL	*(2 cups) milk*
5 mL	*(1 tsp) vanilla*
30 mL	*(2 tbs) sweet butter*
3	*eggs*
175 mL	*(¾ cup) sugar*
825 mL	*(3½ cups) cubed egg bread*
125 mL	*(½ cup) raisins*
3	*kiwis, peeled and sliced in rings*
30 mL	*(2 tbs) brown sugar*

Place milk, vanilla, and butter in glass bowl. Microwave, uncovered, 5 minutes at HIGH.

Place eggs and sugar in electric mixer; beat 2 minutes.

Incorporate hot milk mixture; mix until blended.

Spread bread cubes in buttered casserole. Cover with milk mixture. Sprinkle with raisins; microwave, uncovered, 3 minutes at MEDIUM.

Turn casserole; continue to microwave 4 minutes. Let stand 5 minutes.

Place kiwi slices on pudding and sprinkle with brown sugar. Microwave 1 minute at MEDIUM.

Carrot and Kiwi Cake

Carrot and Kiwi Cake

(serves 6)

Setting: HIGH
Cooking time: 15 minutes
Utensil: 23 cm (9 in) bundt pan

125 mL	*(½ cup) brown sugar*
175 mL	*(¾ cup) sugar*
250 mL	*(1 cup) vegetable oil*
5 mL	*(1 tsp) vanilla*
3	*eggs*
375 mL	*(1½ cups) all-purpose flour*
500 mL	*(2 cups) grated carrots*
2	*kiwis, peeled and diced*
125 mL	*(½ cup) chopped walnuts*
	pinch salt

Place brown sugar, sugar, oil, and vanilla in bowl. Mix 1 minute with electric beater.

Add eggs, one at a time, mixing between additions.

Sift flour and salt into separate bowl; incorporate to egg mixture.

Add carrots, kiwis, and walnuts; incorporate using spatula.

Pour batter into buttered mold. Microwave 15 minutes; turn mold 3 times during cooking.

Ideal with or without icing.

Kiwi Applesauce

(serves 4)

Setting: HIGH
Cooking time: 10 to 11 minutes
Utensil: 3 L casserole

5	*cooking apples*
3	*kiwis*
125 mL	*(½ cup) sugar*
125 mL	*(½ cup) brown sugar*

Core, peel, and dice apples.

Place apples in casserole; cover and microwave 8 to 9 minutes.

Peel kiwis and cube.

Add kiwis to casserole. Sprinkle with both sugars; mix well and microwave, uncovered, 2 minutes.

Let stand 5 minutes.

Serve with heavy cream.

Index

TYPESETTING: ATELIERS
GRAPHITI BARBEAU, TREMBLAY INC.
SAINT-GEORGES-DE-BEAUCE

Printed by
Laflamme et Charrier,
lithographers

PRINTED IN CANADA